THE CAMBRIDGE INTRC
EMMANUEL LE\

This book provides a clear and helpful overview of the thought of Emmanuel Levinas, one of the most significant and interesting philosophers of the late twentieth century. Michael L. Morgan presents an overall interpretation of Levinas's central principle that human existence is fundamentally ethical and that its ethical character is grounded in our face-to-face relationships with other people. He explores the religious, cultural, and political implications of this insight for modern Western culture and how it relates to our conception of selfhood and what it is to be a person, our understanding of the ground of moral values, our experience of time and the meaning of history, and our experience of religious concepts and discourse. The book includes an annotated list of recommended readings and a select bibliography of books by and about Levinas. It will be an excellent introduction to Levinas for readers unfamiliar with his work, even for those without a background in philosophy.

MICHAEL L. MORGAN is Chancellor's Professor of Philosophy and Jewish Studies, Emeritus, at Indiana University in Bloomington. He is the author of numerous books, most recently *Discovering Levinas* (Cambridge, 2007) and *Beyond Auschwitz* (2002), which was a finalist for the Koret Book Award in the category of Jewish Thought. He has also edited several collections of essays and editions of Spinoza's writings, and his articles have appeared in journals including the *Review of Metaphysics*, the *Journal of Religion*, and the *Journal of Jewish Thought and Philosophy*.

THE CAMBRIDGE INTRODUCTION TO EMMANUEL LEVINAS

MICHAEL L. MORGAN
Indiana University

CAMBRIDGE
UNIVERSITY PRESS

32 Avenue of the Americas, New York NY 10013-2473, USA

Cambridge University Press is part of the University of Cambridge.

It furthers the University's mission by disseminating knowledge in the pursuit of education, learning, and research at the highest international levels of excellence

www.cambridge.org
Information on this title: www.cambridge.org/9780521141062

First published 2011
Reprinted 2013

A catalog record for this publication is available from the British Library.

Library of Congress Cataloging in Publication data
Morgan, Michael L., 1944–
The Cambridge introduction to Emmanuel Levinas / Michael L. Morgan.
p. cm.
Includes bibliographical references and index.
ISBN 978-0-521-19302-3 – ISBN 978-0-521-14106-2 (pbk.)
1. Lévinas, Emmanuel. I. Title.
B2430.L484M665 2011
194– dc22 2010033893

ISBN 978-0-521-19302-3 Hardback
ISBN 978-0-521-14106-2 Paperback

Contents

Preface

In 2007 Cambridge University Press published my book *Discovering Levinas*. In that work I sought to accomplish two tasks: to provide an overall interpretation of Emmanuel Levinas's philosophy and to do so by placing Levinas in conversation with the so-called analytic tradition in contemporary Western philosophy. The virtue of the method I used is that it aimed at presenting Levinas in as clear a vocabulary as possible. I tried to explain Levinas's philosophical terminology and to translate his arcane, obscure style into language that could be understood by readers familiar with Anglo-American philosophy and with other developments in modern religious and philosophical thought. At the same time, my first and foremost task was to make a case for reading Levinas in a certain way; I presented a Levinas whose claims about ethics could be appreciated as deep and radical but not incompatible with our ordinary lives – in particular, our moral, political, and religious lives.

When *Discovering Levinas* was about to be published in paperback, the editors at Cambridge suggested that I abridge and revise that book with an eye to introducing Levinas to readers and students who wanted a clear and helpful initial guide to understanding his thinking. The present book is the outcome of that effort. Each of its eight chapters is grounded in that earlier work, but in every case I have made significant modifications in order to streamline the interpretation, to eliminate much of the use of analytic philosophy that would have required special background, and to focus on central texts and themes. Whereas the earlier book was distinctive in the use to which it put analytic philosophy, in this introduction my focus is on presenting Levinas's texts and ideas in as clear a fashion as I can. The result, I hope, is a shorter, more focused book that will be useful for those coming to Levinas for the first time, for readers who are seeking a guide to how to understand his thought and how to read his writings.

Some philosophical writing is distinguished by its argumentation, and there surely are arguments in Levinas's essays and books. But more often, even where there is no evident argument, as one might find in a typical analytic article or paper, there is certainly a very explicit theme and order to Levinas's presentations. Since I have not, however, attempted to provide overall readings of Levinas's works – certainly not of his most important books, *Totality and Infinity* and *Otherwise than Being* – I have not always paid explicit attention to that order or organization. Even in the case of his essays, I have not sought to offer complete readings. Most often, I have focused on concepts and themes, and hence this introduction regularly turns selectively to texts and the careful reading of passages in order to clarify what Levinas is doing and why. In reading him, such careful and attentive reading is mandatory. For the reader first coming to his work, Levinas's style, his terminology, even his sentence structure will seem opaque and utterly impenetrable. He relishes the construction of seemingly paradoxical or at least surprising sentences and descriptions, and he enjoys hyperbole and exaggeration. All of this requires sensitivity and care, if one is going to avoid finding obvious faults with what he is saying. In order to appreciate what he is saying and its significance, there is no substitute for careful translation into an idiom that the reader can understand and then attention to the nuances and caution that such translation always calls for. I have tried to offer a guide to understanding Levinas that is also a guide to how to read him, and hence there is a good deal of quotation and use of phrases and expressions from him, together with paraphrases and interpretations of what I take him to mean.

In the course of working on this book I have taught students at a number of institutions whose eagerness has been a delight to behold and whose questions about Levinas and about my reading of him have been a valuable resource for me. I want to thank students at Indiana University, Yale University, and Northwestern University for all they have taught me. During a semester at Yale, Rabbi Jim Ponet and I spent hours talking about Levinas, and he offered to organize several late-afternoon conversations with students at the Slifka Center, which were as helpful to me as they were enjoyable. I also thank audiences at Yale, the New School, the University of Edinburgh, and the University of Toronto, where I received very valuable comments on talks about Levinas and my reading of him. I especially want to thank Jay Bernstein for an extremely valuable discussion after I presented my paper at the New School. I would also like to thank Nick Alford for preparing the index.

As always, I could not have finished this book without the love and support of my wife, Audrey. Levinas is about teaching us to acknowledge what we owe to others, to be kind, caring, and generous. Aud has always known these lessons – and never needed to study him to learn them, as everyone who knows her well appreciates. Intellectual work has its special joys. However, watching our grandchildren – Gabby, Sasha, Tyler, and now Halle – grow and flourish has brought to both of us delights beyond compare. As I work in my study, they are always in my mind, as are our daughters and sons-in-law – Debbie and Adam, Sara and Marc – who work hard, so that what remains for Aud and myself is to enjoy the rewards of being grandparents.

Introduction

Emmanuel Levinas's life spans the twentieth century. He was born in 1906 and lived his youth in Kovno in Lithuania; he died in 1995 in Paris. Dostoyevsky, Tolstoy, and the great tradition of nineteenth-century Russian literature inspired him to philosophy. In France, his study of philosophy, his career as a Jewish educator and intellectual, and his philosophical teaching and writing were all conducted within the traditions of French and German philosophy, especially the phenomenological tradition of Edmund Husserl, Martin Heidegger, and others such as Jean Wahl. Living in Europe also meant living in the years that led to the Nazi dictatorship and included the horrors of the Nazi atrocities. These events and their aftermath, years of trying to cope with the memories of those horrors, also mark his thinking. His commitment to the French liberal tradition was always powerful, his relationship to Marxism changing and mixed. If Levinas is our teacher, it is because he was a student of, indeed a child of, the twentieth century.

There are four features of Levinas's life and thought that will help us to appreciate his significance: his historical situation, especially the role of the Holocaust in his memory and in his thought; his relationship to Judaism and religious texts, in particular the Bible and the Talmud; his place among those who were critical of Western philosophy and yet found special links to that tradition; and finally, his role in the twentieth-century debates about the place of ethics in our lives and the foundations of ethical value. Let me now say a word about each of these.

The rise of National Socialism and its twelve-year reign had intellectual and personal effects on Levinas. He lost many members of his family in the death camps and the Nazi advance into the east. His own wife and children had to go into hiding in France – his friend Maurice Blanchot arranged for them to be hidden in a monastery – when the Nazis took control and while he was in a prisoner-of-war camp for nearly five years after 1940. And intellectually, it was Martin Heidegger's role as rector of

Freiburg University and his commitment to Nazism that provoked, in 1933, Levinas's lifelong struggle with Heidegger's philosophy and his drive to rethink the character of the human condition and its ethical foundations. Moreover, as the century grew old, in the wake of the Nazi atrocities, Levinas was forever attentive to the evils that we inflict on one another, the threat of nuclear destruction, the continuing genocides – in Cambodia, Bosnia, and Rwanda – and the catastrophes that we wreak of all kinds. To him, the twentieth century, from the First World War through the Rwandan genocide, was a time of human abandonment, injustice of vast scope, inhumanity and suffering. If our thinking often resists acknowledging the horrors of which humankind is capable, our history makes such resistance difficult indeed.

Secondly, Levinas spent much of his life as a Jewish educator and a Jewish intellectual. He published several collections of essays on Jewish subjects and volumes of Talmudic studies, originally presented orally at annual meetings of the organization of French Jewish intellectuals.[1] Moreover, his philosophical writings appropriate biblical and Jewish religious terms and concepts for philosophical purposes. That there is a Jewish side to Levinas's life, intellectual and personal, is well known. However, there are details about his Jewish commitments that are important to keep in mind. His Jewish education as a child and youth in Kovno, while traditional, was nonetheless superseded in his mind by his love for Russian literature and philosophy. Only in the late 1940s, with the encouragement of friends, did he turn to serious Talmudic study under the tutelage of M. Chouchani, the enigmatic Talmudic savant with whom many Jews in Paris studied. That is, he came to serious Talmudic study only from the perspective of his developing philosophical thinking.[2] Furthermore, in the early 1930s, he came to teach in the École Normale Israélite Orientale and eventually to become its director, but this was no doubt because he could not find a university teaching position until completing his second dissertation. This occurred only in 1961, when *Totality and Infinity* was completed and he took a position at the University of Poitiers. In short, his role as a Jewish educator and as Jewish intellectual came to influence his thinking in serious ways only from the late 1940s, as he was developing his own philosophical views and responding against his Heideggerian heritage.

[1] Including *Difficult Freedom*, *In the Time of the Nations*, *Beyond the Verse*, and *Nine Talmudic Readings*. Levinas was a cofounder of the *Colloque des intellectuels juifs de langue française* in 1957.

[2] See, on this theme, Samuel Moyn, *Origins of the Other: Emmanuel Levinas between Revelation and Ethics* (Cornell, 2007).

Third, from literary modernism and the philosophical developments we associate with Heidegger as well as from trends in French philosophy in the interwar period, Levinas inherited a critical stance toward the tradition of Western philosophy. On the one hand, he came to see that tradition as limited; only rarely did figures within it seem able to see beyond its conceptual and linguistic boundaries to features of the human condition that are determinative and yet call for unusual means of access. These features are often referred to with a term like "transcendence," and just as often they are associated with the utterly unique that is of necessity occluded or hidden by systems that always function at the level of generality or universality. On the other hand, Heidegger had sought a more fundamental or primordial investigation into the being of beings in order to place science, philosophy, and more in terms of deeper dimensions of reality. Others challenged philosophical systems – totalizing schemes that sought comprehensiveness and exclusivity – by claiming that they could not, without contradiction, reach out and include the utter particularity of the individual, concrete, living person or the living God. Like such thinkers, Levinas was convinced that all systems reduced genuine multiplicity and diversity to some form of uniformity, to some one source. All totalities reduce the other to the same; they make sameness out of otherness, and since the dominant form of such reductionist accounts, ever since the early seventeenth century, has started with the subjectivity of the self, such totalities have regularly taken the shape of idealisms, reductions of everything to subjective or even mental phenomena. In opposition to all such strategies, Levinas claims that the human condition, intrinsically a social condition where we live together with and in interaction with other persons, has within it something that is irreducibly other. That other, which Plato thought was the Form of the Good, Plotinus the One, and Descartes the infinite and perfect God, Levinas takes to be the utterly particular other person with whom I stand face to face. Levinas's philosophy of the human condition, then, is not just another alternative picture; it is an attempt to replace all accounts of the human condition that fail to appreciate our essential social existence with one that does so and to carry out this task by revolutionizing philosophy, which is the way in which such an account is reflectively identified and disclosed.

Finally, and to my mind most importantly, this project of Levinas's – to revolutionize philosophy and in so doing to disclose the deepest structure of human social existence – yields a remarkable result. That result is the conclusion that, as he often puts it, "ethics is first philosophy." The conclusion – he says something similar when he says that ethics is an optics – has multiple significance. One thing that it means is that philosophy is indeed systematic, in the sense that what it points toward is a study of what is fundamental, that upon which everything else depends. That is, there is a first philosophy, what, ever since the commentators on Aristotle, has been called in the West "metaphysics." There is a study of the most fundamental realities, those things that ground everything else. It may be that philosophy is not constructive or deductive; there are different kinds of systems. It may be, that is, that philosophy is dialectical or probing or interrogative or even imaginative. The issue is not one of method; rather, it is about the outcome. Philosophy discusses all aspects of the human condition, but in so doing there is a philosophical disclosure of the most fundamental things because human existence does have a kind of foundation. In human existence there is something that comes first, so to speak, and for Levinas that something is ethics. We do not yet, of course, know exactly what Levinas means by the expression "ethics." There is every reason to wonder whether that term for him has connections with our everyday use of the expression. Only later will we be able to say more about this. But for the moment, let us assume that "ethics" has something to do with human character and conduct, that it involves in some way our sense that there are actions that we take to be right and good and others that we take to be bad or wrong or harmful. Some things we do increase pain and suffering; others alleviate them. Some things we do are fine and right, respectful and just; others are not. Levinas's slogan that "ethics is first philosophy" seems to suggest that at the bottom of any account of human existence lie these matters – about right and wrong, good and bad, just and harmful. We are not fundamentally beings that are rational or beings that have certain desires or emotions or that are systems of physical processes or bundles of atoms and subatomic particles. Rather, we are fundamentally ethical beings. That, by itself, is an important and rather surprising thing to say.

But there is more to Levinas's slogan. It says that ethics is first or primary, and part of what this means is that ethics is not grounded in anything that is more primary than it. It is not grounded in something else. This means either that it is not grounded at all or that it is, in a sense, self-grounded. On my reading, Levinas clearly advocates the latter. In a provocative way, we might say that for Levinas human existence is ethical all the way down. By saying this, Levinas is making a claim that is, as I see it, tremendously valuable for twentieth-century philosophy. Let me say something here about why that is so; it is an extremely important context in which to understand Levinas's work and his contribution.

In the nineteenth century a variety of critiques of ethics became influential. One came from Kierkegaard, who subordinated ethics, as well as politics, aesthetics, and much else, to the overarching shape of the divine-human relationship and ultimately to the primacy of God. Another came from the sciences. Darwin, for example, suggested that ethical principles and theories, along with religious belief and practices, like all human institutions, were a product of human evolution and ultimately of the drive toward self-preservation. Later, in the early twentieth century, Freud would characterize ethics as a function of the superego that internalized as psychological constraints based on parental relationships. Even earlier, Marx treated the ethical as an expression of fundamental economic needs. A further critique of ethics we associate with Nietzsche and his genealogical or historical account of ethical systems as expressions of class conflict, political confrontations, and historical factors. And furthermore, there was the suggestion that emerged from the development of the human sciences – historiography especially – that all value systems were relative to history, to cultural differences and such. In short, by the turn of the century, ethics had been subjected to doubts from a host of directions – from philosophical critique, from the sciences, and from history and religion. The outcome for some was skepticism about ethics altogether; for others, ethics, like other systems of values, was taken to be relative to historical periods or to cultural, political, or religious traditions. Its authority and content, that is, was localized and made parochial, subordinated to considerations of power or group interests.

At the same time that ethics was being subjected to this multifaceted assault on the universality and absolute or unconditional character of the ethical, philosophers – as well as poets, political theorists, and theologians – sought to come to the rescue of ethics in a number of ways. One response, to the criticism of the logical positivists, was to interpret moral vocabulary in terms of human responses, in particular attitudes of attraction and endorsement or of repulsion and rejection. This development, made more sophisticated as the twentieth century went on, became one foundation for a kind of ethical naturalism that grounded the authority of ethics in our nature, here our psychological nature, and also derived its content from the same source.[3] Another development, present throughout the century, was an attempt to ground the authority and content of ethics in our nature as rational agents. In this case it was Immanuel Kant who

[3] One could include here R. M. Hare, Simon Blackburn, and Alan Gibbard, along with many others.

was the primary historical predecessor; in the twentieth century the heirs were ethical intuitionists, such as W. D. Ross, and later contractualists and other rationalists, from John Rawls to Alan Gewirth, Onora O'Neill, Thomas Hill, Tim Scanlon, Christine Korsgaard, and others. In short, seeking a source of authority for the normative force or the ought-to-be-doneness of the ethical, once a divine source has been subjected to criticisms – from Kant to our own day – these two options, to turn to human nature or to rationality, seem the most likely and compelling alternatives.

In the late twentieth century, by the late 1970s, these developments were deemed by many to be unsatisfactory. In all areas of human endeavor, the ethical, the cognitive, the aesthetic, the political, and even the scientific, arguments had successfully, it seemed to many, challenged the very notion of some foundation or unconditional ground in virtue of which the edifice of principles and commitments was taken to be justified. Debates about what philosophers called "foundationalism" raged in the seventies and eighties, and many took up the banner of one form of anti-foundationalism or other. Some were persuaded by developments in the history and philosophy of science, associated with the work of Thomas Kuhn; others were convinced by the critique of Richard Rorty, which drew on pragmatism to argue against all kinds of foundationalisms, in epistemology, ethics, politics, and elsewhere, in favor of the pluralism of worldviews and positions, to be evaluated in terms of practical considerations alone. Wittgenstein, Heidegger, Foucault, and Derrida – among a host of others – were called to the table as defenders of such pluralism, in part as a response to various forms of colonialism and domination. What began as a defense of minority cultures, of women and gendered concerns, and of the victims of social and political oppression became an attack on all kinds of so-called hegemonic discourses, structures, institutions, and practices. Among the favored objects of such criticism was the philosophy of the Enlightenment, with its emphasis on liberal values, freedom, and rationality, and its seeming dismissal or at least denigration of emotion, feeling, the body, and particularity and distinctiveness. It is no wonder that even the notion of a self with a specified complement of essential features came under attack. Some anti-humanists, as they are called, came to their attack on the self or the person from French structuralism; others came to it from Heidegger's later philosophy of Being, and still others from a form of naturalism. But one result of much of this discussion was a conviction that everything is a text or akin to one, the object of interpretation and understanding and hence relative to the individual or community that engages in this process, as a matter of course or self-consciously.

There is one further feature of this cluster of developments that should be underlined. It is not exclusively a conversation and a debate of one strand of Western philosophy in the twentieth century. Whether the authority of the ethical is grounded in some absolute foundation or not, what is the content of the ethical, and whether the ethical is a primary feature of all human existence – these are common questions in all twentieth-century philosophy and in general intellectual discussion as well. It is well known that during the past century, beginning sometime during the early part of the century, various streams of philosophical thinking began to emerge with enough autonomy and enough of a sense of their own exclusivity to look to us now, from our vantage point in the early twenty-first century, to be distinctive ways of engaging in philosophy. It is commonly said that these streams largely converged into two, what we often call analytic philosophy and continental philosophy. Such a distinction is a simplification, to be sure, and it hides many complexities. But one thing can be said. The concerns I have been discussing about ethics, about the ground of ethical value and the content of ethical obligations and ideals, are issues that have been addressed within both of these traditions. That they are has been seen best by those figures, from both traditions, who in the latter part of the century increasingly ignored the boundary and developed for themselves ways of talking about philosophical issues that draw upon figures from both sides of the so-called divide.[4]

The philosophy of Emmanuel Levinas ought to be understood within this discussion about the foundation and content of the ethical. Levinas can be taken as a foundationalist about the ethical. Responding to Heidegger and the lack of any constraints on what counts as authenticity, and responding too to the horrors of Nazism, Levinas believes that social existence itself incorporates within it, in a primary way, the content and force of the ethical. There is nothing more primary to human existence than the ethical, and the ethical is its own ground, so to speak. On the one hand, of course, as we have seen, Levinas opposes the hegemony of schemes of totalization, comprehensive theories and ways of understanding the world and human experience. In this respect, Levinas seems to begin with a commitment to pluralism, to the openness of languages and conceptual schemes. But, on the other hand, this original commitment to pluralism does not lead Levinas to a form of anti-foundationalism. He knows that even a pluralist can be committed unconditionally to reducing

[4] Here I am thinking of Jurgen Habermas, Stanley Cavell, Charles Taylor, Robert Pippin, Raymond Geuss, Stephen Mulhall, and even Richard Rorty.

suffering, to treating others humanely and with concern, and to fighting for justice and equality. Levinas does not know the work of Richard Rorty, but he knows in principle that pragmatic and wholly interpretive commitments can nonetheless harbor absolute ethical commitments. Rorty knows this, and Levinas knows this. But what distinguishes them is that for Levinas a very careful and philosophically precise understanding of what is required by all our social interactions discloses an ethical need and an ethical imperative that binds us all. In this sense, Levinas believes that ethics is something that occurs between every two particular persons in terms of their face-to-face encounter with one another, and at the same time he believes that this fact is universal. It applies to all our relationships.

Levinas's response to the problem of the authority and content of the ethical is unlike any other twentieth-century response. Indeed, it is unlike any other attempt to deal with similar problems.[5] This is not to say that the *content* of ethical value that he advocates is distinctive. In fact, it is often just what one would expect – that we ought to care for others, respond to their needs, work to feed the hungry and reduce suffering. But what is distinctive of Levinas's account is the role it gives to the ethical in our understanding of human existence and also the *way* in which he accounts for the *force* and content of the ethical. If indeed Levinas does provide a superior way of understanding such matters, then that would count in its favor. It would, if other evidence were also forthcoming, contribute to our taking it seriously and even to our being persuaded by it.

It is worth noting, even at this stage, how this sense of the authority of the ethical and its normative force, as I shall call it, are accounted for. By "authority" I mean the status that the ethical seems to have in our lives, whereby it is regularly thought to count as a dominant reason and sometimes a decisive reason for acting. By "normative force" I mean the kind of influence the ethical is thought to have, in virtue of which it counts as such a reason, its "ought-to-be-doneness," as one might call it. We often distinguish among various kinds of force or necessity – causal, conceptual, deductive or inferential or rational, compulsion, and moral force. Here I am focusing on the latter. For the moment, I take it that this kind of moral force cannot be identified with or reduced to a type of causal or motivational force; nor can it be reduced to a conceptual or inferential force, and it is clearly not a type of compulsion. It does justify our doing something,

[5] It is even unlike the accounts of second-person normativity such as those by Stephen Darwall, R. Jay Wallace, and Michael Thompson.

in a sense, but it also is a reason that carries with it a kind of compellingness, although not one that precludes our choice or our responsibility but somehow incorporates it. It is this normative force, as I shall call it, that philosophers have so often investigated and that Levinas too explores, and it is his way of understanding it that is so unique.

As I have suggested, there have been, in a sense, four twentieth-century responses to this problem that have been most persuasive. Let me call the first the pluralist response, according to which there is no single force or source of authority; it is culturally relative or historically relative or perhaps even tied to the content of particular obligations or ideals. A second is the naturalist response, according to which there is a force, but it is tied to our psychology, either to our preferences or desires or to our needs as identified by a scientific inquiry – evolutionary biology, for example. A third grounds this force in some feature of our rational agency – for example, our ability to deliberate about our desires or reasons reflectively or our ability to choose freely what to do – and a fourth takes the force itself to be conventional, whereby a society takes certain rules and ideals to be compelling. The last is a broadly Wittgensteinian response that is often tied to Aristotle as well.[6]

Unlike the last response, which takes ethics to be conventional and social, and the first, which rejects the idea of a global moral force, Levinas ties the ground of ethics to the utter particularity of the other and the self in their engagement with one another. Since Schelling and Kierkegaard at least, one criticism of philosophical systems is that they cannot reach the uniquely particular, concrete, living individual. They function with concepts, categories, principles, and institutions and hence do not have the capacity to touch the individual and acknowledge her priority. In Marx's terms, such systems deal with species-man and not with individual persons. Ever since Aristotle, philosophers have used various strategies to deal with such particularity. With Levinas, however, the utter particularity of the other person and that of the self are linked; the self's particularity lies in responsibility, which comes into being with the other's claim upon the self. By itself, the other is not utterly particular; nor is the self. But together both are, precisely because the other calls the self into question, that is, cries out to it in need and commands the self to accept it. In short,

[6] See Elizabeth Anscombe, "Modern Moral Philosophy," *Philosophy* 33 (1958), 1–19, reprinted in *Ethics, Religion and Politics* (Minnesota, 1981), 26–42; and Alasdair MacIntyre, *After Virtue* (Notre Dame, 1984) (orig. 1981). Even when one argues that modern moral philosophy is itself grounded in the second-person standpoint and its presuppositions, as does Stephen Darwall in *The Second-Person Standpoint*, it can be shown that Levinas's conclusions differ and function at a different level of understanding.

social existence is the ultimate content of the utter particularity of the self and the other.

Much of Western moral philosophy has it that morality requires of us that we detach ourselves from all that makes us the unique individuals that we are. This criticism of utilitarianism and Kantian moral philosophy is famously associated with someone like Bernard Williams, on the one hand, and with those like Charles Taylor and Michael Sandel, on the other. The criticism is that our selfhood or identity is a complex weaving together of talents, heritages, traditions, practices, and associations. What makes us unique is a highly diverse and rich cluster of features and characteristics. Rationalist moral theory calls upon us to set all that is distinctive aside, to take up a special perspective, that of man in general, or the rational agent in general, and to tie the ethical to that perspective. What is surprising about Levinas, however, is that while he clings to the centrality of our utter particularity, he takes it to be tied to ethical obligation that is prior to all of this complexity and even to the moral universality characteristic of Kantian and utilitarian moral theories.

Levinas refers to the ethical foundation as what is expressed in the relation between two particular persons when they face one another. As we shall see, this is a seemingly simple idea that is deceptively complex and elusive. Its character and its status in our lives are very difficult notions to grasp. In part, however, even here we can notice one feature of this relation. As Levinas wants us to understand, the claim that the other person makes upon me when I encounter his face – indeed, what the face reveals to me – arises out of the other person's need – what Levinas calls vulnerability or nudity or weakness and what I call its dependency-upon-me – and out of the other person's dignity or status – what Levinas calls the face's "height" and I call its authority. That is, the face speaks with authority and out of weakness or need; it commands and petitions at once. This may sound perplexing; how can someone who is destitute or weak make demands of me, and how can one who commands me be vulnerable and deprived? But Levinas's point, in a sense, is that this combination, when understood dialectically, is what is needed to make normativity or the ought-to-be-doneness possible. If the other person were only my superior, then her commands would be compulsion; if she were only destitute or weak, then her pleas would carry no more weight than I choose to give them. Why is it that what the other person needs of me is something that both calls out to me, grips me, moves me, and also makes demands of me, requires me? There must be something about the other person's relation to me that primitively and irreducibly incorporates both these dimensions at once. If it had only one, then its effect would be too much or too little. Only if it has or is both, can the other person be utterly particular for me as the bearer of justified weight, so to speak.

As we shall see later, this response to the question I have raised about the ground of normativity and moral value is unique to Levinas. No other response in the twentieth century (or before) is quite like it. Moreover, it takes seriously the subjective or first-person orientation of human experience and hence the way in which human experience starts with and tracks the concrete individual person's experience. It finds its way to concepts and principles, but it starts with particularity. It is phenomenological and hermeneutical and yet grounded and ethical. It is a foundationalism after anti-foundationalisms, a sense of moral groundedness after Gadamer, Rorty, and Derrida.

To many readers of Levinas, what he has to say about the ethical is extreme and counterintuitive. It appears to require us to be something that it is hard to believe we could or would want to be. Even prior to examining and clarifying Levinas's central idea, the face-to-face encounter, we can prepare ourselves by itemizing some of the perplexities that will confront us.

When we ask ourselves what is essential to ethics or morality, we tend to think about our relationships with other people and what we ought to do for them. That is, we associate ethics with altruism, a concern for the well-being of others. We also think about principles or ideals that we take to be universal, to apply to everyone. To be sure, we note that there are ethical matters that concern only ourselves and how we treat ourselves as the unique persons that we are, but when trying to identify what is central about ethics, we look to others and to what is universal. Levinas does agree with these intuitions, but he gives them a very precise and dramatic formulation. As people tend to read him, they take him to be claiming that our obligations to others always take priority and that they are extreme, in the sense that there are no limits to these obligations. We are responsible for all others, all the time, in every way. This extreme formulation says more than that we ought to care about others; it says that our obligations to them always override any other interest or value we have and that no matter how much we give or share with others, there is always more that we can and should do. Furthermore, it seems to be saying that we should always sacrifice ourselves and any of our own interests or desires in favor of the other person; I should always care more about what others need from me than what I want to do or to have. Indeed, Levinas seems to be saying that everything we do should be judged by this standard. No decision I make should neglect to consider what effect my decision or action would have on the others to whom I am responsible. If an action cannot be justified in terms of what good it can do for others, then it should not be performed.

I am trying to make Levinas sound extraordinarily demanding, daunting, and possibly even incoherent. After all, if my obligations to others have no limits, I must necessarily fail to meet them. Can this be an ethics according to which I am a sinner all the time? Moreover, as if this were not enough to discredit what Levinas says, there is more. He wants us to believe that the other person's claim upon me occurs prior to anything else that is true about me. One feature of this situation is that the other is the active agent; I am totally passive. In fact, Levinas says that this relationship is one that is asymmetrical and unequal and one in which I am passive before I am active. And I am not just passive. I am accused by the other, the other's hostage, substitution for the other, persecuted by the other. All of this sounds violent, oppressive, and dominating. As a result of such a relationship, how can I be elevated in some way? How can I be more noble, a better person, insofar as I am submitting to – indeed, being victimized by – such a relationship? This relationship seems to harm me in some way, to compel me. How can it be the ground of respect and dignity, of what is morally worthwhile?

Within Divine Command moral theories, the individual is the subject of a number of obligations that express divine will. They are, after all, God's commands. But in such theories, God makes these commands out of love and concern for humankind. They are rules that, if followed, will enable human beings to contribute to the social and historical well-being of humankind. Moreover, in such theories, man is given the free will to accept these commands or to reject them, which makes it possible to hold him accountable. The human may live under divine authority, but there is also the recognition that human beings are worthy and beings of value. The commands are rules that express concern for others and respect for all human beings.

In modern rational or naturalist moral theories, the self is at the center. These are individualist theories in one sense or another. But they do differ, of course, in terms of how they understand the centrality of the subject. In some cases, the self or subject is the rational agent. This agent is in one sense a singular individual, but in another she is a representative of all rational agents. It might be that what seems worthy of respect and what is valued here is human rationality and the fact that it is shared by all human beings and that it is worthy of respect. Why this is so, and especially why it is worthy of moral respect, is not often made clear, if indeed it can be made clear. In other cases, the self or subject is a being with desires, needs, and interests who seeks to increase its own and others' well-being. Since it generally makes no difference where these desires or needs are located, so to speak, although their type and character may make a difference, on this kind of theory what is of central value are states in which such needs and desires are satisfied and ultimately world-states in which well-being is maximized. In short, if rationalist theories have reason and rational agency as their real subject, these consequentialist theories have the world or the totality of needful and desiring beings as their subject.

There are moral theories, then, that begin with rationality or freedom and work out from there, and there are theories that begin with desires and needs and work out from there. I say "work out" since in both cases, at least prima facie, the properties apply initially to individuals and only derivatively beyond that. Moreover, some theories have rational beings as their real subject; others have world-states or the states of all sentient beings. Levinas has a different starting place. First, as I have already said, the starting point for him is a relationship between two utterly particular persons who face one another. That is, the starting point is a synthetic whole of two individuals in relationship. Second, the call of the other person to the self incorporates needs and dependency, but it also contains the compellingness of reason. Third, if the other theories begin with reason or dignity or desire and seek limits to these, Levinas begins with unlimited obligation and seeks to limit it and to do so out of the necessary contextual features of each and every situation. There may be general strategies for how to handle such limitation and determination, but there are no fixed and firm rules. What distinguishes Levinas's view, then, is first that it is deontic; it deals with obligations and ethical responsibility toward others. Second, while it is first-personal, it is also second-personal and intrinsically relational. The relations are not tacked on afterward; the subject is situationally embedded to begin with.

As I have tried to point out, Levinas takes the face-to-face and responsibility, no matter what terminology we use for it, to be characteristic of all human social existence. It is not identified as a ground for morality; rather, it is identified as a condition of all human social existence, which turns out to be ethical – moral in character and obligatory in status. On other traditional pictures, human existence is primarily epistemological; we are beings that represent the world and then have beliefs about it. When this is so, our higher-level theorizing about the world – in scientific inquiry, for example – is grounded naturally in our basic epistemological stance toward the world. Where else would that theorizing be grounded? Similarly, in Levinas's case, moral theory and political thinking are grounded naturally in the ethical condition that he identifies. Moreover, just as naturalist views, for example, seek to show that moral obligations and ideals are grounded in natural facts, so Levinas needs to believe, and perhaps can show, that epistemological practices are grounded in the ethical condition that underlies all our existence. In fact, Levinas points in this direction, but does not say very much about it. His interests lie elsewhere.

As one might expect, Levinas continues several strands of thinking that were introduced into modern thought or that have been advanced by others. There is a Kantian strand in Levinas, for example, and also a neo-Orthodox strand – if one might call Barth and other crisis theologians neo-Orthodox. Levinas bears some similarities to Fichte and to certain elements in Hegel and Sartre, and his thinking is akin to that of Foucault and the structuralists in a certain sense. But what I think is especially remarkable in his thinking is the way in which he responds to historical and theoretical problems about human existence in the unique way I have been discussing. In the end, his ethical commitments are pluralistic and situational, but they are also grounded and universal. He is critical of organized and traditional religions – in the spirit of Kierkegaard and Nietzsche and Freud – but he does not eschew religion altogether. Traditional concepts like revelation, eschatology, and redemption play important roles for him, but much of religious orthodoxy he would take to be "childish" and immature. Here he is following in the footsteps of philosophers such as Kant and Hegel, but he does so in his own distinctive way.

Much of the time Levinas employs a surprising and unusual vocabulary and a syntax that seems often to be strange and even ungrammatical. He takes himself to be an iconoclast, a revolutionary; his literary style is calculated to unsettle and disturb, to warn the reader against any facile appropriation of traditional discourse and modes of thought. Hence, like much poetry, literature, and art, Levinas appeals both to our rational ability to reason and to understand and to our imaginative ability to see the world and human existence in a quite different way than is done customarily. His writings are carefully argued; there is no denying this rational structure. But the arguments and reasoning are articulated in such a strange vocabulary and in such an unorthodox way that they are hard to identify and to follow. At the same time, his prose is marked by repetitiveness and hyperbole, exaggeration and blatant paradox, to a degree that may exasperate and confuse. Reading Levinas requires patience; it also requires that we develop a sense about when to relish ambiguities and nuances and when to demand rigor and precision. As we consider his work and his thought, we will have to be careful and bold, at once, careful enough to follow his lines of reasoning and bold enough to imaginatively leap beyond them when he seems to want us to do so.

CHAPTER ONE

Responding to Atrocity in the Twentieth Century

In "Signature," the last piece in *Difficult Freedom*, Levinas tells us that the list of items in the first paragraph, his biography, "is dominated by the presentiment and the memory of the Nazi horror."[1] Hitler, Auschwitz, and Nazi fascism meant a great deal to Levinas – to his life, of course, and also to his philosophical thinking and to his thinking about Judaism. Yet at times Levinas talks about Nazism and Auschwitz in particular, at times about this event as part of or characteristic of a larger phenomenon. That larger phenomenon includes the horrors of the twentieth century overall, before, during, and after the Holocaust. In this chapter I will first discuss what Levinas says about this larger phenomenon and later focus on the Holocaust in particular.

Levinas's ethical and philosophical views provide him with a perspective on human experience and the everyday world that expresses itself often in his occasional writings, interviews, and more popular essays. A particular focus of this perspective is Auschwitz and twentieth-century life. We have not looked yet at his ethics and philosophy, but we can consider one of its manifestations, even prior to examining its details, and that is what I will do here, without any preparation or theorizing. What does Levinas say about life in the twentieth century and especially about the "decline of the West" and the crisis of modernity?

LEVINAS ON GROSSMAN'S *LIFE AND FATE*

During the last ten to fifteen years of his life, Levinas frequently and passionately cited one work as emblematic of this crisis and his own special response to it. He referred to it at least twice in print, in 1984 and 1986, and in 1984 in one of his annual Talmudic lessons.[2] In interviews in the

[1] Levinas, *Difficult Freedom* (1963, 1976), 291; cf. *Is It Righteous to Be?*, 39.

[2] See Levinas, "The Bible and the Greeks," in *In the Time of the Nations* (1988; trans. 1994), 135, published originally in *Cosmopolitique* 4 (February 1986); "Beyond Memory," in *In the Time of the*

eighties, however, he was drawn to it numerous times, almost compulsively. The work is Vasily Grossman's *Life and Fate*, a massive realistic novel about Hitler and Nazism, Stalinism, and the Battle of Stalingrad but more generally about the crisis of European culture and life. Trained as a mathematician and engineer, Grossman began writing in his twenties and by 1934 had written short stories and a first novel that caught the attention of Maxim Gorky. During World War II, while Levinas was in a prisoner-of-war camp, Grossman was a journalist for a Soviet newspaper. He was the first to expose the atrocities of the Nazi death camp at Treblinka. Later he collaborated in the compilation of *The Black Book*, a collection of documents related to the Nazi death camps.[3] Grossman's writing is realistic, direct, and powerful, and while it has a homiletic and didactic quality at times, it is overall riveting. It is no wonder that Levinas was so impressed by Grossman's magnum opus.

Life and Fate was written in the fifties, when Grossman was realizing a good deal of public success, albeit in the wake of postwar attacks on him and a formal letter of repentance. Completed in 1960, the novel was promptly rejected for publication as anti-Soviet, and the manuscript was confiscated by the KGB.[4] Depressed and upset, Grossman died of cancer in 1964.[5] *Life and Fate* was eventually published in Russian by a small Swiss press; translated into French and German, it appeared in an English version in 1987.[6] I would imagine that Levinas, who read it in Russian, did so in 1983 or 1984, when he cites it extensively at the end of his Talmudic lesson "Beyond Memory." It begins to appear in his interviews about 1985–86.[7]

The novel is about large events and tiny ones, and about people, their sufferings, thoughts, actions, hopes, and anguish. The large event is the German siege of Stalingrad in the fall and winter of 1942–43 and the Soviet victory over Hitler's forces.[8] Robert Chandler, who translated the work into English, captures the themes of this large event nicely:

> Like *War and Peace*, *Life and Fate* contains many of [Grossman's] own reflections on history and philosophy.... No other writer has so convincingly established the identity of Nazism and Soviet Communism....

Nations, 88–91. This discussion of *Berachoth* 12b-13a, originally delivered in December 1984, was first published in 1986. See also "Peace and Proximity," in *Alterity and Transcendence* (1984), 140.

3 See Ilya Ehrenburg and Vasily Grossman, *The Complete Black Book of Russian Jewry* (originally completed in 1946; published in Vilnius in 1993; translated and edited by David Patterson in 2002).

4 Garrard and Garrard, *The Bones of Berdichev* (1996), 260–263.

5 Ibid., 263–299.

6 Ibid., 322–323, and *Life and Fate*, 7–11.

7 *Is It Righteous to Be?*, 79, 80–81, 89–90.

8 See Garrard and Garrard, *The Bones of Berdichev*, 236–244.

The real battle portrayed in the battle is not the clash between the Third Reich and Stalin's Russia, but the clash between Freedom and Totalitarianism. At Stalingrad the Russian people believed they were fighting against Totalitarianism in the name of Freedom.... Grossman movingly describes the development of a genuine spirit of camaraderie and egalitarianism among the defenders of Stalingrad; he also shows how this spirit was stamped out by Party functionaries who saw it as a greater danger than the Germans themselves.[9]

But this is the grand scheme. In addition the book contains a smaller, more local and particular one. The novel is also about the very precise decisions, challenges, anxieties, and reflections of its actors and actresses, painted in rich, personal touches by a master observer of humanity. Chandler sees this dimension of *Life and Fate* just as clearly:

'The clash between Freedom and Totalitarianism', however, is too grand and abstract a phrase.... The battle Grossman portrays is the battle we must fight each day in order to preserve our humanity, the battle against the power of ideology, against the power of the state, against all the forces that combine to destroy the possibility of kindness and compassion between individuals.... The true victors [in this battle] ... [are all those] whose actions, however historically insignificant, are motivated by the spirit of senseless, irrational kindness. It is these spontaneous, dangerous acts of kindness that Grossman sees as the truest expression of human freedom.[10]

With grand sweep and extraordinary depth and detail, Grossman "has portrayed the life, not of a few individuals, but of an entire age."[11] Here is realism and scope, scrupulously portrayed individuals against the panorama of history, a throwback to the nineteenth century, a novel untouched by the modernist sensibility of Joyce, Woolf, or Musil, a tapestry of lives, psychology, and events as detailed and concrete as it is broad and expansive.

Setting aside personal associations, we can see at a glance what Grossman's novel might mean to Levinas. It is, in part, about totalitarianism and hence about institutions that seek to surround and dominate everything and everyone. It is also about very concrete events, actions, relationships, and experiences that seem to escape the totality, to grasp what transcends it and yet what enters it as if from the outside – acts of "senseless kindness." *Life and Fate*, moreover, exposes something about Europe and Western history, the immensity of their failures and the horrors and atrocities that have engulfed them in our century. Levinas could

[9] Chandler in Grossman, *Life and Fate*, 11–12.
[10] Ibid., 12.
[11] Ibid., 13.

be expected to take this judgement very seriously, with its sense of loss and despair. But in fact there is no need to speculate. We are fortunate to have many interviews in which Levinas calls our attention to Grossman's great work and to details within it. Let us turn to these themes and details now, in order to see how and why Levinas reads the book.

First, a detail. In the novel, Krymov, an old Bolshevik and once husband of a daughter of the main character, Alexandria Shaposhnikova, is arrested and incarcerated in the Lubyanka prison in Moscow. When Yevgenia, his estranged former wife, hears that Krymov is imprisoned, being interrogated and tortured, she abandons her love affair with Novikov, a tank commander, and moves in order to be near the prison. Daily she stands in long lines to make inquiries, to seek permission to leave a package or a letter. She is among hundreds. Levinas recalls Yevgenia's return to her husband as an "act of goodness, absolutely gratuitous and unforeseen."[12] In addition, he remembers and emphasizes a tiny detail in Grossman's description:

> In *Life and Fate* Grossman tells how in Lubyanka in Moscow, before the infamous gate where one could convey letters or packages to friends and relatives arrested for 'political crimes' or get news of them, people formed a line, each reading on the nape of the person in front of him the feelings and hopes of his misery.[13]

Levinas calls this scene to mind in the course of explaining what he means by "the priority of the other person" and specifically what he means when he refers to meeting the other as "welcoming the face."[14] The face, he says, is not first of all a collection of features, their shapes and the color of its surface, or in general an object of perception. It is rather – *first of all and most significantly* – "expression and appeal," or what he describes as "the nakedness of the other – destitution and misery beneath the adopted countenance."[15] It is at this point that Levinas calls upon Grossman's image, of "human beings who glue their eyes to the nape of the neck of the person in front of them and read on that nape all the anxiety in the world."[16] These are Levinas's words; Grossman had described the situation in these words:

> Yevgenia had never realized that the human back could be so expressive, could so vividly reflect a person's state of mind. People had a particular way of craning

[12] *Is It Righteous to Be?*, 89.

[13] Ibid., 208; cf. Levinas, "Peace and Proximity," in *Alterity and Transcendence*, 140.

[14] *Is It Righteous to Be?*, 191–192.

[15] Ibid., 191.

[16] Ibid., 192.

their necks as they came up to the windows; their backs, with their raised, tensed shoulders, seemed to be crying, to be sobbing and screaming.[17]

These words seem to have led Levinas to envision this line of people, to visualize in his mind's eye what it was like to stand in such a line, to focus on the person before you, and to see his or her pain and suffering in the posture of his back or the curve of his neck.[18]

What is it to be presented with another person in this way? What does it mean for our encounter or engagement with another person for it to be one of being faced with her misery and need first of all and most significantly? Levinas elaborates, in response to Grossman's image:

> In the innocence of our daily lives, the face of the other [or the neck or the back] signifies above all a demand. The face requires you, calls you outside. And already there resounds the word from Sinai, 'thou shalt not kill,' which signifies 'you shall defend the life of the other'.... It is the very articulation of the love of the other. You are indebted to someone from whom you have not borrowed a thing.... And *you* are responsible, the only one who could answer, the noninterchangeable, and the unique one.... In this relation of the unique to the unique there appears, before the purely formal community of the genus, the original sociality.[19]

For now, I want to ignore Levinas's special vocabulary. What is he saying here? Levinas is drawing on Grossman's image to articulate the experience of being faced with another person's pain and misery and realizing how one must respond to it, out of a sense of obligation, a kind of indebtedness, a sense that one cannot avoid acknowledging that misery, that one must care about it, not ignore it, and hence that one must do something. Levinas seems especially interested in the fact that all of this – the experience of the other's misery and the sense of debt and devotion – is what the other's presence, as a face or neck or back, signifies or means. This is what this kind of experience means; the meaning combines an exposure, a plea, a demand, and a recognition, all at once. Moreover, this is not what one sees in the features, the coloration, the shape of the other's face or body; it is what the other person means alongside all of this.

This conclusion leads me to another detail in *Life and Fate* that Levinas frequently calls to mind. Like Yevgenia's senseless abandoning of her love affair with Novikov and her allegiance to Krymov, it is what Levinas calls a "scene of goodness in an inhuman world."[20]

[17] Grossman, *Life and Fate*, 683; cf. 681–685.
[18] See *Is It Righteous to Be?*, 208.
[19] Ibid., 192.
[20] Ibid., 81.

> [T]oward the book's end, when Stalingrad has already been rescued, the German prisoners, including an officer, are cleaning out a basement and removing the decomposing bodies. The officer suffers particularly from this misery. In the crowd, a woman who hates Germans is delighted to see this man more miserable than the others. Then she gives him the last piece of bread she has. This is extraordinary. Even in hatred there exists a mercy stronger than hatred.[21]

If the core meaning of the encounter with another person is a sense of need and demand, the core response to it is an act of goodness or generosity that is beyond explanation, that in fact seems to defy explanation. More than that, as in this case of the woman's act of giving bread to a person whom she hates and whose suffering she seems to be enjoying, there are acts of goodness in a situation that seems to be totally inhumane and insensitive. Levinas emphasizes that acts like Yevgenia's devotion and the woman's gift are "isolated acts." They are not prepared for and seem to surprise rather than to make sense. And they have no larger effect. They do not change things; the world remains as it was; they are anomalies.

Grossman's description of this episode is more gripping, frightening, and complex than Levinas's memory of it.[22] The scene was tense, as the soldiers removed the bodies from the cellar with the crowd of Russians so hostile and threatening. Then they brought out the body of a dead adolescent girl. The woman ran to the girl's body, straightening out her hair, transfixed by her features. She then stood up and walked toward the officer, picked up a brick on the way, hatred radiating from her, without the guard feeling that he could stop her.

> The woman could no longer see anything at all except the face of the German with the handkerchief round his mouth. Not understanding what was happening to her, governed by a power she had just now seemed to control, she felt in the pocket of her jacket for a piece of bread that had been given to her the evening before by a soldier. She held it out to the German officer and said: 'There, have something to eat.'
>
> Afterwards, she was unable to understand what had happened to her, why she had done this. Her life was to be full of moments of humiliation, helplessness and anger, full of petty cruelties that made her lie awake at night, full of brooding resentment.... At one such moment, lying on her bed, full of bitterness, she was to remember that winter morning outside the cellar and think: 'I was a fool then, and I'm still a fool now.'[23]

[21] Ibid., 89; cf. 81.
[22] Grossman, *Life and Fate*, 803–806.
[23] Ibid., 805–806.

Levinas extracts from this episode an act of utterly senseless goodness. Senseless it is: the woman is filled with hatred; she is about to strike the officer, to kill him out of revenge. Instead, she hands him bread to eat. Is it an act of generosity? The bread was given to her by a soldier; perhaps it represented to her that dead girl and giving it to the officer was an act of defiance, of repulsion, of hatred? Or was it more simply a way to avoid killing the officer, a virtually automatic way of preventing herself from doing what she both wanted to do but also could not bring herself to do? And yet it was an act that gave the officer life rather than taking it from him, one that had no effect on her life, miserable and resentful, later remembered with regret that she had not struck and killed him. Perhaps, for all its complexity, the episode has at its core the meaning Levinas found in it: there was an act of goodness, and it was wholly senseless and isolated. It was an act of goodness because it gave life to the officer and even, it appeared, gave out of the little she had to do so. And it was done for no other reason; there was no explanation or justification for it – other than that it was what it was, an act of grace, of giving, of taking responsibility for the other person's need and life. And it was rare, isolated in an inhumane world filled with suffering and misery.

This point brings us to Levinas's other sort of citation of *Life and Fate*. Not only does he call attention to details or episodes; he also points out what Grossman shows us about the twentieth century and about our world. This is a big theme and an important one. I want to discuss it in two steps. First, Levinas reflects on what Grossman's novel means for our understanding of Stalinism, Nazism, and such totalitarian ideologies in the twentieth century. Second, Levinas refers to a letter from a strange figure in the novel, an old Tolstoian, that Grossman presents in what Levinas calls the central chapter of the book.[24] This character, Ikonnikov, Levinas takes to represent Grossman's own views, but whether he does is not as relevant as what these views are, since Levinas clearly finds them very appealing and even, in a way, identifies with them.[25] "The essential teaching," Levinas says, "is articulated by a strange, socially marginal person who has lived through it all. Halfway between simplemindedness and holiness, between madness and wisdom, he doesn't believe in God anymore, nor in the Good that would organize an ideology."[26] Ikonnikov, that is, does not advocate or believe in systems, ideologies, theories, or totalities of any kind. What he does believe in are unique, discrete acts of goodness or kindness.

[24] Ibid., Part II, Chapter 15, 404–411.
[25] See *Is It Righteous to Be?*, 216–218; cf. 89–90, 120.
[26] Ibid., 120.

Levinas summarizes the main points of Ikonnikov's letter on several occasions. In the novel, the letter is read by an old Bolshevik, Mostovsky, in a German concentration camp, alone in his cell, after a lengthy interrogation during which he has been given "Ikonnikov's scribblings" and been questioned about them.[27] Levinas never mentions this context; he calls attention solely to what he takes to be Ikonnikov's view of the world and human goodness:

> The essential thing in this book is simply what the character Ikonnikov says – 'There is neither God nor the Good, but there is goodness' – which is also my thesis. That is all that is left to mankind.... He also says: 'There are acts of goodness which are absolutely gratuitous, unforeseen.'[28]

Levinas gives a fuller account in 1986, when his comments on *Life and Fate* are raised by the interviewer's question about how upsetting Levinas found the book and a lengthy quotation from the novel:

> Grossman's eight hundred pages offer a complete spectacle of desolation and dehumanization.... Yet within that decomposition of human relations, within that sociology of misery, goodness persists. In the relation of one man to an other, goodness is possible. There is a long monologue where Ikonnikov – the character who expresses the ideas of the author – casts doubt upon all social sermonizing, that is, upon all reasonable organization with an ideology, with plans.... Every attempt to organize humanity fails. The only thing that remains undying is the goodness of everyday, ongoing life. Ikonnikov calls that 'the little act of goodness'.... this 'little goodness' is the sole positive thing.... [I]t is a goodness outside of every system, every religion, every social organization.[29]

In the course of Levinas's comments, the interviewer quotes from the text, but the passage makes little difference; he could have cited almost anything from that chapter.[30] No system houses the Good, nor can any evil harm or destroy what is really good. What Grossman calls "petty, thoughtless kindness," "senseless kindness," "a kindness outside any system of social or religious good" or "stupid kindness" is "what is most truly human in a human being." As Levinas notes, "it is as beautiful and powerless as dew." Such acts are not found within systems, that is, not prescribed or justified by systems; nor can systems engulf or annihilate them. "[H]uman qualities persist even on the edge of the grave, even at the door of the gas chamber." "The power of evil ... is impotent in the struggle against man."[31]

[27] Grossman, *Life and Fate*, Part II, Chapter 14, 391–403.
[28] *Is It Righteous to Be?*, 89; cf. 120.
[29] Ibid., 217–218.
[30] The citation is drawn from *Life and Fate*, 407–408.
[31] Grossman, *Life and Fate*, 408–410; cf. *Is It Righteous to Be?*, 218.

Levinas finds this letter extraordinarily congenial. He is moved by its optimism, by its commitment to goodness or kindness outside of systems, institutions, ideologies, something about how one acts toward the other person that is beyond theory, rules, and explanation and that is indestructible and permanent, albeit unique and particular. Furthermore, Levinas agrees that whatever this kindness or goodness is, it occurs in everyday life. It is what the human is all about; it is rare, in one sense, and yet it is fundamental and primary to human life in some sense or other. We can see, then, why it hardly matters for Levinas whether Ikonnikov really speaks for Grossman; what matters is how he seems to speak for Levinas. His is the voice of hope and the humane in the midst of the misery and despair of the twentieth century.

But one cannot and should not forget or mitigate the depth of the despair or the degree of the misery. Grossman does not, nor does Levinas read him that way.[32] Here I come to the last major reason why Levinas cites Grossman, as a true, accurate, and compelling witness to the crisis of the modern world in the twentieth century, of which Auschwitz is a part and the principal paradigm. Grossman paints a vast, grim, horrifying panorama of dehumanization and suffering. It is a world in crisis, where the victors and the victims are mirror images of one another, in which indeed there are no victors, only victims.

> [Grossman] is witness to the end of a certain Europe, the definitive end of the hope of instituting charity in the guise of a regime, the end of the socialist hope. The end of socialism, in the horror of Stalinism, is the greatest spiritual crisis in modern Europe. Marxism represented a generosity, whatever the way in which one understands the materialist doctrine which is its basis. There is in Marxism the recognition of the other.... But the noble hope consists in healing everything, in installing, beyond the chance of individual charity, a regime without evil. And the regime of charity becomes Stalinism and [complicitous] Hitlerian horror. That's what Grossman shows.... An absolutely overwhelming testimony and a complete despair.[33]

Levinas makes a multiple assessment, that Europe has suffered a spiritual crisis, that it involves the failure of socialism or Marxism and the spiraling of socialism into totalitarian violence and atrocity, and finally that this exposes a great truth: "there isn't any solution to the human drama by a change of regime, no system of salvation."[34] Politics must give way

[32] Grossman develops his picture of this despair and misery, starkly, in his subsequent novel, *Forever Flowing*.

[33] *Is It Righteous to Be?*, 80–81; cf. 120, 132; see also Levinas, *Proper Names*, 3.

[34] *Is It Righteous to Be?*, 81; cf. 132.

to something else, to "ethics without ethical system" or individual, discrete acts of goodness. This, moreover, is religion – not as it is, institutionalized and organized, but in spirit, as it might be, what "religion" really means. But here Levinas underlines the negative, what twentieth-century life has shown, that one cannot impose, legislate, or systematize goodness and charity. Grossman's novel shows this in its portrait of Stalinism and Nazism, which are images of each other.[35] If we rely on systems and ideology, the outcome is totalized domination and violence, despair.

> [*Life and Fate*] describes the situation in Europe at the time of Stalin and Hitler. Vassily Grossman represents this society as a completely dehumanized one. There is, of course, the life of the camps; it was the same thing under Hitler and under Stalin. Life seems to be premised upon the total contempt of respect of man, for the human person. Nevertheless, as concerns Stalin, that society came out of the search for a liberated humanity. That Marxism could have turned into Stalinism is the greatest offense to the cause of humanity, for Marxism carried a hope for humanity; this was perhaps one of the greatest psychological shocks for the European of the twentieth century.[36]

Grossman, earlier in his career, in 1946, gave a very early report of the Nazi death camp at Treblinka and later coedited Russian documents dealing with the Nazi persecutions in Russia, *The Black Book*. But here, in these interviews, Levinas seems to focus his attention on Stalinism as the nemesis of Marxist socialism and the larger implication, that even the little, discrete act of goodness that remains is "lost and deformed as soon as it seeks organization and universality and system, as soon as it opts for doctrine, a treatise of politics and theology, a party, a state, and even a church."[37] Hitler, Nazism, and the death camps are not discussed independently or on their own; their significance is swept up by that of Stalinism and its horrors. Levinas sees the twentieth century as a single story, as a failure of "regimes of charity," their transformation into regimes of violence and oppression.[38] This portrait calls to mind an image from Plato's *Republic*: in an unjust polis the philosopher survives by taking shelter in caves and caverns, hidden from the storms of public life.[39] But Levinas's attack on systems, institutions, regimes, and ideologies is more pointed and much more global.

[35] The opposition to all forms of totalitarianism and particularly to Nazi fascism and Stalinism recalls similar themes in Hannah Arendt's famous *The Origins of Totalitarianism*, first published in 1951.

[36] *Is It Righteous to Be?*, 216–217.

[37] Ibid., 206–207.

[38] In *Forever Flowing* Grossman's indictment is even more powerful and direct; see 176–237; cf. Levinas, *Entre Nous*, 119–120.

[39] See *Rep.* 496c-e.

Levinas's attraction to Grossman's great novel is expressed in his recollection of details and his impressions regarding its large themes. My own reading of *Life and Fate*, underscored by reading *Forever Flowing*, suggests that Grossman's great themes were freedom and domination. For Levinas, we might say, they were goodness or kindness and domination. Clearly the novel represented for Levinas a powerful and even decisive teaching about the human condition: the nemesis of totality in "total domination" and the possibility of salvation only in particular, isolated, "senseless" acts of kindness. In short, the twentieth century – Stalinism, Nazism, the labor camps and death camps – exposes, on the one hand, the depths of need, misery, suffering, and atrocity that mark the encounters of people and, on the other, the primordial character of charity and kindness that can arise out of such encounters. These are not the only horrific events of the century – elsewhere Levinas includes nuclear weapons, terrorism, Cambodia, unemployment, and many other features of the past century – but they are emblematic ones.[40]

I have been looking at Levinas's comments on Grossman's *Life and Fate* for several reasons. For a decade or so, at the end of his life, Levinas cited the novel regularly; it meant a good deal to him. He was upset by it and at the same time elevated by it. I wanted to see if we could determine why and to see why he chose to give it such frequent attention, to use it, as it were, as a pedagogical device. We found at least two reasons for Levinas's attraction to the novel. First, he saw examples in Grossman's descriptions of the everyday expression or manifestation of what he calls the "epiphany of the face of the other" and "responsibility for the other," and he takes Grossman to have given these isolated cases a preeminent status in modern life. Levinas is always looking for examples that illustrate responsibility and goodness as he understands it – acts of recognizing the other person's need and demands and responding with acts of gratuitous giving that are unexplainable, almost dissonant, "senseless" in one sense but ultimately meaningful in another. Second, Levinas sees Grossman as an extraordinarily effective witness to the crisis of the modern world as a crisis of "regimes of goodness" that develop into regimes of "total domination."[41] This reflection on Grossman is part of Levinas's own judgement about the failure of modernity and hence about the failure of politics and the importance of ethics and religion. All of these terms – "politics," "ethics," and

[40] For a list of the catastrophes of the twentieth century, see "Peace and Proximity," in *Alterity and Transcendence*, 132, 135.

[41] This expression is Arendt's. It is the title of the famous last subsection of *The Origins of Totalitarianism*.

"religion" – are terms of art for him, so to use them here is anticipatory at best and hence unclear. Perhaps it would be more accurate to say that Levinas finds Grossman congenial for exposing the failures of politics, ethics, and religion as we have known them and for suggesting how ethics and religion might genuinely be understood and revitalized.

In addition, I believe that by looking at Levinas on *Life and Fate*, we see his philosophical views engaged in a task of literary interpretation and political, historical assessment. This discussion, then, enables us to watch Levinas's philosophy function for him personally as a lens through which to judge human conduct and the political realities of the twentieth century prior to and during the Second World War. These judgements become a kind of hypothesis. We can now ask if other things that he writes or says confirm this assessment of the crisis of the modern world. Do they provide a perspective from which that assessment would arise? Does such a perspective justify, contribute to, or elicit this assessment and make sense of it? Moreover, we can ask if his remarks about Auschwitz and Nazi totalitarianism fit the pattern of these remarks and, if so, in what way.

Furthermore, I wanted to begin our examination of Levinas by looking at how Levinas's philosophy expresses itself in and about the everyday world in which we live. How is it a philosophy about ordinary, everyday life? Recently philosophers have thought deeply about everyday life or what some call the ordinary.[42] And not only philosophers. Literary critics too and historians have noted how the development in the twentieth century from modernism to postmodernism involves a set of shifts of concern – from high theory to mundane or prosaic expressions of belief, from the old intellectual history to so-called new intellectual history or *altagsgeschichte* [everyday history], from the development and construction of totalizing theories to the examination of fragmentary cultural expressions of people in the everyday, from the rare to the prosaic, from intellectual life to popular culture, from the mind to the body, from the dominantly male to the plurality of gender diversity, from a Eurocentric perspective to anti-colonialist pluralism, and so forth.[43] One even finds this shift expressed in the general deflationary attitude toward philosophy, associated with Wittgenstein in his later period and more recently with Richard Rorty, Stanley Cavell, and Bernard Williams and also with discussion about the limits of language and thought, the notion of point of view, the examination of skepticism, and much else. Against this background, Levinas

[42] Most explicitly, the everyday and the return to the ordinary are central themes in the work of Stanley Cavell.

[43] I am thinking especially of Michael André Bernstein, in *Foregone Conclusions* and elsewhere.

appears both novel and old-fashioned, modernist in some ways and post-modernist in others. In order to understand him, I believe that we must consider at some point how his philosophy is engaged with and is embedded in the everyday world. By starting with his attraction to Grossman's novel, a vivid and concrete descriptive panorama of people's thoughts and actions in ordinary life, albeit in extraordinary circumstances – the momentous days of fall and winter 1942–43 in Stalingrad, Moscow, and elsewhere in Russia, we have been able to watch Levinas as he appropriates and comments on the everyday or ordinary world. As we move, in later chapters, to direct examination and clarification of his philosophy, we can and should never forget this launching pad. On the one hand, it is in an important sense the origin of his thinking. On the other, it will provide vivid illustrations or examples to which we can return again and again, in order to test our interpretations of his more arcane and technical writings.

AUSCHWITZ AND LEVINAS'S THOUGHT

I want now to turn from Stalingrad to Levinas's discussion of Auschwitz. One of the many venues for *Life and Fate* is an unnamed Nazi death camp that is being constructed and used for the first time. Grossman juxtaposes what goes on there – among the events is the thematically important interrogation of Mostovsky and his reading of Ikonnikov's letter – with events in a Russian Siberian labor camp, and all of this with Stalingrad and Moscow. As the novel develops, we readers are to find it more and more difficult to distinguish how life is lived in them and hence the culture, the mindset of living in these places. But in "Signature" and elsewhere, in terms of Levinas's understanding of anti-Semitism and persecution and suffering, and with regard to his critical approach to Heidegger, the Nazi persecution and extermination of European Jewry, the Holocaust, plays a central role. I want to look at that here. Our questions are: what does the Holocaust mean to Levinas in terms of his historical and political judgments, and how does it fit into his overall understanding of the human condition in the twentieth century? What does Auschwitz tell us about the crisis of the modern world?

Levinas is informed about other treatments of Nazi totalitarianism. In 1985, in a eulogy to his longtime friend Vladimir Jankélévitch, he says,

> [N]o one is unaware that he condemned, beyond any possibility of pardon, the crime and the criminals of the Holocaust or Shoah. Jankélévitch never consented to the trivializing of these atrocities committed by Europeans in a Christian Europe, to view them, as sociologists, as a particular case of xenophobia or racism.

The horror of the crime committed against the human person and human life was no doubt the essence of what prompted the extreme firmness of Jankélévitch's condemnation.[44]

The Holocaust must not be treated as simply another act of hatred or racism; it is "the horror of the crime committed against the human person and human life." Not only does this comment seem to reflect Levinas's own accord; it also alludes to the way in which some German historians and scholars were trivializing the Nazi atrocities – perhaps a reference to the *Historikerstreit* and the kinds of criticisms leveled at Martin Broszat, Andreas Hillgruber, and Ernst Nolte – and not at them alone. Levinas takes these events very seriously; we will learn something by looking at his comments and what he says about what Auschwitz was and what it means. Many of these occur in occasional remarks and in passing.

In his influential anthology, *Face to Face with Levinas*, Richard Cohen includes Richard Kearney's interview with Levinas, first published in 1984. Near the end, Levinas comments on Marxism and socialism as utopian and on the way in which Marxism was "utterly compromised by Stalinism."[45] He sees "Marx's critique of Western idealism" as an "ethical conscience ... demanding that theory be converted into a concrete praxis of concern for the other."[46] Here is the "regime of charity" that Stalinism compromised and abandoned, as we have already seen. But in this remark Levinas goes on to associate this postwar climate of despair with the student revolts of 1968:

The 1968 Revolt in Paris was a revolt of sadness, because it came after the Kruschev Report and the exposure of the corruption of the Communist Church. The year of 1968 epitomized the joy of despair, a last grasping at human justice, happiness, and perfection – after the truth had dawned that the communist ideal had degenerated into totalitarian bureaucracy. By 1968 only dispersed groups and rebellious pockets of individuals remained to seek their surrealist forms of salvation, no longer confident of a collective movement of humanity, no longer assured that Marxism could survive the Stalinist catastrophe as the prophetic messenger of history.[47]

There are clear echoes in this text (or interview) of Levinas's reflections on Grossman – the fall of Marxist socialism into Stalinism with its "totalitarian bureaucracy," the small pockets of group and individual hopes with their "surrealist forms of salvation," the elements of sadness, joy, and

[44] Levinas, *Outside the Subject*, 88.
[45] *Face to Face with Levinas* (ed. Cohen), 33.
[46] Ibid.; cf. Levinas, *Nine Talmudic Readings*, 97–98.
[47] *Face to Face with Levinas* (ed. Cohen), 33.

despair. But the tie to the events of 1968 has an ominous side: it exposes the conflict between ethics and politics, between Judaism and politics, when the forces of revolution become political and turn against the Jews as they did in 1933 and then again in 1968.

The 1969 *Colloques des intellectuels juifs de langue francaise* had, as its theme, "Youth and Revolution in Jewish Consciousness."[48] In the course of his commentary on *Baba Metsia* 83a-83b, Levinas calls attention to the role of the Jewish people in history and the relation between politics and the Jews:

> But those who shouted, a few months ago, 'We are all German Jews' in the streets of Paris were after all not making themselves guilty of petit-bourgeois meanness. German Jews in 1933, foreigners to the course of history and to the world, Jews, in other words, point to that which is most fragile and most persecuted in the world. More persecuted than the proletariat itself, which is exploited but not persecuted. A race cursed, not through its genes, but through its destiny of misfortune, and probably through its books, which call misfortune upon those who are faithful to them and who transmit them outside of any chromosomes.[49]

One of the student leaders of the events of May 1968 was Daniel Cohn-Bendit, a son of German Jews who had emigrated to France in 1933. When, on May 22, 1968, Cohn-Bendit was refused permission to reenter France from Germany, student demonstrators took up the chant "We are all German Jews" as an act of solidarity with him and, as Levinas sees it, as an expression of their role as the persecuted.[50] Stalinism, the decline of Marxism, the student revolt of 1968, and Auschwitz crystallize in Levinas's mind with the role of Jews as persecuted victims.

The point of these twentieth-century events is to expose the depth of persecution and suffering that modern society and culture has generated and to locate the Jew at the center of the crisis of modernity as the site of this persecution. And what does this persecution mean, in Levinas's terms? On the one hand, of course, persecution is oppression and an agency of atrocity and suffering. But, on the other, persecution is what causes this agency or permits it, the failure of concern and care. For Levinas, however,

[48] See *Nine Talmudic Readings*, 94 note. For discussion, see Simon Critchley, "Persecution Before Exploitation: A Non-Jewish Israel," in *Levinas and Politics*, ed. Charmaine Coyle and Simon Critchley, *Parallax* 8:24 (July–September 2002), 71–77.

[49] *Nine Talmudic Readings*, 113.

[50] See ibid., 119 n.5. Discussion of the events of 1968 in Paris, and elsewhere, can be found in: Sylvia Harvey, *May '68 and Film Culture*, which also includes a helpful bibliography; Arthur Marwick, *The Sixties*, 615; George Katsiaficas, *The Imagination of the New Left: A Global Analysis of 1968*, 104; Alain Schnapp and Pierre Vidal-Naquet, *The French Student Uprising November 1967–June 1968*, 211–212.

the notion of "persecution," as we shall see, is a technical one; to be persecuted is to be confronted with the face of the other person and called to respond. To be persecuted, for Levinas, is "to bear responsibility for everything ... to be responsible despite oneself...."[51]

At one level, then, Levinas aligns Nazism as totalitarian and as a dictatorship with Stalinism. Both are emblems of overwhelming domination. But at another level Nazism and the death camps are distinguished by anti-Semitism and unbounded persecution. Auschwitz is about suffering, persecution, and oppression, or, perhaps more accurately, Auschwitz is these things. This is what coordinates Auschwitz with the Jew and the Jew with Jewish books and their critical teaching. I will return to these specifically Jewish issues only later in this book, when we can ask what Levinas takes Judaism to be about in the light of his philosophy and his ethics. Insofar as Auschwitz is linked with Jews, however, we can see even now that its meaning concerns persecution and suffering. In the essays where he deals with Auschwitz explicitly and thematically, it is this association with suffering that is central.[52]

One of the most comprehensive and thoughtful discussions of Levinas on the Holocaust with which I am familiar is an essay by Richard Cohen, "What Good is the Holocaust? On Suffering and Evil."[53] As Cohen points out, Levinas examines evil and suffering in four relatively short articles, and it is in them too that he clarifies what the Holocaust means and how it is associated with evil and suffering.[54] What does Auschwitz indicate about twentieth-century society and culture? Is there something distinctive about the atrocities of Nazi totalitarianism? Is Auschwitz a watershed in history? What characterizes our epoch as post-Holocaust? Cohen identifies one role that the Holocaust plays, according to Levinas, in twentieth-century history and culture: "for Levinas, the 'meaning' – or meaninglessness – of the Holocaust ... is found precisely in the 'end of theodicy'."[55] The Holocaust

[51] Levinas, *Nine Talmudic Readings*, 114–115.

[52] See Levinas, *Beyond the Verse*, xvi; "Ethics and Politics," in *The Levinas Reader* (ed. Hand), 289–291. In American history, culture, and literature, the role that the Jew and anti-Semitism plays for Levinas in France, particularly with the memory of the Dreyfus affair so indelibly marked in his mind, is played by slavery and the memory of the Civil War and the subsequent history of racism in America. This theme is prominent in Stanley Cavell's reading of Thoreau and Emerson. For a fascinating discussion comparing philosophy in French culture and in America in Cavell, see James Conant, "Cavell and the Concept of America," in Russell B. Goodman (ed.), *Contending with Stanley Cavell* (Oxford University Press, 2005), 55–81, especially 70–71.

[53] Richard Cohen, *Ethics, Exegesis and Philosophy*, Chapter 8, 266–282.

[54] The four articles are "Useless Suffering," "Transcendence and Evil," "The Scandal of Evil," and "Loving the Torah More than God."

[55] Cohen, *Ethics, Exegesis and Philosophy*, 268–269; cf. *Is It Righteous to Be?*, 40: "And still, today, I tell myself that Auschwitz was committed by the civilization of transcendental idealism."

has no meaning; its suffering is useless or meaningless. Cohen cites from Levinas's paper "Useless Suffering" to support this claim. This is what Levinas says [my citation is somewhat more extensive than Cohen's]:

> Perhaps the most revolutionary fact of our twentieth-century consciousness – but it is also an event in Sacred History – is that of the destruction of all balance between Western thought's explicit and implicit theodicy and the forms that suffering and its evil are taking on in the very unfolding of the century. This is the century that in thirty years has known two world wars, the totalitarianisms of right and left, Hitlerism and Stalinism, Hiroshima, the Gulag, and the genocides of Auschwitz and Cambodia. This is the century that is drawing to a close in the obsessive fear of the return of everything these barbaric names stood for: suffering and evil inflicted deliberately, but in a manner no reason sets limits to, in the exasperation of a reason become political and detached from ethics.
>
> Among these events the Holocaust of the Jewish people under the reign of Hitler seems to me the paradigm of gratuitous human suffering, in which evil appears in its diabolical horror.... The disproportion between suffering and every theodicy was shown at Auschwitz with a glaring, obvious clarity.[56]

I think that this is a crucial text in Levinas's writings concerning the significance of suffering and evil for Western culture and the special role of Auschwitz in the history of evil. Here Levinas points to the incommensurability of suffering and evil in *reality* – and he names the events and phenomena he has in mind, including the world wars, Stalinism, Hitler, totalitarianisms, genocides, and such – and in *thought*. He points to the challenge Auschwitz makes to our cognitive and systematic capacity to rationalize experience and events, that is, to theodicy. Reason fails to deal with the human reality of suffering and the need for kindness and goodness when it becomes *political* and is *detached* from *ethics*. Auschwitz is the "paradigm" of this extraordinary suffering and evil; it is the primary location of this failure of politics and of reason, of this "end of theodicy."[57]

For Levinas, then, the twentieth century is remarkable for its horrors and atrocities, for its suffering and its evil, which are beyond thought. Moreover, Auschwitz is therefore not unique but rather exemplary. It is a paradigmatic, representative manifestation of evil so extreme that it somehow, as we shall see later, destroys all theodicy. At this point, we can take note of this special role, which we will be able to understand adequately only when we have examined Levinas's ethical metaphysics more fully.

In "Useless Suffering" and in the other essays that Cohen cites, Levinas responds to Emil Fackenheim on the importance of Auschwitz and the

56 Levinas, "Useless Suffering," in *Entre Nous*, 97; cf. 161–162 in Cohen's translation of this essay.

57 I shall return to this theme, "the end of theodicy," in Chapter 8.

obligation to respond to it, and he ties Jewish life to Auschwitz, suffering, and persecution. Setting aside its implications for Jewish life, it is sufficient for now to note Levinas's judgement about twentieth-century culture and the Holocaust and to understand it in a preliminary fashion. Levinas points to several features of the crisis that we have already seen emerge in his comments on Grossman. First, Western culture and society in the twentieth century mark a failure of institutions and theories to realize goodness. Such culture manifests a failure of systems, social and ideological, to bring about the good life – to feed the hungry, reduce poverty and homelessness, care for the sick, and provide the resources and opportunities for living a full and healthy life. In fact, these systems become totalitarian, dominating, and evil. Second, this decline marks a failure of politics itself, of organized, bureaucratic strategies to enhance and support human life. Third, it is about the limits of reason, both actively in practical experience and theoretically in our systems of thought, to comprehend human suffering, to make sense of it and hence "domesticate" it. An honest exposure to the real experience of suffering and evil leaves thought impotent and unsatisfied. The "end of theodicy" refers to a condition in which our attempts to understand and explain everything, including suffering, evil, genocide, and such, simply fail; they reach a limit and cannot go beyond it. We become or should become humble before such suffering, so that the only possible and sensitive response becomes opposition and any kind of acceptance or complacency becomes impossible, inconceivable.

This kind of opposition to suffering is a dimension of what Levinas here calls "ethics." In *Life and Fate*, Levinas saw isolated acts of senseless kindness; he was stirred by the episode of the Russian woman, filled with anger and hatred, handing the piece of bread to the German officer rather than using the rock in her hand to kill him. Here he calls such an incident to mind when he refers to a reason that should give up being political and reattach itself to ethics. What he suggests is that in the face of useless suffering, we need senseless kindness. In place of politics and ideology, we need humanity, goodness, and ethics. In place of systems and totalities, we need an acknowledgment and realization of the utterly particular. This would be a "redemption of the everyday," in a sense, not a new version of the old metaphysics and mythologies, but a new version of a new metaphysics and a new philosophy – a metaphysical ethics of a new kind.

Thus far we have watched Levinas scan some terrain, specifically the political and cultural history of the twentieth century. We have observed him making some large-scale judgements about the "crisis of modernity" in the century. Levinas is not primarily a political thinker or a political, cultural critic. He does not say a great deal or work out a critique in great detail like the Frankfurt school or like Jürgen Habermas, Michael Walzer, John Rawls, and Charles Taylor. His interests lie elsewhere.[58] Nonetheless, as we have watched him, several points of interest have emerged. We would like Levinas to say more about his doubts about theories, ideologies, and systems. We also would like to hear what he means by ethics and small, isolated acts of kindness and why they are "senseless" and yet have the primacy he seems to assume they have. And if Auschwitz and the other horrors of the century mark the "end of theodicy," is this the end of productive, useful, and meaningful thought about the world and especially thought about suffering and evil in it? Is this, in a way, the end of religion and perhaps also the end of philosophy? Why was Levinas so moved by the way in which a person's neck and back can express her misery and suffering and by the act of senseless kindness of giving a hated enemy one's last piece of bread? These are questions that need to be answered.

Levinas's comments on *Life and Fate* might tempt us to think that Levinas is unconditionally opposed to ideologies and systems of thought, political and otherwise, and this temptation might be strengthened by treating his reaction to Auschwitz and his conception of the "end of theodicy" as registering a similar indictment. We might, that is, be persuaded that Levinas has nothing good to say about traditional systems of thought and the role they have played and do play in our lives. Furthermore, his comments on the encounter with the face, the acknowledgment of the other person's suffering and despair, and on the response of gratuitous kindness, uncalled-for and remarkable, might lead us to conclude that the occurrence of such acts ought to be the goal of human life, that what we ought to aim for are such discrete episodes of unexpected, almost "irrational" acts of generosity to others. Interpreting Levinas in this way is tempting indeed, and many have succumbed to just this temptation. Levinas says many things, we shall see, that encourage such a view, and they have led many interpreters to read him as extraordinarily radical and perhaps as a kind of ethical anarchist who opposes systematic thinking,

[58] As we shall see, however, his thinking has important implications for political issues and political life. The most comprehensive treatment of the relationship between his thinking and the political domain, in book form, is Howard Caygill's *Levinas and the Political*. Also of importance are the essays by Simon Critchley, Jacques Derrida, Ernesto Laclau, and Richard Rorty in *Deconstruction and Pragmatism*, edited by Chantal Mouffe.

grand theories, general principles, institutions, and organized ways of life in favor of episodic eruptions of ethical purity that are without reason or preparation or purpose beyond themselves. Hence, in addition to the questions I just raised, we are left with this one, which is perhaps the most important of all: Is this radical reading of Levinas as a kind of irrationalist and "moral saint" a compelling one? Is it required by what he says? Does it capture, best of all, the spirit of his teaching?

CHAPTER TWO

How to Read Levinas: Normativity and Transcendental Philosophy

In Chapter 1, I tried to observe Levinas doing what a philosopher engaged with ethical, political, and religious matters in the twentieth century might be expected to do, to comment on and consider critically the crisis of the century and events and episodes within it. Now it is time to turn to Levinas's philosophical thinking and writings themselves in order later to answer the question: what is the relationship between his philosophy and the judgments and assessments we have seen him making? This will require that we take a brief, preliminary look at the content of his "ethical metaphysics" and begin to examine it by asking what Levinas is doing in the course of that thinking, what kind of thinking it is. In the early part of this chapter, then, I will be making a first pass through his thinking, especially in its early development, a project that will unavoidably use terms yet to be clarified as well as paraphrases that may simplify too much and have a certain impropriety and vagueness about them. I will also avoid argumentation, excessive clarification, problems and questions, and all the trappings of careful analysis. That will come later.

A PRELIMINARY SKETCH

In order to sketch this picture of Levinas's "ethical metaphysics" I am going to begin by drawing on some relatively early works. These include *Time and the Other* (1947) [hereinafter TO], "Is Ontology Fundamental?" (1951), "The Ego and Totality" (1954), "Philosophy and the Idea of the Infinite" (1957), *Totality and Infinity* (1961) [hereinafter TI], and "Transcendence and Height" (1962). At times I may use some terminology that Levinas introduces and develops subsequent to this early period; if I do, I will indicate clearly when the terminology is employed. In the late 1960s and throughout the 1970s, Levinas does modify and expand his basic terms, concepts, and metaphors, at least to a certain extent. Some commentators argue that he does more than modify and expand, that he substantially revises, his philosophy; I will say something about that issue later. For the moment, I set it aside and will call attention to some important modifications as we go along, in subsequent chapters. But on the basic issue of this chapter, his approach to philosophy and the kind of thinking he is engaged in, I believe that he remains firm. For this reason, I think we are best served by outlining his early account, at least for the moment, in as straightforward a way as possible.

In TO and TI Levinas gives an account that appears narrative, like a philosophical story or fable. For all their substantive differences, an account like Hobbes's account of the establishment of the civil state from an original state of nature or the account of John Rawls's social contract theory might seem to be reasonable analogues. Later, we might want to ask how close the analogies are or how inadequate; for now it is sufficient to realize that Levinas's account of the origins of society, ethics, and such is not an anomaly, notwithstanding its own peculiar features. But just as Hobbes never claimed that the state of nature ever existed in a pure form for all of humankind, nor Rawls that anyone actually lived in the "original position" prior to the decision to formulate principles of justice, so Levinas's account does not depend upon treating his narrative as a description of the origins and development of actual life. In fact, like those others, Levinas is giving an account of various features of human experience that are manifest in actual life but can be best illuminated by means of a narrative form, a genetical story.

Suppose we begin with a natural world filled with existing things, natural objects such as trees, rocks, mountains, stars, lakes, wind, and rain. For now, let us omit any items that are constructed or artificial and simply remain with natural things. Each of these things exists in a certain way, and Levinas tries to say something about this "existing" of things, as it is experienced in our lives, at moments when the particular features of things fade and we are left with a sense of sheer, anonymous existence. At this stage in Levinas's story, of course, we have not yet emerged, so in order to identify this basic *existing*, Levinas looks ahead at experiences of ours that point to it, experiences like fatigue and insomnia. This sheer existing is brooding and foreboding, like the relentlessness of being awake to someone who has insomnia and simply cannot sleep; it is an ominous presence – what Levinas calls *il ya* or *there is* – that is inescapable.[1] Now,

[1] Imagine Spinoza's substance in its active sense, as *natura naturans*, but thought of only as manifest at a certain level of complexity, not yet including human beings, who are percipient, cognitive, rational, and reflective. This is the pulse of existence that is manifest in each and every particular thing, everywhere in nature.

Levinas suggests, let us think of consciousness as "standing out from" this natural existing plenum. "Consciousness is the power to sleep," of tearing itself away or withdrawing from the insomnia attuned to and plagued by sheer existing, and even though Levinas presents this emergence as a state of pure sleepfulness, it in fact represents the state of being able to think about itself and its existence, of reflection. What arises with this emergence of consciousness is the "I" or the self.[2]

At this stage, then, we have the I, the particular self, a natural organic being with consciousness, living in the world, and a world of things in which this I lives. Levinas's next step is to consider how this living self responds to or lives in its world, amid the natural things that surround it. My primary way of living in the world, Levinas calls "enjoyment." "The world is an ensemble of nourishment.... To stroll is to enjoy the fresh air, not for health but for the air.... It is an ecstatic experience – being outside oneself – but limited by the object."[3] Such enjoyment involves sensation and thought, but it is fuller than mere sensation or mere thought. It is a kind of involvement with the world, not use but satisfaction, incorporation, and proximity. In a sense, I am at home in the world around me, not unqualifiedly, of course, but sufficiently to appreciate eating, breathing, exploring, viewing, feeling, and enjoying what is there for me.[4]

At first I am totally invested in myself. Then I turn to the world, that is, to things around me, for enjoyment and nourishment; I sense it too and think about it and what it means to me. But I am still alone, as it were. I may now have some perspective on the world and on myself in it, but I am alone, and I even tend to lose myself in a universal view of the world.[5] "The world offers the subject participating in existing in the form of enjoyment, and consequently permits it to exist at a distance from itself. The subject is absorbed in the object it absorbs, and nevertheless keeps a distance with regard to that object.... It is not just the disappearance of the self, but self-forgetfulness, as a first abnegation."[6] Levinas calls this state, in which "knowledge never encounters anything truly other in the world," "the profound truth of idealism."[7] That is, what we later, philosophically, call idealism, the view that assimilates the world to the self or to a cosmic self or spirit or mind, is in fact already grounded in this fundamental

[2] See TO, Part I, 39–57. For a helpful account, see Michael Purcell, *Levinas and Theology* (Cambridge, 2006), 88–94, 95–98, 128–130.

[3] TO, Part II, 63.

[4] Cf. TI, 109–121.

[5] TO, Part III, 67.

[6] Ibid.

[7] Ibid., 68.

feature of the human condition, that it includes a "moment" in which the self is alone in the world and even takes the world into itself from a wholly detached, nonparticular point of view.

As I pointed out earlier, Levinas does not mean that as individuals we are ever alone in the world, as if existing in some Eden or state of nature. Nor does he mean that we are ever actually alone. But there are these features in our existence or these dimensions of our inhabiting the world, living within and from it, becoming aware of it and coming to know it and ourselves in it.[8] What does Levinas mean, however, when he calls our knowledge of this world an "idealism?" For now, it is sufficient to recognize that this claim is associated with Levinas's use of the word "totality" and the ideas of same and other. That is, when I am fully at home in the world and achieve some understanding of it, I grasp it as a totality or as a systematic, orderly whole, from my point of view as a knowing agent, but in terms of general concepts, ideas, principles, and so forth. I organize and order the world and comprehend it; Levinas calls the "I" the "same" and says that in this way the same absorbs the other into itself or forms the other to itself. Particular as my existence is, I think in generalities, commonalities, and I grasp the world by incorporating everything into these concepts and ideas as if into a container. In this sense, all such knowing is a kind of idealism, of taming the world and domesticating it to my capacities and venue, as if my capacities were wholly general and detached and impersonal. I make everything thinkable and knowable by drawing everything within the borders of these conceptual capacities. This achievement of sameness or homogeneity is one outcome of my inhabiting the world.

I skip to Levinas's main idea:[9] this solitude of the I inhabiting the world is shattered or interrupted. The I is not alone; there is an other person whose face I confront and experience. In *Time and the Other*, Levinas puts it this way: "... the Other is what I myself am not. The Other is this, not because of the Other's character, or physiognomy, or psychology, but because of the Other's very alterity. The Other is, for example, the weak, the poor, 'the orphan and the widow,' whereas I am the rich or the powerful."[10] In social life, I am always confronted by another particular person, who is near or far, friend or foe, present or absent, but always in the world with me and more importantly over against me or before me.

[8] TI, 109–174.

[9] In the text, Levinas moves from the same to the other via consideration of suffering, evil, and death; only then does he arrive at the other person, as an unconditionally other that completely negates the self when it is encountered. We shall say more about this later.

[10] TO, 83.

This person is different from me fundamentally – prior to considering her features or character, her height, complexion, her features, or the color of her hair, her humor and mood, whatever. She is a person like me, but because her perspective, her experiences, are inaccessible to me, she is radically separated from me and different from me. And her difference is all about what she imposes upon me simply in virtue of being there, before me. What she imposes is dependence and need, integrity and demand. Her presence, before it says anything else to me, says "let me live," "let me be here too," "feed me," "allow me to share the world and be nourished by it too." I am imposed upon, called into question, beseeched and commanded, and thereby I am responsible, Levinas says. In *Totality and Infinity*, Levinas says: "I must have been in relation with something I do not live from." This relation occurs as an "encounter [with] the indiscrete face of the Other that calls me into question. The Other … paralyzes possession, which he contests by his epiphany in the face.… I welcome the Other who presents himself in my home by opening my home to him."[11] My thinking about the world and understanding it is also, in this way, like my inhabiting and enjoying what nature provides me, interrupted. Something outside or prior to my thinking confronts me: it is the demand and need of another person, of each and every other person. In this way, I am responsible before I am an observer or explainer or interpreter; I am, in a sense, a moral agent before I am a cognitive one. Levinas even associates this "epiphany of the face of the other" or encounter with the other person's need and demand with "language." What he means is that words, communication, and speech all arise out of and are embedded in a prelinguistic relationship of encounter between myself and a particular other person. This relationship, moreover, has an ethical character; it is a relationship with the other person's "face," not with her appearance or features or whatever; it is with the fragility and dependence on me of her very being.[12]

I have been trying, in these paragraphs, to construct a very spare sketch of Levinas's account of what the human condition is, based on some early texts of his. Let me reiterate: this is a very preliminary outline and merely that. My intention is a limited one, to provide us with enough detail to ask the question that I now want to pose: what is the *status* of this account? In giving it and developing it, *what is Levinas doing*? Is this a philosophical account? Is it empirical in one way or other? Is it more than empirical? Is it

[11] TI, 170–171.

[12] TI, 171–174, 197–201, 204–214.

an "ethical metaphysics," and what might it mean to say that for Levinas this account frames an "ethics as first philosophy?"[13]

INTERPRETING LEVINAS'S APPROACH

Commentators often note that Levinas does not thematically discuss methodological questions; he even goes so far as to denigrate any over-indulgence in such matters. This judgment is correct. Levinas may have many reasons for his dismissal of methodological questions. But there are just as many reasons, if not more, why we need to think about them. If we are to understand his writing and his thinking, we need to understand the precise context for what he says and does. We need to understand what he is claiming and under what constraints. Even at this stage, before we have examined more fully his views, his analyses and arguments, and more, we can see that the assessments and observations we watched Levinas make in the public and political domain ought to be related to the sketch we have just given. But it is not clear or obvious how that relationship should be or might be conceived. This is the sort of thing we now need to consider.

Levinas may be thought to have answered our concerns explicitly and precisely. In the "Preface" to *Totality and Infinity*, he says that his method is the "phenomenological method" and that "the way we are describing to work back and remain this side of objective certitude resembles what has come to be called the transcendental method...."[14] Moreover, referring to Edmund Husserl, he notes that "intentional analysis is the search for the concrete."[15] He clarifies what this intentional analysis involves: "notions held under the direct gaze of the thought that defines them are nevertheless, unbeknown to this naive thought, revealed to be implanted in horizons unsuspected by thought; these horizons endow them with a meaning." Levinas says that in this way "an objectifying thought"

[13] At a crucial moment in TO, a kind of turning point in the development of the work, Levinas stops to make a remark about method that is very revealing. Having developed part of the story that I have outlined, he says: "I have just described a dialectical situation. I am now going to show a concrete situation where this dialectic is accomplished. It is impossible for me to explain this method at length here; I have resorted to it again and again. One sees in any event that it is not phenomenological to the end." Like Hegel's dialectic in *The Phenomenology of Spirit*, Levinas has set out an itinerary or developmental account that reveals the layers or dimensions of human existence and finally arrives at a primordial level; he now proposes to identify and examine in a way like the "phenomenological" a concrete situation that reveals the most fundamental and primordial level in an especially perspicuous way, even though, as he warns, at a certain point it ceases to be phenomenological, strictly speaking. We shall see exactly what he means in what follows.

[14] TI, 28, 25.

[15] TI, 28.

overflows with "a forgotten experience from which it lives." This is called a "deduction" – whereby "the formal structure of thought" is broken up "into events which this structure dissimulates, but which sustain it and restore its concrete significance."[16] Here we have an explicit admission that Levinas's method is transcendental phenomenology or something akin to it and that its goal is to expose forgotten or hidden horizons of meaning that underlie our normal, objective experience of things and our thoughts about them. Would that things were so simple!

I do not think that there is any doubt that throughout his career Levinas thought of his thinking as a mode or development of Husserlian phenomenology.[17] Broadly speaking, he saw himself as casting light on a forgotten or hidden, hitherto unnoticed, layer or level of meaning within our everyday experience that has a primacy for human (social) living. In a sense, he saw himself as calling attention to a "regime of meaning" that we take for granted, pay insufficient attention to, depend upon, and should attend to more fully in order to become as human as we can become. One way to clarify what his method is and what status his thinking has, what he is doing in thinking as he does, would be to look substantively at his analyses and to clarify how they work and what they seem to accomplish. In a sense, the remainder of this book will seek to do that, not always explicitly but at least indirectly. In this chapter, I want to set the stage for any attempt to clarify these matters.[18]

I will begin by discussing an important paper by Robert Bernasconi on reading *Totality and Infinity* published in 1989. In returning to that work after twenty-five years, Bernasconi notices that Levinas's face-to-face relation is treated in two ways by interpreters.[19] "Some interpreters understand it as a concrete experience that we can recognize in our lives. Other commentators have understood the face-to-face relation to be the condition for the possibility of ethics and indeed of all economic existence and

[16] TI, 28; cf. 44–45. See also *Of God Who Comes to Mind*, 152–165 and especially 15–32.

[17] For a very interesting and helpful discussion of these issues, see John E. Drabinski, *Sensibility and Singularity: The Problem of Phenomenology in Levinas*. Drabinski focuses on Levinas's later work *Otherwise Than Being*, although he does touch on the earlier writings. There are, as one might expect, numerous treatments of Levinas's debt to Husserl.

[18] A standard way of doing that would be to discuss the phenomenological method in Husserl and Heidegger, especially in the light of what Levinas wrote about both, including his Husserl book and his essays on Husserl and on Heidegger. I may say a little about these matters but only a little. My approach will largely, however, be a different one.

[19] The distinction between these two interpretations of the status of the face-to-face relation, as drawn by Bernasconi, is appropriated and employed, for their own purposes, by Tamra Wright, *The Twilight of Jewish Philosophy*, 16–22, and by Robert Drabinski, *Sensibility and Singularity*, passim.

knowledge."[20] Bernasconi calls the former an "empirical" reading and the latter a "transcendental" one, and he remarks that "Levinas himself seems unable to decide between these rival interpretations."[21] Let me use this distinction, between an *empirical* reading and a *transcendental* one, not as a device for characterizing differences in the interpretation of Levinas but rather as an instrument for investigating what Levinas himself is doing.

Is the face-to-face encounter a "concrete experience," or is it a "transcendental condition," or is it neither or both? What would it mean to say that the face-to-face encounter between the self and the other person, for each and every other, is a concrete experience?[22] I think that the point of this question is to ask whether the event of one person confronting another particular person in the way Levinas describes as face-to-face occurs, or can occur, in ordinary everyday life. Is it something that happens in the course of such life, intentionally or by happenstance? Can we aim to engage the other this way or aim to create opportunities for such encounters to occur? Are our lives diminished if we fail to have face-to-face encounters?

At first glance, we might be inclined to think that Levinas clearly acknowledges this possibility and might even be thought to idealize such encounters. We need only recall the two episodes from *Life and Fate* that he cites so frequently, the act of the Russian woman who hands a piece of bread to the German officer and Yevgenia's encounter with the necks and backs of those in line in front of her at the Lubyanka prison. Both seem to be episodes of a particular face-to-face encounter. Or more accurately, one is an engagement with the face, the other the kind and generous response to such an engagement. Furthermore, if human life is meaningful because it is oriented in terms of responsibility to and for the other, it must be a demand experienced in life that provides that orientation. Where, if not from particular experiences, would this sense of responsibility come from?[23]

20 Robert Bernasconi, "Re-reading *Totality and Infinity*," in *The Question of the Other*, ed. Charles Scott and Arlene Dallery (SUNY, 1989), 23.

21 See ibid. and also see Levinas, *Of God Who Comes to Mind*, 86–90, which is a response to an article on the subject of method by Theodore De Boer. We shall discuss De Boer later.

22 I prefer to call this the "episodic" interpretation of the face-to-face rather than the "empirical" or concrete-experience interpretation. The issue is not whether one self experiences another but rather whether the experience of the face of the other is a discrete, identifiable, singular event or episode. Does it occur? On this reading, which takes the face-to-face as an analogue to episodes like Martin Buber's I-Thou encounters or meetings, Levinas's view seems almost quasi-mystical, insofar as the experience or episode has a transcendent quality and is an event of a rare and special kind.

23 I think that it is unavoidable that in some sense or other the face-to-face does occur as an actually lived experience or, perhaps better, as one dimension of actually lived social experience. Levinas invests himself in examining experiences like insomnia, fatigue, and eros, precisely because they

At the same time, however, it seems utterly impossible that the face-to-face could occur in ordinary life. There are several reasons to be suspicious. First, Levinas says that the encounter with the face is somehow originary and promordial, prior to ontology and being, in his terms "an-archic." Ontology is the study of being or the thinking about being, and the domain of being is the world of everyday existence, of objects, life, experience, sensation, thought, and practical affairs. Any theoretical understanding we have is grounded in this world and is about it, in one sense or another. Only in the world of being do objects disclose themselves to us, and only there are they grasped by us. Hence, thought, language, and explanation are exclusive to the world of existing things, as are sensory experience and activity. But if the face is prior to or more original than what exists and presents itself to us, then it cannot be experienced, sensed, analyzed, grasped in concepts, thematized, and so forth. In short, it cannot be encountered in ordinary life; the "epiphany of the face" and the responsibility it calls forth are not episodes that occur. Levinas stretches his terminology in order to emphasize this fact; he denies that the face appears to us or is a phenomenon. Rather it *reveals* itself or is an *epiphany*.[24] It is *like* an appearance but not one. It is pre-perceptual, pre-linguistic, pre-conceptual, and pre-theoretical. Nonetheless, the individual self does engage with or encounter the face of the other person. Given this framework, however, it is hard to believe that this engagement is an everyday event or an ordinary – or even extraordinary – concrete experience.

Second, Levinas calls the epiphany of the face of the other "the infinite" or "exteriority," and he contrasts it with totality, which is the domain circumscribed, encompassed, and to a degree constructed by the self or the agent. In effect, what Levinas means is that the face is outside whatever is the object of our experience and thought. Totality is the domain of reason or mind or culture or theory. Hence, Levinas's point about the face and its presence to us is that it does not reveal itself in the ordinary ways, as an object of normal perception or of everyday concepts and thought. To be

are concrete, ordinary experiences and yet show us to be in touch with what he calls transcendence or the other, in one sense or another. Furthermore, it is precisely such episodes or concrete experiences that he subjects to phenomenological or quasi-phenomenological investigation, in order to expose what is regularly hidden from view. It is very clear, therefore, that the face-to-face is part of our ordinary lives and not some eccentric or anomalous experience, such as a mystical experience or an ecstatic one.

[24] "Epiphany" is a theological expression for God's revelation. Levinas often uses it to refer to the way in which the face of the other person is revealed to the self. Like all the religious and theological vocabulary Levinas employs, this term is meant to call attention to the fact that the face-to-face and human responsibility are matters of the highest importance to us and worthy of our loftiest sentiments, our sense of awe and aspiration.

sure, he says, we do encounter the face – in a sense – and Descartes's claim that we have an idea of the infinite is a groping in the direction of saying this and affirming it, as Levinas sees it.[25] But Descartes does not appreciate either what the infinite is or what it means to have an idea of it, that is, to grasp it. Descartes thinks that the idea of the infinite is an idea like other ideas, at least in many ways, and also an idea of God. Levinas not only reinterprets the sense in which the idea of the infinite is an encounter with God, but also argues that as an idea it is unique, that is, unlike having other ideas. The idea of the infinite just *is* the encounter with the face of the other. Basically, then, if ordinary life occurs within the broad confines of totality, the face cannot be encountered therein or in that way. Descartes's notion of having an idea of the infinite, as Levinas sees it, cannot designate an everyday experience even if it can designate some kind of experience – or quasi-experience.

Moreover, for these reasons, Levinas's method cannot be phenomenological, strictly speaking; it can only be like it, one might argue. This is a third reason for doubting that the face-to-face can occur in ordinary life as a discrete episode. As Levinas points out, phenomenology is the study of intentionality, of consciousness as directed at objects or, perhaps more accurately, at the meaning of objects or objects as meaning something in our experience of them. It is a descriptive examination of both the subjective and objective dimensions or aspects of things as they appear to us – exactly how this appearing occurs, for various types of intentionality or consciousness, for various types of things, and so forth.[26] Fundamentally, then, phenomenology is the study of appearing, but, as we have seen, Levinas goes to great lengths to distinguish the face from an appearance. Now, one reason for this distinction is that the face is hidden or occluded in normal experience. This could mean that the face is a hidden horizon or aspect of an actual perception or experience, analogous to the backside of a cube seen from the front or to other features of Napoleon known only as the general who fought and was defeated at Waterloo. But this interpretation hardly seems radical enough for the status Levinas ascribes to the face. It cannot just be a hidden or undisclosed dimension of an actually perceived person. It is hidden, but it is not contingently hidden; in a sense, the face is *necessarily hidden*. It does not just happen to be the case that because of circumstances one does not encounter the other

[25] We will discuss Levinas's reading of Descartes more fully in Chapter 4.

[26] For a clear and succinct account, see Robert Sokolowski, *Introduction to Phenomenology*, passim; see also Dan Zahavi, *Husserl's Phenomenology*.

person's face where that means to perceive the other as a face, as the one who beseeches and demands of me. There is a sense, for Levinas, in which one cannot ever possibly *perceive* the other as a face or the face of the other person; rather, what one does is encounter the face of the other, and these are very different modes of relation. Or, more precisely, one is a mode of relation; the other is something else, something unique and originary and determinative.[27]

Husserl called the object of the intentionality of consciousness a *noema* and the intentional act a *noesis*.[28] The terminology is confusing and has led to major controversy. Part of the point of exploring the intentionality of consciousness is to appreciate that the self and the world, or better, individual selves and particular things in the world, are not given or do not exist as independent, enclosed, isolated entities, all of whose relations with other things need to be grounded and explained and justified solely by virtue of attention to features of the isolated, enclosed things to be related. Rather, the doctrine of intentionality claims, selves or persons are embedded primordially in a world of things, persons, and so forth. Selves occur in various forms of a self-world nexus. People are not like marbles in a bag; they live in the world. Phenomenological analysis explores these forms of nexus from both sides and in terms of the features constitutive of each type of nexus – sense perception, enjoyment, work, use, and so forth. From the side of the world in these nexes, the thing presented in various ways – given its profiles, aspects, and so forth – is called a *noema*. This term has led to several interpretations, but two are especially important. To some, the *noema* is an entity present to consciousness, yet distinguishable from the thing itself. It is a *sense* or *meaning*, grasped by consciousness as a perceptual profile or as a meaning of a concept or word or whatever. To others, the *noema* is the object intended but precisely as it is intended; it is, in perception, the perceived object precisely as it is perceived or as it appears from a particular point of view, in certain conditions, and so on.

If, for Levinas, the face reveals itself to the self and the study of the encounter with the face is a kind of, or similar to, phenomenology, then is the face a kind of or like a *noema*? Is it meaning or sense?[29] Or is it

[27] See Theodore De Boer, *The Rationality of Transcendence*, 25.

[28] There is an important and fascinating debate about the nature of the Husserlian *noema*. For discussion, see Sokolowski, *Introduction to Phenomenology*; the essays by Føllesdal, McIntyre and Smith, and Dreyfus in *Husserl, Intentionality, and Cognitive Science*, ed. Hubert L. Dreyfus and Harrison Hall; D. Smith and R. McIntyre, *Husserl and Intentionality*; Robert Cobb-Stevens, *Husserl and Analytic Philosophy*; and *The Cambridge Companion to Husserl*.

[29] In an important passage, near the end of *Totality and Infinity*, Levinas says: "One of the principal theses of this work is that the noesis-noema structure is not the primordial structure of

the other person when that person is encountered as a face? When one examines another person in everyday life, engages with that person, and so forth, these events occur within the natural attitude, as Husserl calls it. Examination of the intentionality of consciousness, of the modes of engagement with that person, however, occurs within the phenomenological attitude, in Husserl's terms. This requires a shift of perspective and focus, what he calls "bracketing" or "*epoche*." If encountering the face is to be explored, then, that exploration will have to require a shift of perspective from the everyday to something else. But does this mean that the face-to-face itself cannot occur in the everyday? Surely not. But if the exploration is *like* phenomenological examination but not exactly a case of it, then it might be that neither it nor its exploration are everyday matters.[30]

TRANSCENDENTAL PHILOSOPHY

We have seen enough to appreciate how difficult it is to say what Levinas's disclosure of the encounter with the face of the other person is supposed to amount to. Especially given doubts about its empirical or episodic character, and in particular doubts that it is an extraordinary or anomalous experience, one is tempted to give it a different status altogether. Probably the most powerful case of this kind has been developed by the Dutch commentator Theodore De Boer in a classic essay, "An Ethical Transcendental Philosophy."[31] De Boer's basic point is that "Levinas integrates phenomenological ontology into dialogical thought. Only the philosophy of the Other, 'metaphysics,' is able to provide a foundation for this ontology. Dialogue is the transcendental framework for the intentional relation to the world...."[32] Later he says that "the transcendental condition is not a necessary ontological structure which can be reconstructed from the

intentionality...." (294). Throughout the work, of course, Levinas does say that the face-to-face is in fact "the primordial structure of intentionality." That is, if we take the notion of intentionality broadly enough, then the face-to-face is a mode of person-other relation that is more basic, more determinative than the noesis-noema relation. Insofar as intentionality, however, is a matter of the structure of appearing, then strictly speaking the face-to-face is a quasi-intentionality and not literally a mode of intentionality at all. As we shall see, Levinas works hard to use language and yet to stretch it, to clarify the dimension of human existence he is seeking to disclose.

30 In interviews, Levinas refers to phenomenology as an opening to contexts not present to view and as a search for *mise-en-scène*; see *Is It Righteous To Be?*, 150–151, 159–160, 227. See also "Transcendence and Intelligibility," in *Basic Philosophical Writings*, 158; this essay, first given as a lecture in 1983, was published in 1984.

31 See Bernasconi's comments in "Re-reading *Totality and Infinity*," 26–27, and De Boer's essay, Chapter 1 in *The Rationality of Transcendence*, also in Cohen (ed.), *Face to Face with Levinas*. See also Levinas's response, *Of God Who Comes to Mind*, 86–90.

32 De Boer, *The Rationality of Transcendence*, 2.

empirical phenomena; it is an unrecoverable event or ontic incident which intersects the ontological order."[33] That is, there is something real about the face-to-face; it is an event and not a structure. But that reality also has the status of a transcendental condition of our everyday lives. In order to understand what this might mean, however, we need to clarify what it means for a philosophical inquiry to be transcendental.

Philosophers interested in transcendental arguments often focus, as we might expect, on Kant's use of transcendental methods, especially in the transcendental deduction in the first *Critique*, and on Kant's transcendental views.[34] The philosophical issues concern the employment of transcendental arguments against skepticism and, specifically, Kant's use of them against Hume's skepticism.[35] The skeptic could be denying the existence of the external world, the fact of causality, the existence of other minds, or the objectivity of moral values, among other things. Philosophical discussion predominantly has focused on skepticism about the existence of the external world and about knowledge of that world. These were Kant's concerns in the first *Critique*. In this case, then, commentators seek to show that Kant's transcendental arguments are an attempt to refute the skeptic who denies the existence of the external world. Against the skeptic, these arguments begin from positions or claims that the skeptic must accept if there is going to be conversation at all, and they proceed to conclusions about conditions that must be true claims and that refute the skeptic or, more accurately, that lead the skeptic to the abandonment of his skepticism.

Ostensibly Levinas's transcendental philosophy, if he has one or if it is helpful to characterize his thinking as transcendental, is more indebted to Husserl than it is to Kant. Still, from about 1906, Husserl himself began to see his phenomenology as akin to Kant's inquiry and to take it as transcendental in a Kantian sense. It is reasonable to consider the way or ways in which Levinas's thinking might be akin to Kant's as a transcendental enterprise.

Kant argues that the categories of the understanding, a specific set of concepts, on the one hand, and space and time, on the other, are necessary conditions for knowledge of the world and for sensory experience of it.

33 Ibid., 30.

34 Some commentators claim that it was a return to Kant by Husserl around 1906 that facilitated his claims that his own phenomenological method was transcendental in something like the Kantian sense. If Levinas is methodologically indebted to Husserl – and to Heidegger – and if both are indebted to Kant for their understanding of transcendental argumentation, then there is some reason to turn to recent discussion of Kant and German Idealism and the role and character of transcendental argumentation to clarify what Levinas is doing.

35 Contemporary analytic discussion stems from P. F. Strawson's interpretation of Kant and Barry Stroud's criticism of it.

Moreover, Kant's transcendental deduction of the categories comes to even deeper conclusions about what makes possible the applicability of these categories and forms of intuition to the sensory manifold in the first place. In a sense, all of Kant's results begin with the self's experience and hence with the I's conscious activity, and his outcomes concern the contributions of the I, the world, and their relationship that make this experience possible.

Levinas's commitment to Husserlian intentionality situates him differently. For him, the I and the world begin as interrelated; the self experiences the world in various ways, is situated in the world in many ways, and the world means various things to the self. Levinas is not concerned with skepticism about the existence of the world or of other minds. If Levinas is concerned with skepticism, it is skepticism about the absolute or unconditional character of ethics. Or, to put it differently, Levinas is concerned with our social experience in the world and how it is possible. The question for Levinas is how the manifold interrelations between self and world occur and what makes them possible. How can the face-to-face be an ultimate answer to this question?

For the moment, let me set aside the question whether Levinas employs or formulates any transcendental arguments per se, and instead let me ask whether his conclusions, about the primordial and determinative character of the face-to-face, have transcendental status. How might the encounter with the face be related to everyday experiences or events such that it makes sense to call it a transcendental condition of those experiences or events? Paul Franks calls attention to the fact that some transcendental accounts are regressive, others progressive.[36] That is, in some cases we begin with experience, language, belief, and so on and recover the necessary condition or conditions that make the original phenomenon (experience, language, etc.) possible; such an account is regressive. In other cases, we begin with the necessary condition and proceed to show how the original phenomenon is derived from it; these accounts are progressive.[37] Kant takes the former route, his German Idealist descendants the latter. Generally, in both cases, the conditioned state or experience is empirical; the condition is nonempirical or at least nonpsychological.[38]

[36] Paul Franks, "Transcendental Arguments, Reason, and Skepticism: Contemporary Debates and the Origins of Post-Kantianism," in Robert Stern (ed.), *Transcendental Arguments. Problems and Projects*, 116–117 and n.9.

[37] We might also call this form of transcendental arguments "constructive," as in deductive systems based on necessary foundations or premises.

[38] Ralph C. S. Walker, "Induction and Transcendental Arguments," in Stern (ed.), *Transcendental Arguments*, 20; cf. Robert Stern, "On Kant's Response to Hume: The Second Analogy as Transcendental Argument," in Stern (ed.), *Transcendental Arguments*, 48.

Commentators differ about whether Kant's account is realist or coherentist, about whether his transcendental philosophy grounds experience (etc.) in facts beyond our normal grasp or whether it demonstrates the internal coherence of our experiences and beliefs without an external foundation.[39] If Levinas's indentification of the face-to-face as basic and determinative is a transcendental outcome, it is certainly in the former or realist sense; it would be a case of grounding our ordinary experience in a fact (or event, as De Boer calls it) that is beyond our normal grasp, that is, beyond the orbit of totality. Quassim Cassam calls one group of transcendental arguments "world-directed": "they start with the assumption that there is thought or experience of some particular kind, and argue that for thought or experience of this kind to be possible, the world on which these thoughts or experiences occur must be a certain way."[40] Other transcendental arguments, he says, are "self-directed": they "tell us something about the cognitive faculties of the thinking and knowing self."[41] Levinas's face-to-face would, in these terms, be both. Hence, it would be a kind of realist condition – a fact or event – that is beyond our normal grasp, that tells us how the world is and what the self is, and how they are related, in order for certain experiences, thoughts, and so on to be possible.

Transcendental grounds are necessary conditions that make certain experiences possible. It is regularly pointed out that transcendental arguments have a close link to skepticism, as I indicated earlier, but skepticism can be epistemic or other than epistemic.[42] Levinas, we might propose, is primarily or at least initially provoked by moral skepticism or the threat of moral doubt, insecurity, and even nihilism. This sense of worry or threat is part of Levinas's reaction to Heidegger's Nazism and hence a central motivation for Levinas's critique of Heidegger in the years after 1933 and continuing through the publication of *Totality and Infinity* in 1961 and even through *Otherwise than Being* in 1974.[43] The moral skeptic doubts that we live with firm moral beliefs, that we make defensible moral decisions, that morality is a universally grounded mode of life, and that human life

[39] See Robert Stern, "On Kant's Response to Hume," in Stern (ed.), *Transcendental Arguments*, Chapter 4, especially 56–66; Mark Sacks, "Transcendental Arguments and the Inference to Reality: A Reply to Stern," in Stern (ed.), *Transcendental Arguments*, Chapter 5, 67–82.

[40] Quassim Cassam, "Self-Directed Transcendental Arguments," in Stern (ed.), *Transcendental Arguments*, 83.

[41] Ibid., 85.

[42] See Stern (ed.), *Transcendental Arguments*, passim, especially Franks, "Transcendental Arguments, Reason, and Skepticism," 113–114.

[43] See also Levinas's short comment on Heidegger's failure, "As If Consenting to Horror," *Critical Inquiry* 15 (Winter 1989), 485–488.

is morally meaningful. Levinas, as a defender of the moral and the ethical, begins by setting out how life proceeds, but he must do so in a way that the moral skeptic will accept. He then seeks to show what this life – which is "possible or even actual" – requires in order to occur. As Franks puts it, the transcendental philosopher "has learned from skepticism that there is a pressing question as to *how* this can be the case, and that an answer to the question would provide philosophical insight."[44] To be sure, as Franks subtly points out, the defender or believer can have many different goals in mind, and to refute the skeptic outright is or might be only one. But the general point is well taken, that transcendental philosophy may begin with skepticism only to work toward an insight that is somehow beyond that philosophy's grasp.

What does that insight provide? Cassam, in discussing "self-directed" transcendental arguments, distinguishes between two ways in which the necessary conditions contribute to the original experience, beliefs, and so forth. I take it that the two are not exclusive; the same outcome could teach more than one lesson. For Cassam, the two ways clarify two different types of argument; for me, they are different purposes the outcomes can be thought to serve. The first is *revelatory*; the arguments can seek to "uncover" what is necessary, to bring it to our attention.[45] In this way, the transcendental condition that is identified is a philosophical and epistemic outcome; it discloses what is or has been hidden. Second, however, the argument can also seek to *validate* the experience by showing "that we are justified in operating in the ways we actually operate when thinking about or experiencing the world." Cassam points to how Kant's transcendental deduction of the categories serves this function by showing how our use of concepts in sensory experience is legitimate.[46] Here the outcome or necessary condition serves a *rational* or justificatory role. It shows why we can live as we in fact do live, and the condition is normative, in a sense, insofar as it shows why the possible is possible.

I think that it is clear that if Levinas's face-to-face is a kind of necessary condition or ground for our moral conduct, or if it is akin to such a ground and plays a transcendental role, it would have a normative or justificatory force. In fact, given its content, as we shall see, it would be not merely a justification for why moral and meaningful human life is possible but also

[44] Franks, "Transcendental Arguments, Reason, and Skepticism," in Stern (ed.), *Transcendental Arguments*, 113.

[45] Quassim Cassam, "Self-Directed Transcendental Arguments," in Stern (ed.), *Transcendental Arguments*, 85–86.

[46] Ibid., 86.

a reason why a *certain kind of moral life is necessary*. It would constitute a kind of duty or obligation. At the same time, in Cassam's terms, the face-to-face would also be *revelatory*, or, perhaps more precisely, the exposure of it would be revelatory, disclosing the face-to-face as the transcendental and normative condition for social life.

Franks also notes, in his discussion of Idealist responses to Kant, that these figures sought "not only a ground of everything, but an absolute unconditioned ground for all grounds."[47] Levinas speaks of the face-to-face as originary, primordial, and an-archic. There is a suggestion here that its status is uncompromised or unconditioned, that it is in a sense independent and underived, whereas all else derives from it, in one way or another, directly or indirectly. I do not want to suggest that Levinas is doing metaphysics in a traditional way, like Hegel, Fichte, Spinoza, or Aristotle, but there is a sense that nothing, for human existence, is prior to the face of the other person, and that eventually we need to make sense of this priority, if we are to understand Levinas deeply enough.[48]

There are a number of issues that would have to be clarified before we could confidently call Levinas's philosophy transcendental in any useful way. As I have suggested, it is possible to take him to be responding to a kind of moral skepticism. But this is merely a suggestion at this point and needs to be developed and justified. Then, we should consider whether Levinas's thinking does have this second-person or dialectical quality, that is, whether it carries out its inquiry consistently from this perspective, as if Levinas were engaging in a dialogue with the moral skeptic. This issue is connected, I think, to the question of Levinas's use of the phenomenological method. If his inquiry does involve a phenomenological or at least quasi-phenomenological examination of modes of intentionality, then it must take place within the so-called phenomenological attitude, with the natural attitude bracketed or suspended. There is a notorious problem, however, about what motivates this act of suspension and the shift from the natural to the phenomenological attitude, from ordinary experience to philosophical inquiry.[49] This is akin to the problem of what motivates

[47] Franks, "Transcendental Arguments, Reason, and Skepticism," in Stern (ed.), *Transcendental Arguments*, 116; cf. 122–132.

[48] As we shall see, Levinas does see the normativity of the face-to-face as absolute, and while not "grounded" in anything else, it has a characteristic, which he calls "height," that links this absolute normativity with our everyday vocabulary of the divine, "God," and traditional theology, at least in the West. But more of this later.

[49] This problem is regularly discussed in the literature on Husserlian phenomenology; the classic treatment is Eugene Fink, "The Phenomenological Philosophy of Edmund Husserl and Contemporary Criticism," translated in R. O. Elveton (ed.), *The Phenomenology of Husserl*

skepticism itself and what in fact motivates philosophy. For Levinas, we might take Heidegger's moral skepticism, as it were, or the threat of such skepticism or nihilism, as Levinas's motive for his own shift of attitude.[50] But once he has shifted his point of view, he would be responding to the skeptic in the skeptic's own terms, and need we believe that the skeptic will follow Levinas in his dialogue with him? This needs to be clarified and our question resolved.

Even if we follow Levinas this far, there is much to be done. If the encounter with the face of the other person is the transcendental ground of what I will call the moral or meaningful human life, how is it identified, and what is its relationship to that life? It may reveal how certain features of life are possible and indeed why they occur as actual, but how does it justify them or even mandate, demand, and require them? Furthermore, is there a sense in which this ground is present in ordinary everyday experience and enters into it? In what way, if at all, can one consider the ground from within ordinary life? Can the object of phenomenological inquiry be identified, discussed, and understood from within the natural attitude, that is, with the linguistic resources employed in ordinary life and in theorizing about it? Can the infinite be described, discussed, and grasped from within totality, as Levinas calls it, and still remain, in a sense, infinite?

I have tried thus far to promote the idea, championed by De Boer among others, that Levinas's inquiry should be understood as a transcendental enterprise of a certain sort. There are reasons, of course, for thinking that it is not only that – an inquiry into the fact that the face-to-face is not an event in everyday experience but rather a dimension of (or fact about) all of social life – but I have paid attention most of all to proposing that it is at least such a transcendental philosophy. Much of the rest of this book will elaborate this case, in one sense or another, although it is not aimed only at doing so, and I will clarify how it is not as well.

AN OBJECTION

There is, however, an objection to this transcendental reading of Levinas that I want to address now. It will lead us to consider another type of reading altogether, albeit one that I shall try to show has transcendental

(Quadrangle Books, 1970), 73–147. For discussion, see Sokolowski, *Introduction to Phenomenology*; Zahavi, *Husserl's Phenomenology*, and Dermot Moran, *Introduction to Phenomenology*.

50 Later Levinas treats deconstruction as a form of skepticism and Derrida as a skeptic; for an excellent discussion, see Simon Critchley, *The Ethics of Deconstruction*, 156–169.

features. The objection is this. Broadly speaking, transcendental arguments aim to derive *metaphysical* results from *psychological* premises. Typically, they originate from premises about our ordinary experiences, thoughts, beliefs, and knowledge, and they terminate by proving the existence of certain features of the world or the self or both, without which the original experiences are not possible. But, the objection goes, even if we can identify what Levinas and his skeptical opponent take those original, ordinary experiences to be, it is surely wrong to take Levinas to have sought or arrived at new metaphysical results. The face of the other person and the responsibility of the self are hardly new entities or new features of the world; they are hardly new constituents of our ontology. They are hidden or forgotten "horizons of meaning" and somehow beyond ontology, being, presence, appearance, and such. They are not new items or features, for they are neither *new* nor *entities* or *features* at all. Hence, they cannot be transcendental grounds in any meaningful sense. The face and responsibility are the core of Levinas's insight into human existence, but they are hardly transcendental grounds for that existence.

I have been trying to mitigate this kind of objection, but its thrust is potent indeed and direct. It suggests that "transcendental philosophy" is at best a metaphor for what Levinas is doing and, because of its connotations, perhaps a misleading metaphor at that. Like words such as "phenomenological," "analytical," and "synthetic," it is a term used within systems or domains of thought, but Levinas's project decidedly reaches outside such domains. His philosophy is more like Plato and Neo-Platonism than it is like Aristotle, scholastic systems, Spinoza, Leibniz, Hegel, and Fichte; more like Augustine, Jacobi, Kierkegaard, Barth, and Rosenzweig, too. In each of these cases, what is ultimate is genuinely transcendent and not simply a preeminent feature of the whole of nature or the cosmos. Levinas's thought begins within the everyday and then reaches beyond it, but the task is not simply metaphysical or epistemological. It is not aimed at discovery of new entities; it is not aimed at discovery at all. Neither the face of the other person nor our responsibility to and for the other is unknown or absent in the ordinary everyday world. They are present but in a sense hidden or forgotten or, perhaps better, misunderstood and distorted. To learn about them, then, is not a matter of being introduced to new things or being given a new faculty or capacity; it is to see the old from a new perspective, in a new light. It is a bit like Plato's conception, in the *Republic*, of true *paideia*, a kind of *periagoge* or conversion, a change of perspective or direction of vision in terms of which something once hidden comes into view. What Levinas is doing, one might claim, is to provide a new perspective on the ordinary world as we live in it. He could be said to be opening our eyes to the way we are, but in a way that we do not now adequately realize or understand. His philosophy gives us a new way of understanding human existence in the world that takes its origin from an appreciation of what kind of beings we are most of all. He does not say that he is the first to see things in this way, but he does believe that this understanding, which he thinks is accurate and true, has been occluded, distorted, and obscured and needs to be recovered.

One might still want to call this philosophical approach "transcendental." But there is a difference between a realist and an idealist reading of this transcendental project. Peculiar as it sounds, given Levinas's opposition to the imperialism of totalities and the role of the subject in them, the kind of transcendental project I am describing should be understood idealistically, that is, as a matter of viewing things differently rather than as a matter of discovering new realities or features in the world. To be sure, Levinas wants to introduce or reintroduce us to a way of understanding life in this world, human existence, that we have forgotten or misunderstood. His philosophy is about this world and our lives in it. But it is not a matter of locating entities beyond this world on which it is grounded or which determine it, as much as it is about disclosing features of this world that we do not currently appreciate. When we consider other persons, that is, we use concepts, roles, and rules; we perceive how they look, implicitly grasp similarities and differences, take them into view and react to them in terms of patterns, in terms of common features or distinctive ones, and so forth. In everyday circumstances, however, we do not regularly see their faces. For each face is unique to the particular other; it is sheer plea and command, at once; it beseeches and demands. That is all – until then, in the world, it accumulates its characteristics, features, and so on. We do grasp the latter; we do not, as Levinas sees it, grasp the former adequately or perhaps at all. Levinas wants to teach us to do so, to take up this perspective, and to show us as well what it means for our lives, for grasping the face of the other is not to take up an epistemic stance but rather to respond to the suffering, need, and destitution that the face expresses to us.

How might the face be taken realistically and how idealistically? Every feature of the other person whom I encounter, every profile, role, and so forth, in the terminology of phenomenology, is a *noema*, the other person precisely as he or she appears to me in a particular mode of intentionality – as an object of seeing, hearing, as a conversational partner, as an object of my action, my affection, my hatred, or whatever. Is the face of the other person a *noema*?[51] Is it a sense or meaning that mediates between my self and the other person? Or, alternatively, is the face of the other present to me as plea and command? The first reading is realist, and it is not Levinas's meaning; the second is idealist, as it were. Levinas's understanding is more like the idealist reading, although not exactly it. The *noema* is the object as it is presented to the self, the thing-qua-x, but it is not the object of a double grasping. The self does not grasp the thing and also its feature or profile, x. It grasps the whole at once, the thing-qua-x. Similarly, when I encounter the face of the other, I do not encounter the other and his face; I encounter the other person as face, as plea and command, to be responded to independently of and, as Levinas claims, prior to seeing, describing, and thinking about the other. If the face is a *noema*, then, it is one not present to the self, as the "look" of the other is; nor does it have the same *status* as the *noemata* grasped in the remainder of everyday experience.

There are many questions to be asked about Levinas's idea of the face of the other. We have been considering one: what is it? It is, one might say, a hidden or obscured perspective on the other person, but in addition it is a primary or determinative and grounding perspective or profile. It is what the other person means to me first and foremost, more than anything else, before that person means anything else to me. Why is this so? What makes the face more primary than the other person's kinship with me, than her posture or shape or height or complexion? While part of Levinas's project in its transcendental sense, I think, is to expose the face and responsibility, part is to show this priority. How does he accomplish this task? How does he clarify why the face is somehow primordial and fundamental? By showing how the face is beyond totality and ontology, that it comes with a certain force or *gravitas*, and that all human experience derives from it or is grounded in it, whereas it – the need and vulnerability and force of the face – derives from nothing. It simply is in all its brute particularity – as an epiphany or revelation to the self. In later chapters we will have to see how Levinas accomplishes these tasks.

If Levinas's philosophy is transcendental, then, it is so in a rather distinctive way. Jonathan Lear, in two well-known essays, has argued that Wittgenstein's project in the *Philosophical Investigations* is a kind of transcendental philosophy.[52] Is Levinas's transcendental enterprise anything

[51] See Levinas, *Totality and Infinity*, 294, where Levinas answers this question explicitly with a denial; no – the face is not a *noema*.

[52] Jonathan Lear, "Transcendental Anthropology" in Philip Petit and John McDowell (eds.), *Subject, Thought, and Context*, 267–298, and "The Disappearing 'We'," *Proceedings of the Aristotelian Society* 58 (1984), 219–242. I have been arguing that the face-to-face is, in one sense, an

like Wittgenstein's, as Lear understands it? One of the lessons of this chapter is that Levinas's accomplishment does not fit comfortably into categories that have been proposed for it or that might seem appropriate for describing it. It is and is not phenomenology; it is and is not empirical or episodic; it is and is not transcendental. Lear argues something similar about Wittgenstein. If he is to be regarded as a transcendental philosopher, that notion must be modified from its classical, Kantian sense. Lear is especially interested in what Wittgenstein helps us to understand about how we follow rules and what it is we do when we communicate in language. Lear claims that, in a suitably extended sense, Wittgenstein's investigation of rule following in the *Philosophical Investigations* "can plausibly be considered a transcendental inquiry," for the outcome of this inquiry is a "non-empirical insight into how we go on."[53] According to Lear, this investigation is transcendental not because it seeks to identify "the necessary structure of the mind, of the world, or of both," for it "displays no interest in necessary structures" and looks unabashedly at "ordinary activities like speaking language."[54] What Lear proposes is a "loosening" of the Kantian definition, so that a "transcendental argument for x is concerned with establishing the legitimacy of x ... by revealing in its broadest and deepest context what it is to be x," freed of the skeptical context and of the need to disclose what are, strictly speaking, necessary conditions.[55] Wittgenstein's attention is on language, psychological states, rule following, philosophy, and such themes, and especially on how philosophy obscures rather than clarifies what is going on in language speaking and human affairs. Moreover, according to Lear, Wittgenstein's inquiry is anthropological as well as transcendental, empirical and nonempirical at once. His analysis of Wittgenstein that claims to show this need not be examined here, but the point is of interest.

Is it possible that Levinas too is both an empirical and a transcendental thinker, but neither in a conventional sense? Levinas's philosophy is about ordinary life, but it is also about what it is to live that life meaningfully and morally. Like Wittgenstein, Levinas seems to assign to philosophy a therapeutic role, to cure us and to cure Western philosophy from mistaken and ultimately destructive ways of understanding and living life in

essential feature of all social existence. For a similar account of Heidegger, see Robert Brandom, *Tales of the Mighty Dead* (Harvard, 2002), Chapter 11, especially 328–342.

[53] Jonathan Lear, "Transcendental Anthropology," in Petit and McDowell (eds.), *Subject, Thought and Content*, 269.

[54] Ibid., 270.

[55] Lear, "The Disappearing 'We'," 222–223.

the world. But to serve this function, Levinas's thinking must be both transcendental and empirical. It must be immersed in that life and also reflective about it. I do not believe that Wittgenstein and Levinas carry out their projects in the same way, but there are similarities, and Lear's attention to the empirical and nonempirical dimensions of Wittgenstein's approach helps to remind us of them.[56]

Having said this much about method and approach, it is time to consider Levinas's central ethical insight in a substantive way. The questions we have raised and suggestions we have made can be addressed only if we leave our detached view and move into the core of his thinking.

[56] Bob Plant's discussion of Wittgenstein, Levinas, and Derrida, *Wittgenstein and Levinas: Ethical and Religious Thought* (Routledge, 2005), reached me too late to consider here. Indeed, its subtle and complex argument deserves special treatment. To my knowledge, it is the first book-length attempt to think about Wittgenstein and Levinas together, a task that it carries out in a deep and fascinating way.

CHAPTER THREE

The Ethical Content of the Face-to-Face

The first things to remember about the face-to-face encounter between the self and the other person are that it is concrete and particular. It is not an idea or concept, nor a type of action or event. It is a concrete reality, an event; it occurs. Furthermore, it occurs as utterly particular: the self is a particular person, and the face-of-the-other is a particular revelation of a particular person. What is occluded, hidden, or forgotten in our ordinary lives is not some idea or value; it is this presence of the other's face to me – and my responsibility to and for this person.[1] Moreover, this reality or event or encounter, which in a sense is beyond our thinking, our concepts, and our rules, and prior to them, is determinative and unconditional. It is all plea and command, made again and again, in episode after episode. It is not like a single clash that occurred sometime in the past and that is heard only in its continuing echoes; it is more like echoes themselves always present without any such crash or origin.

What does the face reveal? Why is its content ethical? How does Levinas clarify and argue for this content? What does the face mean? Is its meaning absolute?

In order to answer these and other questions about the ethical content and the character of the face-to-face encounter that Levinas calls attention to, I want to look first at his writings from 1947 to 1961, from *Time and the Other* to *Totality and Infinity*. Moreover, it will be helpful to compare what Levinas says to an early discussion of Stanley Cavell's that introduces the notion of acknowledgment as a way to characterize the self's relation to the other person. Once Levinas comes to describe this fundamental event in a certain way in these works, he repeats and refines that formulation. If later he modifies his account, it is a

[1] Cohen emphasizes the concreteness especially in his book *Ethics, Exegesis and Philosophy*; he reminds us again and again that responsibility is not a reflective grasp of the other or an epistemic attitude. It is action; it is doing something for someone.

modification of this early description. We need to have its basic features in hand.

THE SOCIAL, THE FACE, AND THE ETHICAL

We begin with everyday life, a life of people living with one another. Here, Levinas says, "the solitude and fundamental alterity of the other are already veiled by decency."[2] In the course of ordinary daily experience, we live together, sympathize, care about one another or offend, are angry with another, and do her injury. There are social relationships or etiquette and, he says, a certain kind of reciprocity. "But already, in the very heart of the relationship with the other that characterizes our social life, alterity appears as a nonreciprocal relationship – that is, as contrasting strongly with contemporaneousness." That is, within these ordinary social relationships there is a dimension that is nonreciprocal, and it is always "already" there, although hidden from view or, in his words, "veiled by decency." In life, I join you for a movie; we leave the house together, go to the theater, purchase tickets, and watch the film together. But more basic to our experience and our relationship than these features, something not in sight, is a relationship between us, whereby you confront me and I am called to respond, to reject or accept you; this is a relatedness that is "already" present in the midst of all this, "veiled" by the features and formalities of our everyday encounter. There, at that level, you are other than I; you stand over against me: "the Other as Other" – in this case, you – "is not only an alter ego" – another person different from me who joins me from his own point of view – "the Other is what I myself am not. The Other is, for example, the weak, the poor, 'the widow and the orphan,' whereas I am the rich or the powerful." You are exterior, other, and outside, and your sheer otherness is not a function of or constituted by spatial difference, nonidentity of features or properties, or any other such things. Your otherness is a brute fact; it is wholly made up of your being poor, my being rich, your need and my capacity to respond to you and your need.[3] That is, the brute otherness is constituted by dependence and what the dependence aims at, what Levinas calls "vulnerability" and "nudity." "In civilized life there are traces of this relationship with the other," for example, in sexual

[2] Levinas, *Time and the Other*, 82.

[3] Ibid., 83–84. Commentators on Levinas have been tempted to look in various directions to identify antecedents for Levinas's view about the primacy of the call or summons of the other and to clarify his thinking by comparison to similar accounts. They have turned to Fichte, Marcel, Sartre, and the Marburg Neo-Kantian Hermann Cohen.

difference, what Levinas calls "modesty" and "mystery," and which he also calls "eros" or love.[4] The alterity of the feminine is constituted by this withdrawal and attraction, nothing else. "Love," he says, "is not a possibility, is not due to our initiative, is without reason; it invades and wounds us, and nevertheless the I survives it."[5]

Below the surface of the social, in a sense, hidden from view, is a layer of relationship, a dimension of how we are related to one another, the I and the other person as other, where the otherness is wholly a matter of status, what Levinas calls rich and poor, powerful and weak. This is not one person being together with or alongside another; it is something else. Moreover, it is unlike Martin Buber's I-Thou encounter, Levinas says, "where reciprocity remains the tie between two separate freedoms, and the ineluctable character of isolated subjectivity is underestimated.... It is a collectivity that is not a communion. It is the face-to-face without intermediary...."[6] Here, then, is Levinas's starting point, as it were. The self, the I, in normal everyday life, experiences intimations or hints of otherness; in social life the self experiences "traces" of a primordial relationship between itself and the particular other person. But while those traces include sexuality and love, what is the character of the otherness itself? What metaphors can we use, what further hints, to describe its content? What gives that otherness its dynamic rather than static character, its force? What is its ethical content?

In his important essay of 1951, "Is Ontology Fundamental?," Levinas answers these questions.[7] In this essay Levinas approaches the relation to the other through language, comprehension, and a discussion of Heidegger.[8] "Language is founded on a relation anterior to comprehension," and it is this "prior" relation that Levinas seeks to expose. I want to ignore for now the role of language, conversation, and such issues and move to Levinas's description of the encounter in ethical terms, an encounter that Levinas says is prior to and irreducible to comprehension or thought.[9]

The first thing that Levinas says about this relation between the self and the other person, that is, between each particular self and each and every other person, is that it occurs in the vocative. He calls it "religion," which

[4] Ibid., 84–90.
[5] Ibid., 89.
[6] Ibid., 93–94.
[7] See Levinas, "Is Ontology Fundamental?," in Robert Bernasconi, Simon Critchley and Adriaan Peperzak (eds.), *Basic Philosophical Writings*.
[8] Ibid., 5.
[9] Ibid., 7.

he associates with imploring and prayer.[10] It is an "event of sociality," and he says that the word "religion" has an "ethical resonance" and "Kantian echoes." Why does Levinas introduce the kinship with Kant? For Kant, the highest form of religion is a moral faith intimately tied to human rationality, autonomous selfhood, self-determination, and the moral law. Levinas will differ with Kant dramatically about the core of ethics, its character, the role of autonomy and freedom, and much else, but he agrees with Kant about the centrality of the ethical to human existence.[11] It is this notion of moral religiosity that Levinas has in mind when he calls the basic "event of sociality," of the I encountering the other person, "religion." The term does not refer, of course, to a positive or instituted religion, for it is an event or relation, not a practice or structure of practices. Nor is it a matter of doctrine, of creed, or even of moral theory. What Levinas is referring to with expressions like "religion" is a fact-event that is at the core of both ethics and religion, in what he takes to be their most basic and primordial senses.[12] The hidden, ignored, or forgotten dimension of everyday life, of which we have only hints or traces in that life, is this ethico-religious event that is what constitutes the otherness of the other person for the I. It is an event, a relation, in one sense; in another, it is a dimension or aspect of everyday interpersonal and social life that is hidden from view and that Levinas is opening to our gaze, bringing into the open, as it were. It is an

10 Ibid.; cf. Levinas, "Freedom and Command," in Alphonso Lingis (trans.), *Collected Philosophical Papers*, 23; see also *Totality and Infinity*, 80. Notice that Levinas does not say that the face-to-face is "religious." Rather, he calls it "religion," i.e., it is the locus of what is genuine and fundamental about religion as it occurs in our ordinary experience.

11 See Levinas, "Is Ontology Fundamental?," in *Basic Philosophical Writings*, 10: "that which we catch sight of seems suggested by the practical philosophy of Kant, to which we feel particularly close." As one might expect, given comments such as this and the centrality of the ethical for Levinas, there has been a great deal of discussion concerning his relation to Kant. A good treatment can be found in Catherine Chalier, *What Ought I to Do? Morality in Kant and Levinas* (Cornell, 2002); see also Anthony F. Beavers, "Kant and the Problem of Ethical Metaphysics," and Peter Atterton, "From Transcendental Freedom to the Other: Levinas and Kant," in Melvyn New with Robert Bernasconi and Richard Cohen (eds.), *In Proximity: Emmanuel Levinas and the 18th Century*.

12 As Paul Franks has shown, the term *Tatsache* (fact-event) was introduced in the eighteenth century as a technical term not for a "matter of fact" but more precisely for an "act-event." It was used by Kant to explain the *Factum der Vernunft* (fact of reason) in 1790. Franks emphasizes the active feature of the expression, but since for Levinas the face-to-face is first of all passive, although the subject's posture as responsibility is in a sense an active response, I am not here using the idea with that same emphasis. Hence, I call it a "fact-event" and not an "act-event." See Paul Franks, "Freedom, *Tatsache*, and *Tathandlung* in the Development of Fichte's Jena *Wissenschaftslehre*," *Archiv für Gerschichte der Philosophie* 79:3 (1997), 331–344; also Paul Franks, *All or Nothing: Systematicity, Transcendental Arguments, and Skepticism in German Idealism* (Harvard University Press, 2005), 278.

event that constitutes, more precisely, a perspective on the ordinary or an aspect of the ordinary.

The last section of "Is Ontology Fundamental?" is entitled "The Ethical Significance of the Other (= the human other)."[13] In everyday life, my first-person point of view orients me to the world and to other persons. I desire them, name them, classify them, take hold of them, and hence dominate them. They belong to me. This Hobbesian situation is at the core of Levinas's understanding of totality, which we shall discuss in the next chapter. Here the issue I want to focus on is the limited one of how the world, including the other person, fulfills my needs or at least serves those needs. Levinas says that the other is possessed. "As consumable, it [the world] is nourishment, and in enjoyment, it offers itself, gives itself, belongs to me."[14] These terms come from *Time and the Other*; they will be elaborated and explored in *Totality and Infinity*. In the ordinary world of everyday life, things and people are there for me, the I, to use, consume, enjoy, and thereby to become nourished. But, Levinas then says, "the encounter with the other (*autrui*) consists in the fact that despite the extent of my domination and his slavery [i.e., despite the extent of the other's enslavement to me], I do not possess him." At a fundamental level, Levinas claims, the other person is more than a thing; she confronts me with an uncircumscribed, absolute choice: either to let her live or to murder her or, in some circumstances, to support her living or to let her die. "The other (*autrui*) is the sole being I can wish to kill." With the other person comes this possibility: to desire its death or to allow it to live.

Things – natural sources of nourishment and enjoyment and use, from fruits and vegetables to flowers and sunsets – are there for me, and my first choice, with regard to them, is whether to appropriate them at all, after which I set about determining how. But with persons a new situation arises.[15] When the other person faces me, *before* I choose to use or dominate the other person, I must respond to her being a person by allowing her to live or not. She comes on the scene, comes into my venue, not for me to do something with; she comes with a need to share the world with me. First she needs my acceptance and risks my rejection. I am tempted,

[13] Levinas, "Is Ontology Fundamental?," in *Basic Philosophical Writings*, 9–10.

[14] Ibid., 9.

[15] I am inclined to think that for Levinas, while this "new situation," the fact of the ethical, so to speak, only comes about with the relationship with the other person, it is not confined to that relationship. That is, there is room here to introduce concern for animals as well as concern for the earth and its resources. These are, however, large and widely contested issues among students and critics of Levinas that I do not discuss in this book.

Levinas says; I *can* choose to kill her; I *can* desire her death. But in this *can*, this temptation, this capacity, there is already an acceptance of the other, an acknowledgment of her facing me, needing me, risking me. "At the very moment when my power to kill realizes itself, the other (*autrui*) has escaped me." I have already, at that instant, engaged her, accepted her, or better, been engaged by her and responded. "The temptation of total negation, measuring the infinity of this attempt and its impossibility – this is the presence of the face. To be in relation with the other (*autrui*) face to face is to be unable to kill."[16] This, Levinas says, is a "depth" rather than a horizon, "a breach in the horizon," if we take "horizon" to be an expression for unperceived, unattended profiles in everyday life itself but ones that could be grasped or seen.[17] What does the face, this breach, signify? "In it the infinite resistance of a being to our power affirms itself precisely against the murderous will that it defies; because, completely naked, the face signifies itself."[18] The face does not point beyond itself; it simply is what it is.

Levinas employs the word "face" with the greatest care. The face of the other person is not the appearance of that person; it is not a collection of features given to visual perception. It has no parts, no components. It is basic and, as he says, "self-signifying." The face means what it is – imploring, a plea of the weak to the powerful, of the poor to the rich. The face is the way the other person, as the imposing presence I just described, presents herself to me. It is not the object of everyday intentional consciousness but a "breach" in that intentionality. "To comprehension and signification grasped within a horizon [of meanings], we oppose the signifyingness of the face."[19] By "oppose" Levinas means that the special significance of the face of the other challenges and shapes the status of everyday meanings and sense; it is more basic than they are, more original, presumed by them as an engagement of the self with the other that lies hidden within every other interpersonal relationship. It is, from the self's side, the responsibility to acknowledge and accept the other that is always already present in ordinary life – pre-conceptual, pre-articulate, pre-reflective.

Levinas's term "face," then, has something of the nuance of what Bernard Williams called "thick" moral concepts. These concepts do not

[16] Levinas, "Is Ontology Fundamental?," in *Basic Philosophical Writings*, 9.

[17] Ibid., 10. What Levinas means here is that the face is like a horizon, but because it is deep and primordial and fundamental, in a metaphorical sense, we should think of it as a "depth" rather than strictly speaking a hidden horizon or one that is contingently unattended to. Alternatively, it is a breach or break in the horizons of everyday experience.

[18] Ibid.

[19] Ibid.

solely announce moral correctness, as the concepts of right and wrong do, or obligation and permission. Rather, they are moral concepts such that their descriptive and prescriptive dimensions cannot be separated, even for conceptual purposes; honor, shame, humiliation, and pride are examples.[20] In a similar way, Levinas's term "face" refers to an aspect of *one person's being present to another* that has its descriptive features, to be sure, but that also has those other features I call "appeal" and "command." That is, in addition to however the other person appears to me – as tall or short, burly or slim, light- or dark-skinned, and so forth – the other person presents a vulnerability and destitution, a sense of dependence, that appeals or petitions me and at the same time addresses me and makes a demand upon me. This particular young girl, with curly dark hair, smiling, and gangly, whatever else she means to me, also and even "before" in a sense calls out to me, burdens me with responsibility, singles me out for an appeal and a demand. Moreover, there is no way correctly and precisely to sever that appeal and command from the way she looks to me; the appeal and demand is *in* the look, so to speak; it is something that the look means, something primary and fundamental.[21] It is in this way that Levinas's "face" is like Williams's "thick" moral concepts. It is the way in which each of us is a "thick" moral presence for each and every other person. In later works, Levinas will call my posture toward each person "responsibility," and hence this relatedness too can be thought of along the lines of such "thick" moral concepts. The one caveat we should enter, however, is that technically speaking, both thin and thick moral concepts, in Levinas's terms, occur within the domains of totality, that is, occur within everyday life and our theoretical and explanatory articulations of it. Levinas's face, on the other hand, is technically speaking a breach in totality and not a part of it. Nonetheless, even if, in general, Levinas is more inclined to characterize the face by using "thin" moral concepts, as when he talks about the face-to-face and

[20] See Bernard Williams, *Ethics and the Limits of Philosophy* (Harvard University Press, 1985), 129, 140, 143–145. Williams' examples are *coward, lie, brutality, gratitude*, and *courage*, among others.

[21] In the second book, *Useless Knowledge*, of Charlotte Delbo's imaginative memoir of her time in Auschwitz and release from Ravensbrück, *Auschwitz and After* (Yale University Press, 1995), 204–205, when the liberation of the camps was imminent, the camp organization was deteriorating, and the prisoners clung to life in the midst of the chaotic conditions, Delbo says: "One never met a face that wasn't a question, a face burning with questions: 'Do you think we're going to leave? What's your opinion?' … She was looking at me with supplicating eyes, her voice hardly perceptible, her lips retracted, her pupils enlarged: 'I'm going to die,' her eyes said. 'I'm going to die if I don't leave this place at once.' " Here we have a very vivid portrayal, in the face with the "supplicating eyes," of what Levinas means by the *face*; it was a look of "questioning" that Delbo felt compelled to "answer."

responsibility as the good rather than the right and when in later writings he avoids calling it "justice," saving that term for political and social rules and programs that are developments of them, it is helpful to understand what he means by "face" as having a kinship with "thick" moral concepts.

By 1962, when Levinas seeks to summarize the exposition that he gives in the early sections of *Totality and Infinity*, his account of the encounter with the face of the other person has become richer and fuller.[22]

> The epiphany of the Absolutely Other is a face by which the Other challenges and commands me through his nakedness, through his destitution. He challenges me from his humility and from his height.... The absolutely Other is the human Other (*autrui*). And the putting into question of the Same by the Other is a summons to respond.... Hence, to be I signifies not being able to escape responsibility.[23]

The Same is the self or I; the Other is the other person. The "epiphany" – notice the theological vocabulary that Levinas appropriates – is the event of the other person engaging the I as a face, and the content of that engagement is, from the other person's side, a plea born out of need and destitution and a summons to respond to that plea, and, from the self's side, an unlimited responsibility toward that other person in virtue of that plea and that command. At this level, if we were to speak of it in such terms, the self *is* wholly responsibility, and the other person *is* wholly plea and command. More correctly, perhaps, in everyday life every social interaction, every encounter between one person and another, is always *already* such a nexus of plea, command, and inescapable responsibility, *before* it is anything else – which it always is. Only once the self is confronted by a face can it be responsible and must it be responsible – for and to that other person. But if Levinas can say this in 1962, it is because in the intervening decade, his reflection on the face and its philosophical articulation has become nuanced and deep. It is worth looking briefly at how this process unfolded.

22 Why does Levinas use the word "face" to express the way the other person encounters or engages with the self? Negatively, of course, Levinas appropriates a nontechnical word that is not used in traditional epistemological contexts, e.g., the word "impression" or "appearance" or "idea." Moreover, the face is a perspective or aspect, e.g., the face of a cube or triangle. Furthermore, the face is characteristic of a living thing, an animal or person, and its bodily presence. The face is the most expressive physical manifestation of such a living being's inner self, its feelings and thoughts and attitudes. It reveals most vividly its needs, pain and joy, sorrow and suffering. Above all, in its eyes, one sees how the other feels. For such reasons and more, then, Levinas chooses this term to indicate the mode of presence of the other person to the self.

23 Levinas, "Transcendence and Height," in *Basic Philosophical Writings*, 17.

THE CALL OF THE FACE

We have seen that as early as 1951, Kant was on Levinas's mind. Levinas was attracted to the commitment to the priority of the ethical in Kant's philosophy. Hence, it was natural for him to try to clarify his notion of the ethical character of the face, its ethical meaning, by looking at Kant or at least by looking at Kantian issues. To a certain degree, he does this in "Freedom and Command" (1953), an essay also written with Plato in mind and especially the priority of the Good in Plato's *Republic*.[24] I will focus only on what the essay says about the ethical content of the face. We should not forget, however, that the essay, if only indirectly, is also a response to Nazi fascism and domination.[25]

Levinas asks, "Does not impersonal discourse presuppose discourse in the sense of this face-to-face situation? In other words, is there not *always* between one will and another a *relationship of command* without tyranny, which is *not yet* an obedience to an impersonal law, but is the *indispensable condition* for the institution of such a law?"[26] Levinas calls this situation or event a "discourse before discourse" and a "relationship between particulars prior to the institution of rational law," a "condition for even the commands of the State" and "the condition for freedom." This is familiar territory. Engagement with the face is, we have seen, a relationship of command, albeit one of plea and command. It is particular and prior to law, both moral and political. It is presumed by all social interaction.

Next Levinas turns to everyday social interaction in an extreme form: war. War is violence, use, domination; it is – and we have already seen this theme – work, enjoyment, and domination but here applied to other persons rather than to worldly things. War, however, seeks to violate and dominate what it ignores – it seeks to annihilate an opposing force, but it "does not see the face in the other."[27] Levinas distinguishes the *force* of the other person, its resisting force that lies in its freedom to oppose, from its *face*, which he calls its "pacific opposition." The face is "what resists me by its opposition [i.e., its pacific opposition – plea and destitution] and not what is opposed to me by its resistance."[28] This is an opposition that is prior to its freedom or mine. Levinas uses language he will later refuse himself to describe this opposition: "it opposes itself to me insofar as it turns to

[24] Levinas, "Freedom and Command," in *Collected Philosophical Papers*, Chapter 2, 15–23.

[25] See especially ibid., 16–17, and the attention to tyranny.

[26] Ibid., 18, italics mine.

[27] Ibid., 19.

[28] Ibid.

me." Moreover, real violence is not war, domination, and so forth; real violence is "ignoring this opposition, ignoring the face of a being, avoiding the gaze," and this means denying its plea to live and to be acknowledged, aided, and sustained, to ignore its suffering, to kill the face and the other person, and hence to avoid all responsibility. Here, "pacific opposition" is what earlier, in "Is Ontology Fundamental?," Levinas called the "otherness" of the other person or the other as "negation." It incorporates or is constituted by a command, prior to the commands of moral rules, of law, or of political sovereignty, and the command – "do not kill me" – is also a plea, something like "make room for me" or "feed me" or "share the world with me" or "reduce my suffering."

Levinas works at how to formulate the way the face presents itself, its "epiphany." In this essay he uses the language of expression. "Expression renders present what is communicated and the one who is communicating; they are both in the expression. But that does not mean that expression provides us with knowledge about the other." The other person who is present in expression "appeals" to the self and dominates it. In expression there is already sociality.[29]

Levinas then turns to another way of clarifying the "originality of the encounter with the face."[30] Thus far he has, in this essay, emphasized the dimension of command in the encounter with the face. He has argued that politics requires discourse, and discourse requires the encounter, with its command prior to all command.[31] Levinas now turns to the other dimension of the encounter, its character as plea and the face as expressive of misery and destitution:

> The absolute nakedness of a face, the absolutely defenseless face, without covering, clothing or mask, is what opposes my power over it, my violence, and opposes it in an absolute way, with an opposition that is opposition itself. The being that expresses itself, that faces me, says *no* to me by his very expression.... [I]t is not the *no* of a hostile force or a threat; it is the impossibility of killing him who presents that face.... The face is the fact that a being affects us not in the indicative, but in the imperative.[32]

This face-to-face, then, is a "metaphysical relationship that is ethical," "the ethical impossibility of killing" as the other's resistance to the I.

It is helpful here, as we have regularly done, to consider this passage from the perspective of everyday life, as proposing an insight into an

[29] Ibid., 20–21.
[30] Ibid., 21.
[31] See ibid., 23, for a summary of the essay.
[32] Ibid., 21.

aspect or dimension of ordinary experience that is generally hidden from view. What Levinas is saying, from this point of view, is that in every social encounter, whether violent or benign, the other person stands as other than the self, as a *no* to the I. But, at this basic level, the *no* is not one of hostility or anger or threat. It is, as it were, the *no* of need, of defenselessness, and of dependence; the other says "no" to my unchecked desire, to unbridled self-interest. The I has the power of its sheer presence, and the other stands over against it as a plea for acknowledgment, permission, assistance, concern, for a "piece of bread" from the I's mouth.[33]

Levinas talks of the impossibility of killing.[34] But is this right? Why is it not the case that for the other standing before the I, there is both the possibility and the impossibility of killing the other? The reason, I think, is that even the choice to kill or the act of killing itself *already* in some sense incorporates an acknowledgment, an acceptance, so that one can say that all social encounters, even the most violent and destructive, are acts of responsibility, albeit ones that do not necessarily *express* and *develop* that sense of responsibility but may rather corrupt and nullify it. In every social interaction, then, there is a plea to be supported in life and, by its sheer otherness, the other issues a command to be supported. The plea of the other person makes me responsible for her, and the command makes me responsible or accountable to her. Hence, in every social encounter, each person begins *already* with a responsibility to the other person, which is a standard that is undeniable and demanding to live up to. However the interaction goes, whatever its special features or character, this responsibility is already there, and insofar as it is an ethical matter, an imperative, its directiveness or force permeates the encounter. It is in this sense that sociality is ethical through and through, or from the ground up. Even

33 An obvious comparison to Levinas's face-to-face with the other is the idea of recognition in Fichte and Hegel. Fichte, in his *Foundations of Natural Right*, argues that I must have the concept of the other in order to have self-consciousness and the grasp of myself as a self. I become a self only insofar as I am summoned to free action by an other, whom I take to be a self in the very act of taking myself to be summoned by it. See J. G. Fichte, *Foundations of Natural Right* (Cambridge, 2000), I, Section 3, 32–37. Paul Franks explains that Fichte takes this process to be the historical genesis of self-consciousness and the notion of the self; the self becomes a self in becoming free, i.e., in coming to have the ability to determine itself in order to comply with the summons of the other or to resist it. See Franks, "The Discovery of the Other: Cavell, Fichte and Skepticism," in Crary and Shieh (eds.), *Reading Cavell* (Routledge, 2006), 176–177; also Paul Franks, *All or Nothing* (Harvard, 2005), 323–325. Franks points out that Fichte's transcendental project takes the process of the genesis of the self to be historical, unlike Kant, whose transcendental argument is aimed at a justification and not at a genetic account of the self's actual emergence. Levinas's account differs from Fichte's – and from Hegel's later version – at least in not being historical.

34 This theme, the impossiblity of murder, is also discussed in an important passage in "Is Ontology Fundamental?" See *Basic Philosophical Writings*, 9–10.

the most casual meeting, then, includes at its deepest level the command for each party to heed the misery, the plight of the other person and to take responsibility to and for that person. Here is a "metaphysical" layer of human existence at its deepest, which is particular, imperative, and ethical.[35] In this sense, then, murder is impossible.

THE FACE-TO-FACE AS SUMMONS

Much of this account of the ethical content of the face-to-face remains firmly in Levinas's grasp throughout his career. It is often affirmed in what becomes an almost standard terminology for him – in technical essays on various themes, in occasional writings, and in interviews. What I propose to do here is first to see how it takes shape in *Totality and Infinity*. Then I want to raise some questions about the account and the very character of the face-to-face as a primordial ethical event or relational experience. Some of these are questions that Levinas deals with or tries to deal with. Others he does not or at least not in ways we might find helpful. In the course of introducing and discussing these problems, I will turn to recent philosophical discussion to help us grapple with his ideas, in particular to Stanley Cavell's discussion of acknowledgment. Finally, we will take a preliminary look at some later modifications and developments of this account. We should be forewarned, however, that what we have sketched in this chapter is not yet a full account or even a sufficiently developed one. There are terms and features of the face-to-face encounter that Levinas elaborates but that we must temporarily set aside. Some of them we will return to in subsequent chapters – for example, the notion of height; the way in which Levinas understands terms like "God," the "sacred," and "holiness"; and the primordial or originary status of the event. For the moment, however, I want to focus on its ethical character.

The central section of *Totality and Infinity* is Section III, "Exteriority and the Face" and especially IIIB, "Ethics and the Face." While I will look primarily at this section, I will call attention to phrases and passages elsewhere that tell us important things about the face-to-face encounter as an ethical event, encounter, or experience. To begin with, the "epiphany as a face" is not a form of perception; this phrase does not refer to the way one person appears to another, nor even to the way a particular other

[35] For similar accounts, see Levinas, "The Ego and Totality" (1954), in *Collected Philosophical Papers*, 39–44; "Philosophy and the Idea of the Infinite," in *Collected Philosophical Papers*, especially 54–56; and "Ethics as First Philosophy" in *The Levinas Reader*, 82–83.

person appears to the I. It refers rather to a "putting in question" of the I that "emanates from the other."[36] It is a "moral summons" that "calls into question" the self's powers. That is, as we saw when we surveyed the dialectical story that Levinas gives in *Time and the Other* and that *Totality and Infinity* here elaborates, it is as if the self's power or capacity to work and appropriate worldly things for its enjoyment and nourishment is now challenged by the sheer fact that another person, who also needs those things for her nourishment and enjoyment, presents herself to the I and registers what Levinas here calls a "moral summons," the content of which is to share, to be generous, and most fundamentally to acknowledge and accept that other person.

"The face resists possession, resists my powers. In its epiphany, in expression, the sensible, still graspable, turns into total resistance to the grasp."[37] This resistance, as we have seen, is a resistance in the extreme to the I's wish to kill or at least to its power to kill, and the other person resists that wish or that power with the "primordial *expression* … 'you shall not commit murder'!"[38] The face does not literally say this, of course; it does not issue an imperative; rather, its presence expresses a summons that we as philosophers can otherwise articulate in these terms. The biblical text, in uttering this commandment as an expression of divine revelation, is giving everyday form to the most fundamental character of social interaction, which is, intrinsically, outside the domain of everyday formulation. In this sense, "the epiphany of the face is ethical." Levinas calls the face, as he had elsewhere, "destitute" and "hungry" and "naked" or "nude" and says that it "arouses" the self's goodness, through its plea and command.[39] Moreover, once again calling upon biblical and religious motifs, Levinas says that it is an event of "election" or a "call" to serve "the poor, the stranger, the widow, and the orphan."[40] This picturesque, rhetorical language is of course metonymy; the primordial relation to the other via the epiphany of the other's face applies not just to these types of people; in fact, it applies to each and every person, insofar as that person addresses the I out of her weakness, her need, and her intrinsic poverty. When one person faces another, she does so as a dependent person but not as dependent in general; rather, she confronts the particular self as wholly dependent upon that self. It is a targeted dependence, my dependency upon you.

[36] *Totality and Infinity*, 195; 196; cf. 171.
[37] Ibid., 197.
[38] Ibid., 198–199; cf. 178.
[39] Ibid., 200; cf. 213, 247.
[40] Ibid., 245–246.

This account, which emerges in *Totality and Infinity*, has a transcendental character. In this section, Levinas shows how various ordinary experiences and practices presuppose this original, deep level of meaning or hidden dimension, and, as we have seen, in "Freedom and Command" Levinas had argued that politics involves commanding and that commanding is speech, but that speech and discourse presuppose the face-to-face. This line of thought has a heroic quality about it; it is most likely part of Levinas's effort to outdo Heidegger on his own ground and even to overturn him. In recent philosophy, there have been very influential attempts to articulate transcendental arguments for the conditions that make communication possible, but none that would better satisfy Levinas. For they are either idealist or realist in ways that Levinas would surely claim are inadequate or insufficient, more akin to Heidegger's conclusions than to his own.

Exactly how does Levinas attempt to show that discourse and communication are transcendentally grounded in the face-to-face and thereby in the ethical, in some sense? In fact, Levinas does provide us with an argument that discourse is possible only on the basis of the face-to-face.[41] How does this argument develop, and why – and how – does it result in an ethical foundation or ground for the possibility of language and communication? Levinas's basic argument is rather direct. Language presupposes interlocutors, persons engaged in discourse one with another. Discourse is a "struggle between thinkers" and hence implies "transcendence, radical separation, the strangeness of the interlocutors, the revelation of the other to me."[42] Language and discourse, then, presuppose an encounter between myself and the "nudity of the face," which is different from the way a thing is disclosed to me in everyday life.[43] The face is naked, destitute, a plea and a command, that "supplicates and demands, that can supplicate only because it demands … which one recognizes in giving – … the epiphany of the face as face.… To recognize the Other is to recognize a hunger. To recognize the Other is to give."[44] It is "calling into question of my joyous possession of the world."[45]

Here is an epitome of Levinas's regressive argument, from language to what is its basic condition: discourse requires two interlocutors in relation

[41] Here I will be looking primarily at "Discourse and Ethics," section IB5 in *Totality and Infinity*, 72–77.

[42] *Totality and Infinity*, 73.

[43] Ibid., 74–75.

[44] Ibid., 75.

[45] Ibid., 76.

to one another; their relation – no matter what else it is – involves the face-to-face encounter, and what that face-to-face reveals is the other's need, plea, and so forth and the self's responsibility. Levinas then adds a progressive argument, which he develops more fully elsewhere, that shows how "this initial dispossession conditions the subsequent generalization of money," the process of generalization, conceptualization, objectivization, and ultimately the realization of "community and universality."[46] Levinas's line of thought begins with this basic event of encounter, plea, command, and generosity, leads through my making of what is mine common, to the universal, to conceptualization, and then to language, community, and thought itself.[47] "Language does not exteriorize a representation preexisting in me: it puts in common a world hitherto mine."[48] Hence, the face and language are inextricably connected.

This is a very rudimentary sketch of what Levinas says about language and discourse, on the one hand, and the face-to-face encounter, on the other, in *Totality and Infinity*. The gist of his reasoning is that language requires two elements that are both grounded in the face-to-face: first, the otherness or separateness of a dialogical partner or interlocutor, another person to talk with; and second, universality or commonality. For Levinas, there is no private language, and there is no universality not grounded in the encounter with the other's plea and demand in virtue of which I make common what is originally only mine.

Another way to look at this two-dimensional argument, with its regressive and progressive strands, is this. We live in society and communicate with one another, and the latter is possible only because of the former. But what is it about our sociality that makes communication and discourse possible? It is not simply the normal features of social interaction that we experience and are aware of in ordinary experience. It is not merely that we share features or capacities with one another or that we enjoy the same things or feel kinship with some, animosity toward others. All of this may be true, but it is derivative, and while language may enable us to describe these things or capitalize on them, they are not fundamental conditions. What is it then? If language is tied to commonality and universality and possible only in social life, where do these features come from? What is their ground? Levinas's answer is that they derive from a dimension of ordinary life hidden from view but hinted at – the nexus of the other's "supplication

46 Ibid.

47 See ibid., 100–101, 170–174, 209–212, and 296–297.

48 Ibid., 174.

and demand" and my responsibility and generosity. Only because of this nexus or event is the world ours and not mine; only because of it is there you and I and not just me. This condition is by itself not sufficient for language – we do need words, syntax, and so forth – but it is necessary.

One might object that prior to this encounter or event there is an I and then its recognition of the other person. Before the plea is the I and the other, and before responsible generosity is the recognition. Levinas denies both, in a sense. He says explicitly, "To recognize the Other is to recognize a hunger. To recognize the Other is to give."[49] The encounter with the face is not an act of seeing; it is not perceptual or judgmental. What confronts me is the other person's need, misery, destitution, and I do not see them, for I do not see yet at all. I sense and respond. I sense the suffering and give or withhold, that is, I respond, and my sensing, my responding, and my recognizing – acknowledging and accepting – the other are all one. Moreover, in a sense that we shall examine later, at that instant, so to speak, I am wholly this sensing, this responding, and this recognizing, and that is all I am as a human being; it is the totality of my humanity. In ordinary life, of course, I am much else, and since the encounter with the face occurs, if never purely but only in context, in the everyday, I am always many things in addition to responsible – at any given moment. But this is what I am primordially and fundamentally, in a sense before I am anything else. Hence, ethics comes first. My ethical character precedes all else that I am, and ethics is the ground of language and community.[50]

CAVELL ON ACKNOWLEDGMENT

Levinas's face-to-face as sensing and responding to the other's suffering and destitution, which is distinguishable from perception and knowledge of the other person but always occurs "alongside" our daily experience,

[49] Ibid., 75.

[50] Is Levinas's conception of the primacy of the ethical and the self's relation to the other too simplistic? Does it ignore too much about human interaction by focusing on just one feature of our relation to others, their vulnerability and suffering? I shall consider a criticism along these lines later, but it is interesting to notice that such an objection sounds similar to one that has often been raised against utilitarianism. W. D. Ross, for example, in *The Right and the Good* (1930), charges that "The theory of … utilitarianism … seems to simplify unduly our relations to our fellows. It says, in effect, that the only morally significant relation in which my neighbours stand to me is that of being possible beneficiaries of my action. But they may also stand to me in the relation of promisee to promisor, of creditor to debtor, of wife to husband, of fellow countryman to fellow countryman, and the like; and each of these relations is the foundation of a … duty …" (19), quoted by David McNaughton, *Moral Vision*, 177. As we shall see, Levinas does not ignore or reject the moral relevance of such relationships, but he does believe that all of them supervene on the fundamental social relationship of summons and responsibility, what Ross calls "beneficence."

may not seem wholly unfamiliar to us. Something like it has played an important role for Stanley Cavell in his reading of the later Wittgenstein and in his own philosophical thinking. I am referring to Cavell's notion of "acknowledgment." This idea arises for Cavell in his thinking about Wittgenstein's reflections on psychological states and about the problem of other minds. It then takes on other roles and a wider scope, eventually playing a central role in Cavell's thinking about skepticism, romanticism, and larger questions about the human condition.[51]

Cavell's early discussion of Wittgenstein on psychological states, other minds, and such themes, although it is obviously aimed at clarifying issues that are not central for Levinas, nonetheless does draw close to Levinasian themes. Just as Levinas, as we shall see, seeks to expose the limits of Western philosophy, Cavell seems to be working his way toward a view of how we live in the world and how we live with other people that breaks sharply with the traditional Cartesian view or any variation of it. He does this by considering skeptical challenges to our knowledge of other minds and by glossing that knowledge as a kind of acknowledgment and acceptance of responsibility for the other person.[52] This can be seen clearly in an early essay on these themes. His basic strategy is this. We should, he says, distinguish between the statements "I know I am in pain" and "I know you are in pain" in the following way. Although they appear to be syntactically similar, the two statements differ significantly. The first claim is

51 Simon Critchley explicitly associates Cavell's conception of acknowledgment with Levinas's notion of justice (in *Totality and Infinity*) in "Cavell's 'Romanticism' and Cavell's Romanticism," in Russell Goodman (ed.), *Contending with Stanley Cavell* (Oxford, 2005), 50: "... in Cavell's terms, tragedy is the dramatization of the failure to acknowledge others. The skeptical teaching of tragedy – and the tragic teaching of skepticism – is the fact that I cannot know the other.... [*The Claim of Reason*] closes with the image of Othello and Desdamona dead on their nuptial bed. For Cavell, this image constitutes an emblem for the truth of skepticism.... [Othello] could not accept the tragic wisdom of the limitedness of his knowledge of Desdemona and consequently he failed to acknowledge her separateness, her alterity. This is why Othello kills Desdemona" (50). Critchley calls the relationship with the other that Othello fails to engage "what Levinas, and Derrida after him, call justice" (50). We live, in Cavell's terms, between love and avoidance. Tragedy, skepticism, and acknowledgment are the central themes of Part IV of *The Claim of Reason*.

In a discussion of Cavell on the moral of skepticism and moral perfectionism, Hilary Putnam notes that "if Othello's is a pathology, it is an exaggerated form of, so to speak, a *normal* pathology. The point of saying this is not simply to awaken us to the suffering of others, as Levinas does (although I have heard Cavell speak about Levinas with deep respect); it is also to get us to see that an idea of being totally free of skepticism, in this deep sense, is itself a *form* of skepticism" ("Philosophy as the Education of Grownups: Stanley Cavell and Skepticism," in Crary and Shieh (eds.), *Reading Cavell*, 127). I would just like to point out that Levinas would doubtless object to the word "simply" and the suggestion that what Putnam is ascribing to Cavell is not also something that Levinas understands in a very serious way.

52 See Stanley Cavell, "Knowing and Acknowledging," in *Must We Mean What We Say?*, Chapter 9, 238–266. The theme is also pervasive in many of Cavell's later works, e.g., *The Claim of Reason*.

really an expression of pain, an exhibiting of me, as suffering, to another, while the second is "a response to this exhibiting; it is an expression of *sympathy*.... But why is sympathy expressed this way? Because your suffering makes a *claim* on me. It is not enough that I *know* (am certain) that you suffer – I must do or reveal something (whatever can be done). In a word, I must *acknowledge* it." To be sure, as Cavell goes on to point out, "the claim of suffering may go unanswered.... The point, however, is that the concept of acknowledgment is evidenced equally by its failure as by its success."[53] Cavell's point, which he gets from his reading of Wittgenstein, is that "pain" language is not about knowledge claims. Its uses both express pain and acknowledge it, and the acknowledgment is a response to a claim made on me, not by the other person's statement or utterance but rather by the other's pain or suffering. As Cavell puts it, when I am presented with that suffering "I must do or reveal something." I cannot avoid it; whatever I do or say is a response to it. Pain and suffering – and perhaps, or even probably, not them alone – *must be* acknowledged when exhibited.[54]

This bit is important to Cavell, although it is not the end of the matter. It is only part of his discussion of criteria, psychological concepts, other minds, and many other themes. But for my purposes, it is a central, revealing passage. Notice some of its features. First, the notion of acknowledging another person's suffering or pain is part of a larger project of clarifying psychological concepts in their first-, second-, and third-person uses. In a sense, then, Cavell begins with an interest in epistemology, language, and cognitive psychology. Second, it applies to a whole variety of such concepts, not just to pain and suffering.[55] Third, it will eventually coordinate acknowledging with imagination, in order to tie together the first-person use and the second- and third-person uses.[56] Finally, acknowledgment will eventually become central to Cavell's romantic conception of how we live in the world and with the world.[57] These features remind us that the relevance of Cavell for understanding Levinas, while limited, is important, and the text we looked at is very helpful. Clearly, for Levinas, the suffering of the other person, present to me in her face, is not simply one psychological state among others. It is somehow basic and original, for

[53] Cavell, "Knowing and Acknowledging" in *Must We Mean What We Say?*, 263.

[54] See Stephen Mulhall, *Stanley Cavell: Philosophy's Recounting of the Ordinary*, 110–111, 119; see also Stanley Cavell, *The Claim of Reason*, 82–85. For a very helpful discussion of the relevance of this asymmetry between first- and third-person experience, especially with regard to the conceptual problem of other minds, see Anita Avramides, *Other Minds* (Routledge, 2001), passim.

[55] See Stephen Mulhall, *Stanley Cavell*, 130–138.

[56] See ibid., 119–122.

[57] See ibid., 158–163; see also Stanley Cavell, *In Quest of the Ordinary* (Chicago, 1988), passim.

its everyday occurrences as pain, hunger, or loneliness, for example, are indications or hints of a more basic fact, that the other person's very presence in my world, over against me, is both a plea to share my possessions, my space, and my bread, and a demand that I respond to that plea. In this early essay, Cavell does not see things this way, or at least his purposes in reading Wittgenstein against Descartes and others do not lead him in this direction. His is still a romantic, subject-oriented conception. What it does capture nonetheless is the way in which the other's pain is present and is received, so to speak.[58] That is, once we accept the situation as one of another person's pain or need being exhibited for me or being expressed to me, Cavell helps us to see how that exhibition or expression actually constitutes a *claim*: it includes a supplication and a demand that I respond in some way or other. This is what acknowledging the other's pain is: sensing that claim and that demand. Hence the statement "I know you are in pain" or "I know she is in pain" are not knowledge claims, assertions based on sensory evidence, or anything of this sort. They are acts of sympathy that *express* this acknowledgment; they are public expressions of the face-to-face. If Levinas can show how this encounter is fundamental or primary, Cavell has helped us to see that such an encounter is not strange, extraordinary, or ineffable. Indeed, if Cavell is right, as a category, the face-to-face encounter is exemplified regularly in everyday life. What is remarkable would be how basic the role of suffering is and how regularly our respect or sensitivity to it is occluded or ignored.

In a sense, Cavell's account has the outcome that we are tied into the world and tied together with other people in ways more fundamental than the cognitive, epistemic, and presentational. This is a kind of Heideggerian insight, which Cavell himself acknowledges. It is Husserlian, too, to the degree that what Heideggerian calls *existentale* (existential ways of being) are modes of intentionality broadly in Husserl's sense. Levinas would of course deny that the encounter with the face of the other person is simply a mode of intentionality or even, strictly speaking, such a mode at all, but it is quasi-intentional at least in the sense that it is not a kind

[58] Because of the orientation of the philosophical tradition out of which Cavell speaks, the focus, at one level, is on language and the syntactic similarity between the statements "I know I am in pain" and "I know you are in pain." What he proceeds to do, of course, is to show that the two statements serve very different purposes in terms of the interpersonal interaction between parties who utter them. What begins as a narrowly linguistic issue becomes a larger issue about human existence. This larger perspective already emerges in essays such as "The Avoidance of Love" on *King Lear*, in *Must We Mean What We Say?*, and then in *The Claim of Reason*, especially Part Four, on tragedy, and Chapter 13, "Between Acknowledgment and Avoidance" (Oxford University Press, 1979).

of external relation between the other person and the self.[59] This too is a feature of Cavell's insight; part of disclosing, not solving, the problem of other minds is to appreciate how fundamentally the I and the other person are tied together. The concepts of expression or exhibition and acknowledgment are intended in part to expose this linkage and to suggest that epistemic "distance" and "detachment," which generates the traditional problem of other minds, is already a particular mode of that linkage.[60]

What makes the epiphany of the face ethical, then, is that intrinsically it involves a claim – what I have called "plea and command" – on me by the other to acknowledge her, to respond to the other person's suffering, to her claim upon me and her "election" of me. As we have seen, at times Levinas puts this in biblical terms: the face says to me, in the imperative, "thou shalt not kill." In Cavell's terms, the imperative is: acknowledge me. But this is no rule or principle in the normal sense; it is nothing general, but rather a precise, particular, utterly unique directive. Any rule or principle must come later, so to speak; that is, moral rules and legal principles do occur, but they arise out of the dimension of the face-to-face and are "indebted" to that dimension. What the utterly particular face says to the utterly particular me is "do not kill *me*" or "make room for *me*," "help *me*," "give *me* a share of your bread." It is, as Cavell puts it, a claim or demand, but it is not a rule. That comes only with universality or generality, which we have yet to discuss. What underlies every social relation we have is an utterly unique relation between each and every other person and me. To be sure, in everyday affairs, our relationship is also defined and shaped by a host of rules, regularized patterns, and principles of conduct – social, moral, legal, and otherwise. But it is Levinas's point that all of these "derive" from the encounter with the face, which is particular and determinative.[61] Moreover, every act of following a moral principle is always a way of responding to another person. Knowing is but one way of acknowledging. In other words, the priority of the face is not temporal; in a sense, it is incorporated into ordinary life, but only in qualified, obscured, or distorted ways. Neither the face nor the many other ways the other person appears to me occur on their own, in isolation. The other may be my friend, my companion on a trip, an excellent chess player, a

[59] Levinas, *Totality and Infinity*, 49: "The 'intentionality' of transcendence is unique in its kind."

[60] See Avramides, *Other Minds*, for discussion of the difference between lived context and Cartesian detachment for the problem of other minds.

[61] We shall discuss this relationship, in part the relationship between ethics (in Levinas's deep sense) and politics, later. For the moment, we should note that this account is *not* a genetic account; social relationships with moral and legal rules do not *come from* the face-to-face, but they are "grounded" in it.

lover of Kiarostami's films, and the claimant of my responsibility, all at once. Some of these relations arise out of conventions, popular culture, common practices, and traditional roles, but one relation is constituted by our most fundamental engagement with one another, and that one is Levinas's primary concern.[62]

LATER THOUGHTS ON ETHICS AND THE FACE

We do not yet know why the face has the primacy that it does, why Levinas takes it to be the infinite or transcendent that breaches the totality of our lives and our thinking, and what this idea means. Nor do we know in what sense the face has meaning or sense, how it can be approached in language, what gives it the force to make the claim it does, how it gives rise to society, moral rules, and politics, and exactly why it is called "religion" and what Levinas's extensive use of religious and theological vocabulary means. Nor do we understand Levinas's conception of the self and the paradoxical claim that it is originally passive and responsible before it is anything else and that its freedom is derivative and not original. These are among the themes of chapters yet to come. What we do understand is that the epiphany of the face has an ethical force and an ethical content. Before we move on, however, I want to consider some of the developments we find in Levinas's later treatment of the face-to-face and the terminology he comes to use to designate it. In these later works, Levinas attends more and more to the face-to-face from the point of the view of the self or subject. In Chapter 5, I will discuss Levinas's conception of subjectivity and the self, what one might call the "subjective side" of the encounter with the other. Here, even as I turn to Levinas's later writings, I will try to remain focused on the ethical content of the face

62 Levinas's understanding of the ethical has some similarities to what is currently called "moral particularism," but it is distinctive. As we shall see, for example, Levinas argues that each ethical situation has its own features that need to be identified and examined with the greatest care and attention to detail. In this same spirit, David McNaughton points out that the moral particularist holds that "what is required is the correct conception of the particular case in hand, with its unique set of properties. There is thus no substitute for a sensitive and detailed examination of each individual case" (*Moral Vision* [Blackwell's, 1988], 190). But the particularist associates this attention to detail with a skepticism "about the role of moral principles in moral reasoning.... Moral particularism takes the view that moral principles are at best useless, and at worst a hindrance, in trying to find out which is the right action" (*Moral Vision*, 190; cf. Jonathan Dancy, *Ethics Without Principles* [Oxford, 2004]). Many commentators read Levinas as endorsing such a view as well, if not an even more radically critical view of moral rules, but I doubt that this is correct, as I shall try to show. Moral rules may not be fundamental in Levinas's eyes, but neither are they totally useless or an obstacle to determining what is right or just.

and its "objective side," that is, the ethical character of the impact of the other on the self.

Regularly, after *Totality and Infinity*, Levinas continues to describe the face and its impact as he has: it puts the self in question or calls it into question; it speaks out of nakedness, destitution, and weakness; it forbids murder; it challenges the self from its humility and height; it summons the self to respond.[63] In interviews, when asked about the face, his responses reflect these same themes.[64] The nudity of the face is a call, an appeal, and also an imperative, he says in 1989.[65] And in his interview with Richard Kearney, published in 1984, he says that "the face is the other who asks me not to let him die alone, as if to do so were to become an accomplice in his death. Thus the face says to me: you shall not kill."[66] Finally, in *Ethics and Infinity*, his conversations with Philippe Nemo, published in 1982, he describes the face as "exposed, menaced, as if inviting us to an act of violence. At the same time, the face is what forbids us to kill.... The face is what one cannot kill, or at least it is that whose *meaning* consists in saying: 'thou shalt not kill'."[67] This account, then, remains a consistent background to Levinas's understanding of the face-to-face. But against that background there are modifications, new emphases, and new dimensions. These developments are often tied to the use of new terminology. As I indicated, I will restrict present comments to the ethical character of the "objective" side of the encounter with the face, that is, to the ethical import of the face for the self.[68] I will leave discussion of such matters as the religious character of the encounter and its subjective side for later.

In his essay "Substitution" (1968), later modified as the core of *Otherwise than Being* (1974), we find several new terms associated with the face. The encounter is now called "proximity" and is characterized as "my relationship with the neighbor" and as "the summoning of myself by the other (*autrui*) ... a summons of extreme urgency.... The term *obsession*

[63] See Levinas, "Phenomenon and Enigma," in *Collected Philosophical Papers*, 69–70; "Transcendence and Height," in *Basic Philosophical Writings*, 16–19; "Meaning and Sense," in *Basic Philosophical Writings*, 54; "Language and Proximity," in *Collected Philosophical Papers*, 120–121; "Transcendence and Evil," in *Collected Philosophical Papers*, 185; "Philosophy, Justice and Love," in *Entre Nous*, 103–105; and "From One to the Other," in *Entre Nous*, 144–146.

[64] See in *Is It Righteous To Be?*, 48–49, 114–115, 127–128, 135–136, 144–145, 215.

[65] Levinas, "Being for the Other," in *Is It Righteous To Be?*, 115.

[66] "Dialogue with Emmanuel Levinas," in Cohen (ed.), *Face to Face with Levinas*, 24.

[67] *Ethics and Infinity*, 86–87; cf. 85–92.

[68] That is, I will set aside until later discussion of responsibility and the selfhood constituted by it, i.e., the subjective side of the face-to-face.

designates this relation which is irreducible to consciousness."[69] On the one hand, Levinas takes the other not to be alien and distant as much as close and nearby. On the other, the emphasis now is on the "urgency" that the face evinces and its alien and yet unavoidable character, which Levinas goes on to describe "as something foreign, as disequilibrium, as delirium, undoing thematization, eluding *principle*, origin, and will."[70] The face not only pleas and commands; it is strange and disorienting; it unsettles – and overwhelms.

Levinas also calls it "an-archic" but not simply as disordering, which involves one order replacing another.[71] The face is "beyond these alternatives." It is somehow independent of order or principle altogether, prior to them, wholly oblique and disruptive. Moreover, since an *arche* is a beginning or starting point, an original principle, the face is something "prior" to beginning and to what, in everyday life or theoretical understanding, is a starting point or founding principle. It is, then, an obsession that is an-archic *persecution*, "a placing in question anterior to questioning, a responsibility beyond the logos of response, as though persecution by the other (*autrui*) were the basis of solidarity with the other (*autrui*)."[72] The face as persecution, moreover, is an *accusation*: "it strips the Ego of its self-conceit and its dominating imperialism."[73] The Ego returns to its true, original self by being accused, and hence through its tie to the other person, spontaneity – the freedom we have as subjects – returns to passivity – the responsibility we have as objects, as it were. "Obsessed with responsibilities, which do not result from decisions taken by a 'freely contemplating' subject, consequently accused of what it never willed or decreed, accused of what it did not do, subjectivity is thrown back on itself – in itself – by a persecuting accusation."[74] The result for the self, engaged by the other via accusation and persecution, is what Levinas calls "substitution" and "being a hostage," "the fact of human fellowship, prior to freedom."[75]

[69] Levinas, "Substitution," in *Basic Philosophical Writings*, 81.

[70] Ibid.

[71] The Greek word *arche* means starting point, beginning, or principle. The English word "anarchy" is derived from it, with the alpha privative, *an*, which means "without." In the text I point out that Levinas does not mean, by an-archic, "anarchic" in our sense, chaotic or without order. He wants us to think about the word's original Greek sense, without a beginning, but in a special way.

[72] Levinas, "Substitution," in *Basic Philosophical Writings*, 82.

[73] Ibid., 88.

[74] Ibid.

[75] Ibid., 90–91.

Levinas's new vocabulary is intended in part to show that the encounter with the face of the other person is ethically prior to language, thought, reflection, and the everyday. For the moment I want to notice especially the *tonality* of the terminology.[76] Many of the new expressions – obsession, persecution, accusation, hostage – take the earlier themes of calling into question, summoning, and demanding and modulate them into a disturbing, almost assaulting, register. From one point of view, the terms call attention to the way in which the face-to-face indicts our everyday sense of ourselves, our priorities, and our freedom, and pulls us back to our origins, indeed to a point prior to our origins, against our will, as it were. From another point of view, these terms remind us of what we originally are – accused before we have done anything, obsessed before we have chosen at all and in a sense overcome, persecuted by the demand made of us before we have accepted it. And, in a sense, this is also what we always are – unjust, inadequately caring and attentive, out of control. Moreover, the new vocabulary – the terms all virtual metaphors – already marks a shift in Levinas's attention, a development widely appreciated by commentators, from the objective side of the face-to-face, the suffering and misery of the other person, to the subjective side, the kind of self I am as accused by that face. Nonetheless, from either perspective, the face is seen as disruptive and demanding; our interpersonal relationships always have this character, and in this sense Levinas's new expressions only underscore the imperative force of the primordial relationship. Ethics at this level is an assault; we are deluged by responsibility.[77] Whether we think of the

[76] Levinas's terminology for the encounter with the other person capitalizes on the richness of the terms, their multiple meanings and suggestiveness. In the case of *hostage*, for example, the other holds the self hostage in the sense that it imposes itself with a kind of force, binds the self, and seeks help in exchange. To hold someone hostage, after all, is to confine that person by force or against his will with an offer of release only in exchange for money or goods of some kind. Levinas says that the other *accuses* the self. An accusation is a charge leveled against someone for a harm or injury committed or for having done something wrong, but the term *accusation* also suggests grammatically the *accusative* case. What is in the accusative is the direct object of the verb and hence is passive. As a final example, the other person *persecutes* the self. To persecute someone is to insult, harm, or inflict a wrong in a continuous or consistent way, over a significant period of time, but, more generally, it is to dominate or impose oneself on them. We associate *persecution*, historically, with the mistreatment of minorities of one kind or another, and in Europe the paradigmatic persecution was anti-Semitism, just as in the United States it has been the mistreatment of African Americans, Indians, and other racial minorities. Levinas applies these verbs to the way the other person is related to the subject, but the connotations he is drawing upon are broader and deeper than some one specific sense.

[77] An entire literature has grown up around the so-called life-saving analogy, utilized in a classic way by Peter Singer in "Famine, Affluence and Morality," *Philosophy and Public Affairs* 1 (1972), 229–243. One development is argument in behalf of a morality of beneficence. An excellent discussion occurs in Garrett Cullity, *The Moral Demands of Affluence* (Oxford, 2004). Cullity

disruption caused by the face as original or as a return to origins, it is still unsettling, oblique to the calm confines of cognitive experience and its associated ordinary way of life. As Levinas sees it, human existence does not start out on still waters but rather in a turbulent sea, and that turbulence persists. Our humanity emerges for us with the cries of hungry children and the agony of destitute neighbors, floundering and calling for help.[78] At that urgent moment, we are human beings for the first time, so to speak, before we have done a thing.[79]

In Western philosophy, certainly since Hume, the fact/value distinction or the distinction between the descriptive and the prescriptive or normative has played a central role and is contested to this day.[80] To some, a feature of the distinction is the special force of the ethical. Levinas does not use this distinction in any explicit way; it is not a feature of his philosophical vocabulary. To him, it would be a distinction used by philosophers and others within everyday life and our theoretical reflection on it, a characteristic of the domain of being or ontology. But it is illuminating to take his increasingly dramatic and urgent vocabulary for the way the face imposes itself on the self as an expression of his appreciation for the "excessive" and "extraordinary" way in which ethical value intrudes into our natural lives. Moreover, it is illuminating too to see the relationship with the face as a dimension of human social experience that complements our existence as natural beings and introduces the sense of value and goodness that we believe human life has. Ethics may be elevating and hence one reason for calling it "religion" and later "the holy," but it is also a venue for

characterizes a "failure of *beneficence*" as "the failure to display an adequate practical concern for other people's interests" insofar as "other people's interests in receiving our help give us a clear reason to help them" and "the failure to respond to this reason by going ahead and helping them can be morally wrong" (13, cf. 16). This sounds very much like Levinas. There are affinities between what Levinas has to say and such moral thinking, affinities worth pursuing on another occasion.

78 For Levinas, the historical paradigm of one who understands the primacy of the ethical character of human existence is the Jew; the Bible and the Talmud are the earliest Jewish texts that teach this lesson. Later examples of people abandoned by others and subject to injustice, persecution, and assault are all "honorary" Jews, for Levinas. As we shall see, the Jewish people is an historical reality, to be sure, but the "Jew" is also a philosophical trope or figure, a term that stands for the primacy of the ethical for human existence. This holds as well for the figure of the prophet.

79 We will return to this point: even though I have used temporal and developmental language, as Levinas often does, I want to emphasize that the face-to-face does not occur "before" the rest of social life. It is a permanent dimension of it, even when it is ignored or hidden from view. For Levinas, as I shall argue later, all human life is ethical and political at once. There is no avoiding the face and no avoiding compromising our responsibility to the other person, ever.

80 See Hilary Putnam, *The Collapse of the Fact/Value Dichotomy and Other Essays* (Harvard University Press, 2002).

disturbance, a locale for an anomaly. It is in this sense that ethics is a kind of persecution and accusation. It holds us hostage; we are in its grip, and because it is an unavoidable feature of our existence, we are not duped by it; it is no trick, no distortion. Levinas expresses these sentiments about the primacy and yet the difficulty of ethical obligation when he employs such dramatic terms for the way the "face of the other" confronts the self and calls it into question.

CHAPTER FOUR

Philosophy, Totality, and the Everyday

PHILOSOPHY AND THE EVERYDAY

Most often, when Levinas turns to the encounter with the face of the other in order to shed light on its objective or subjective side, he does so within the context of everyday life and ordinary experience.[1] His accounts are abstract and metaphorical, but they arise out of everyday experiences of misery and suffering, of the orphan, the stranger, the poor, and the widow. Their biblical overtones notwithstanding, such figures are ones whom we meet in ordinary life. As we have pointed out, it is as if he is locating a dimension of experience largely hidden from view, obscured by our habits and ways of conducting affairs, or distorted by culturally and historically grounded attitudes, as a reminder of the fundamental meaning of our humanity. The face is both in our lives and somehow not in them; it confronts us in ordinary life and yet also from outside it. The face is not a phenomenon, but rather, as Levinas comes to put it, an *enigma* or riddle, a challenge to what is customary and accepted, and yet also in some ways a foundation of the ordinary.[2]

Philosophy reaches out and locates the face-to-face, describes and clarifies it, and hence philosophy arises at least in part for moral reasons, because that clarification and that articulation are needed.[3] But philosophy

[1] By the "subjective" side of the face-to-face, I mean the self's point of view and any features that Levinas ascribes to the self, such as its responsibility; by the "objective" side of the face-to-face, I mean the other person's point of view and any features Levinas ascribes to it, e.g., that it is present as a face or that it is vulnerable, nude, and weak.

[2] See "Enigma and Phenomenon" in *Basic Philosophical Writings*, and "Phenomenon and Enigma" in *Collected Philosophical Papers*. The face also breaches or disrupts our everyday experience, Levinas says; in a sense, it enters it from the outside. These expressions, however, cannot be taken literally; the words and concepts of disrupting and such are used within everyday life; they cannot be applied literally to whatever enters the everyday sphere from the outside, so to speak. Like all terms for the face-to-face, these have a metaphorical quality.

[3] What philosophy aims at and accomplishes, then, at least in part, is an act of disclosure, of clarification or illumination of what is "dark" or hidden, of articulation – to use an expression that both

is located in the everyday and always returns to it. One wonders, however, if and in what sense it really leaves it. What philosophy does, as ethical metaphysics, is to see the role of the face-to-face in life and in thought. But in order to do this, does it reach beyond life and beyond thought? In one sense, it does, but in another it does not. In this chapter we will say something about why and how both are so.

Why is the face primordial? One reason is that it is infinite, and as infinite the face ruptures or breaches totality, which cannot encompass it. In a sense, then, the face is unconditioned, absolute, unjustified, given prior to everything else in our lives, our experience, and our thinking. In this chapter, we need to try to clarify these matters. It is a dark saying that the face is the infinite. What does it mean? What did Levinas learn from Franz Rosenzweig, the Weimar Jewish philosopher whom he credits in the Preface to *Totality and Infinity* with having preceded him in opposing "the idea of totality?" Why is the face exteriority, the transcendent, and the other?

From one point of view, this discussion about totality, infinity, ethics, and the face takes the downward route, from the everyday to its primordial condition or ground. Another route leads up, from the face to the everyday world, a world of society, moral systems, and politics. If Levinas's ethical metaphysics incorporates a critique of Western society and culture and judgments about episodes of generosity and kindness, then it does so because the face somehow marks our ordinary lives. In the everyday there are hints or traces of genuine humanity because life and thought, morality and politics, are ultimately grounded in the encounter with the face of the other person. We need to explore this route too, from the particularity of the face-to-face to the institutions and practices of social life.

One way of distinguishing the movements that scholars call modernism and postmodernism is to point out how they respond to ordinary everyday affairs. Modernism is redemptive and elevating. It seeks to transcend the limitations of the everyday through heroic action, creativity, and extraordinary religious experience. Modernism is a kind of heroic romanticism. Postmodernism, on the other hand, and some who anticipated it – I am thinking of Robert Musil, Siegfried Kracauer, and Walter Benjamin – invoke a redemptive realism and an affirmation of the mundane, the prosaic. Unlike modernism, this trend claims that seeking transcendence tends to malign or demean everyday experience and

Charles Taylor and Robert Brandom employ in technical ways; see Taylor, *Sources of the Self*, and Brandom, *The Articulation of Practical Reasoning* and *Making It Explicit*.

to reduce the importance of all the common items and experiences that fill up our everyday lives and that give our lives the meaning they have. One might associate modernism, then, with transcendence and a metaphysical realism of a Platonist kind, an insecurity about the everyday and an elevation of the extraordinary. Postmodernism is, on the other hand, a kind of idealism, confined to our web of beliefs and practices, reverent of revealing more and more of what lies within it. In which camp should we expect to find Levinas? Or does he perhaps straddle both? Is there a sense in which the face is both a condition for ordinary life and an ideal that ordinary people are called to realize? There are modern philosophers who honor ordinary life and natural existence but who seek to find standards of human flourishing within it. Is there a way in which Levinas is both one of their party and also a critic of their inadequacies?

To mark these issues, Levinas uses the terms "totality" and "infinity," terms that we shall try to clarify as this chapter proceeds. The everyday world, our lives and our thinking, is the domain of totality. What is the infinite, and how does it rupture or breach that world? Here I turn to two essays – "Philosophy and the Idea of Infinity" (1957) and "Transcendence and Height" (1962) – and *Totality and Infinity* (1961) in order to clarify these issues and answer these questions. The issues and questions are central for Levinas and might be seen as the starting point of his thinking. Among other things, investigating totality and infinity will shed light on Levinas's relation to the Western philosophical tradition as well as to everyday experience, history, beliefs, and actions.

The infinite, exteriority, the transcendent, the Other – these are all expressions for what is outside or what is different, but outside of what? Different from what? And in what way outside or different? Moreover, why is this issue at all significant or perhaps even important? Why does it matter whether there is something outside?

These are not new questions. Plato wondered if there was anything outside the everyday world of sensory experience, the world of nature, motion, and change. Aristotle wondered if there was anything outside the natural world, the world of scientific knowledge, of the terrestrial and celestial domains. Plotinus wondered whether there were not a pure unity beyond being. Medieval religious philosophers and theologians – Arabic, Christian, and Jewish – wondered if there was anything outside of the natural or ordered world, and modern Cartesian skeptics if there was anything outside the domain of appearances, ideas, or impressions. Kant proposed that outside the domain of sensory experience and scientific knowledge there lies the *thing-in-itself*, and his contemporaries wondered whether this did not conduce to skepticism, leaving the knowable permanently beyond our grasp. Some twentieth-century philosophers and their eighteenth- and nineteenth-century ancestors wondered whether there were minds outside each of our own, and idealists like Berkeley whether there were material things outside minds. Others wondered whether perception requires the presence of some pre-conceptual given outside the bounds of the "space of reasons" and thought. Against this background, Levinas stands. He does not wonder; he believes that the infinite is outside totality and yet breaches it, like the traditional providential God of Western faiths who exists as transcendent and yet reveals Himself, in speech and in act, to human beings within the natural world. But Levinas's infinite is not God, and its breaking into totality is only metaphorically a revelation or epiphany. What, then, is totality and what the infinite?

In his 1987 Preface to the German edition of *Totality and Infinity*, Levinas comments on the themes of that book:

> This book challenges the synthesis of knowledge, the totality of being that is embraced by the *transcendental ego*, presence grasped in the representation and the concept … – inevitable stations of Reason – as the ultimate authorities in deciding what is *meaningful*.... Beyond the *in-itself* and *for-itself* of the disclosed, there is human nakedness, more exterior than the outside of the world – landscapes, things, institutions – the nakedness that cries out its strangeness to the world.... Within the world of appearances, it cries out the shame of its hidden misery....[4]

Levinas's book challenges an old and conventional way of looking at our lives, our world, and our experience. What he challenges about this picture is not its sufficiency within its own domain; rather, what he challenges is its assumption of its own completeness and comprehensiveness, its conviction that its meaning is wholly self-contained. In fact, his charge is that what it omits or ignores is fundamental to everything within it.

According to the view that Levinas opposes, what is meaningful about human life is determined by thought or reason, in a broad sense. That reason is either personal or impersonal, subjective or absolute. It is the individual's rational capacities of synthesis, conceptualization, and organization or those capacities as the ordering principles of the whole of nature; reason is individual and personal or cosmic and unconditional. This tradition of thinking permeates our everyday lives, but its emblem is the tradition of Western philosophy from Parmenides and Plato, through the medievals to Spinoza, Leibniz, Kant, the German Idealists, Husserl, and even, Levinas argues, Heidegger. In this tradition, relative exteriority

[4] Levinas, Preface to the German edition of *Totality and Infinity*, in *Entre Nous*, 198.

or otherness is eventually assimilated into an ultimate, comprehensive unity or whole. Only occasionally is there a hint of an absolute exteriority, something unqualifiedly outside the domain of reason, albeit not necessarily outside the domain of our actual experience and our actual lives. This domain of reason is what Levinas calls "totality"; it is the "world of appearances," and it is Levinas's claim that an ultimate ground of what is *meaningful* in it comes from the outside, in a sense, from the crying out of the face of suffering, out of its "hidden misery."

TOTALITY AND THE INFINITE

Levinas gives an excellent early account of this kind of totality and the infinity that breaches it in his 1957 essay "Philosophy and the Idea of Infinity."[5] Levinas begins by identifying two impulses of Western philosophy and of the aspiration for knowledge, what he calls "heteronomy" and "autonomy." "Heteronomy" refers to the aspiration, especially philosophical, to move from this world to another, from the everyday to the beyond. Heteronomy, then, is characteristic of metaphysics and philosophical theology. Autonomy is the opposite tendency, aimed at "the reduction of the other to the same"; it is the movement of human thought to "domesticate" everything and incorporate it into its own venue – concepts, principles, and theories. Typically, Levinas claims, Western philosophy has inclined toward the side of autonomy, from Ionia to Jena; it has seemed "to exclude the transcendent, encompass every other in the same, and proclaim the philosophical birthright of autonomy."[6]

Levinas uses Plato's terms from the *Sophist* and the *Timaeus*, the "same" and the "other." Basically, the same is the self, mind, thought, and reason; in one sense or another, everything outside the self becomes the same as the self or spirit. The other is everything different or other than the same. Western philosophy's primary impulse is imperialistic, to reduce the other to the same, to think everything.[7]

Before we proceed with Levinas's own exposition, it is worth stopping to notice that there are, as we have suggested earlier, two ways of understanding these impulses and their goals. There is what we might call an

[5] There are several translations of this important essay and a detailed commentary by Adriaan Peperzak in his book *To the Other*. I will cite the translation in *Collected Philosophical Papers*.

[6] Levinas, "Philosophy and the Idea of Infinity," in *Collected Philosophical Papers*, 47–48, especially 48.

[7] In principle, reductive materialism or naturalism, as well as idealism, also reduces everything to one sort of thing, but in this case it is matter rather than idea, physical rather than mental (or spiritual) events.

empirical reading, according to which heteronomy seems involved in a virtually incoherent task, to reach beyond the bounds of thought and consciousness to identify and acknowledge something that may seem to be necessary to make sense of the natural order but that is itself beyond thought and awareness. On this reading, then, philosophy claims to experience what cannot in principle be experienced. Levinas pinpoints one such goal as the divine, which must be understood as somehow indentifiable while being beyond thought, experience, and language. An analogue, in a different context, would be Kant's thing-in-itself or, in more recent epistemology, the target of what Sellars calls the "myth of the given," some kind of pre-conceptual, brute perceptual sensa or data. All of this, no matter how common in the philosophical tradition, certainly has struck many as smacking of mysticism or obscurantism.

But there is another reading of Levinas's conception of heteronomy and autonomy, one we might call "perspectivalist." According to this view, all that is included in the notion of the same are the typical, regularly accepted, and even mythologized perspectives that we take on things and people in the world. The things called "the other" are not new entities as much as they are or represent unnoticed or repressed perspectives, dimensions, or aspects of the world as we already experience and think about it. The divine, on this reading, represents a perspective on nature – say, that it is dependent or ordered – that we might regularly ignore but that, with greater attention and direction, we might better notice and appreciate. Another example comes from the theory of knowledge. Just as intellectualist approaches to knowledge neglect or distort our emotional lives, for example, recognition of the role of institutions and practices would open up a social perspective that has tended to be ignored or reduced to a kind of individual construction. On this account, the other calls upon us to see things we had not seen before, so to speak, although even to speak of "seeing" might at best be a metaphor.[8] Moreover, if the other were treated as something prior or determinative or fundamental, this would mean that the repressed perspective was meaningful in a basic and especially significant way, in a way that is foundational and that shapes other ways in which we relate to people and things.

It may very well be that Levinas shifts back and forth in his discussion of totality, infinity, and the face, from this empirical reading to this perspectival one.[9] At the very least, we should keep in mind that Levinas does

[8] The other could be diverse, e.g., the material and economic character of human experience or the Unconscious.

[9] We might compare his practice to Kant's and the shifting in Kant from the transcendental or critical to the empirical or material standpoint.

not have to be read as an obscurantist or a mystic. He is a philosopher and an ethical thinker and a critic of modern society and culture. And his thinking is ineluctably ordinary and concrete, even where it might seem to be obscure and distractingly abstract.

In Levinas's view, then, Western philosophy is fundamentally a form of reduction, in particular a reduction to the self or what he calls egology, attempting unwaveringly to swallow every other into thought or reason. Hence, in religious terms, it is atheism (nontheism) – or, as we might put it, humanism.[10] This is the dominant pitch of what Franz Rosenzweig called "the old thinking," what both Wittgenstein and Heidegger, each in his own way, charged with distortion and obfuscation.[11] Levinas explicitly acknowledges his debt to Rosenzweig, and indirectly then to other critics of traditional philosophy such as Schelling, Kierkegaard, and Nietzsche, and his commitment to expose the shortcomings of this philosophical tradition. But Levinas realizes or at least claims that the alternative tendency – toward heteronomy rather than autonomy – is as old and as venerated. It is found, he here notes, in Plato and Descartes at certain crucial moments.[12] He sets about to explore that moment in Descartes's thought; it is a moment he cites regularly to the end of his career.

This heteronomous moment is indeed a *crucial* one, to Descartes and to the entire Cartesian project as well as to Levinas. It occurs in Meditation III. Descartes's reasoning is familiar and famous. In order to prove the veracity of clear and distinct ideas, Descartes seeks to prove the existence of an infinite, perfect, and benevolent God. Only if such a perfect, nondeceiving God exists can we trust the accuracy of our rational understanding of nature. The argument begins with the premise that I have an idea of an infinite and perfect being. Levinas is interested only in this first premise, what he calls "the *formal* design" of the structure that Descartes's analysis outlines.[13] In the *Meditations* Descartes argues that in having this idea, that is, in being conscious of an infinite being, we do not create the idea or imagine it. Rather, it must come to us from a source independent of us, and furthermore the source must have as much "formal reality" as the idea has "objective reality." What this means, roughly speaking, is that the "cause" of the idea's being in the mind must have as high a degree of being as the idea depicts, and since the idea depicts a perfect and infinite being, the cause of the idea must *be* a perfect and infinite being. Levinas focuses

[10] See "Philosophy and the Idea of Infinity," in *Collected Philosophical Papers*, 49–51.

[11] See Hilary Putnam's introduction to Rosenzweig's *Understanding the Sick and the Healthy*.

[12] "Philosophy and the Idea of Infinity," in *Collected Philosophical Papers*, 53. See Stephen Menn on the Platonism of Descartes in his *Descartes and Augustine*.

[13] "Philosophy and the Idea of Infinity," in *Collected Philosophical Papers*, 53.

his attention on these two features: we grasp the infinite, and it comes to us from a source independent of us. This event or fact, then, is *philosophical testimony* to what Levinas had called our heteronomous impulse, to our grasping something that is wholly other.[14]

Levinas proceeds to try to describe what is involved in this *having the idea of the infinite*. It is a relationship but not of "a container to a content" or of "a content to a container." It is not like other cases in which we have a mental act or representation of an object. Its intentionality is "not comparable with any other," for "it aims at what it cannot embrace." "The alterity of the infinite is not cancelled, is not extinguished in the thought that thinks it." Having the idea, then, is a relationship with an absolute alterity, an exterior or other, "without this exteriority being able to be integrated into the same."[15] Levinas then goes on to ask what this infinite is such that our relationship to it is of this kind.

For Levinas, then, Descartes testifies to there being a nontotalizing relation between the infinite and myself, between the infinite and every self. No standard terminology taken from everyday life or philosophical reflection can describe this relationship literally and adequately. The terms are metaphors, and it is best, perhaps, to use an expression that is not normally a part of the epistemological vocabulary and one that marks the fact that the event occurs from the outside, so to speak. Descartes uses his most general, standard expression for a mental grasping, to have an "idea." We might better say that the infinite "engages" the I or, as Levinas puts it, that the infinite "calls the I into question."

We expect that Levinas will go on to identify the infinite as the "face" of the other person that engages me in this way. It is not another thing, wholly different from things in the world. If the intentionality is unique, it is because the engagement by the face gives us a standpoint or perspective on my relation to the other person wholly unlike my normal relations. "The idea of infinity is the social relationship." Levinas calls it the "epiphany" of the face, and says that its logos or content is: "You shall not kill." It is an engagement that "puts an end to the irresistible imperialism of the same and the I," the resistance to murder. It is the "first given of moral consciousness."[16] We have here arrived on familiar ground.

Since this relation is not cognitive, Levinas argues, it has about it a kind of dynamic, driven quality. Hence Levinas calls it, from the subjective

[14] He cites Plato in the *Republic* and the Idea of the Good as well; "Philosophy and the Idea of Infinity," in *Collected Philosophical Papers*, 53.

[15] Ibid., 54.

[16] Ibid., 54–56.

side, "desire," which marks its character as the "propulsion, the inflation, of this going beyond. . . ." It is an "unquenchable" dynamism or aspiration, without satisfaction.[17] The word "desire" is a central one in moral theory and moral psychology; it plays an especially prominent role in the interpretation of Plato, Aristotle, Hellenistic ethics, Hobbes, Hume, Kant, and then in contemporary naturalist moral theory. On the "standard," Humean model of moral psychology, desire provides the causally effective component in moral action, its motivation; it provides a kind of propulsion. The term therefore has a host of implications and is very suggestive.[18] Levinas contrasts it with thought; what he wants to underline is that we do not think or cognitively grasp the face of the other; our relation to it is of a different order. We aspire to it, reach out and respond to it. I am not happy with the language of desire, and there is reason to think that later Levinas has his own doubts about it. Even for him, it is too self-oriented, rather than other-oriented, an expression. But the crucial points are evident, that the relationship between the self and the other is not cognitive and that its manifestation in everyday life is in the domain of love, eros, concern, generosity, and sensitivity rather than knowing and believing. It is, as it were, a kind of passive striving or aspiring.[19]

The face, then, as the infinite, is an original breach in the self's world, or, alternatively, it is a wholly unique perspective on our relations with other people, a wholly unique dimension or aspect of these relations.[20] But there is more. It is not just a *different* perspective or dimension; it is a *determinative* one. The relationship with the other is a measure of our injustice, as Levinas puts it, for it "puts into question the naive right

[17] Ibid., 56–57. I suspect that Levinas has in mind Plato's notion of *eros*, especially as it occurs in the *Symposium*.

[18] One of the connotations of desire is that having desire is passive, unlike beliefs or judgments, which are active states. Indeed, even rationalist accounts of motivation, which take deliberative judgments or decisions to be motivating, typically take desires to be passive. In this spirit, Levinas's calling the self as responsibility "desire" is quite consistent with the way desire is treated in Western philosophy, at least from Aristotle and the Stoics and perhaps even earlier from Plato and Socrates. On desire, motivation, and internalism, see David McNaughton, *Moral Vision*, and R. Jay Wallace, *Normativity and the Will*.

[19] In *German Idealism*, Fred Beiser suggests something similar about Fichte.

[20] My use of the expressions "aspect" and "dimension" are intended to suggest the Husserlian notion of *noema* or adumbration; as we have seen, Levinas himself takes his method to be one of exposing or disclosing hidden horizons of meaning. Two other terminologies might also be used to suggest the same status. One is Anscombe's discourse of treating actions or events "under a description"; the other is Wittgenstein's notion of "seeing-as" or "aspectual seeing." The point, I take it, is in this case, where we are dealing with the relationship between a unique person and a unique other, to consider that relationship in terms that do not reify some property or feature but do draw attention to a nonetheless real constituent of the overall relationship.

of my powers."[21] It is tempting to say that the face's infinity is that it unsettles us. It tells us what we ought to do and hence always questions what we are doing. It is completely normative, although, to be precise, *norms* are general rules or principles while the face is a unique presence. We might better see the face as an imperative force entering *into* the *finite* from the outside, from beyond the ordinary or philosophical perspective; in this sense, as revealed by its face, the suffering of the other person is *in* the *finite*. Social existence, then, carries with it a direction to act, and its content is generosity that is unbounded because the need is unbounded. Moreover, when I realize who and what I am in terms of the suffering or misery or need of the other, I am disturbed. My response must involve a sense of my own failure in generosity, a sense of *shame*.[22]

Levinas's notion of shame is distinctive, or at least its role is distinctive, unlike the use that someone like Charles Taylor, for example, makes of it. Taylor argues that human beings are distinctive as self-interpreting animals. What this means is that they have attitudes, states, or emotions that incorporate within them a sense of their own character and identity; in this sense, human beings have states that have a special kind of reflexivity. Shame is such an emotion.[23] To feel shame one must have an understanding of an ideal that one holds to and a grasp of oneself as failing to fulfill that ideal; moreover, one realizes that the other person is aware of one's failure. The special significance of shame, for Taylor, is that it, like other similar emotional or attitudinal states, reveals something distinctive about human self-understanding and self-interpretation, the acknowledgment of a value or standard to which one holds oneself and which is constitutive of one's sense of identity or one's character. Alternatively, for Levinas, one dimension of this complex emotion stands out: the realization that one's own freedom is "murderous and usurpatory in its exercise."[24] But this sense of being capable of murder and injustice requires a moral standard against which we and our freedom are measured. From where do we arrive at such a standard? This most fundamental expression of one's freedom

[21] "Philosophy and the Idea of Infinity," in *Collected Philosophical Papers*, 57–58. Here I emphasize the sense in which the "face" discloses a standard for judging the self's responsibility and generosity; later I will deal with another dimension of its determinativeness, that judgment, language, concepts, discourse, and more are in a sense grounded in the face-to-face.

[22] Ibid., 58; see also *Totality and Infinity*, 83–84. Levinas gives an early account of shame as involving a sense of one's own nakedness to oneself, a kind of self-exposure that is unavoidable, in *On Escape*, 63–65.

[23] Taylor in several places discusses the notion of self-interpretation and the way it is involved in emotions and states such as shame. See, for example, Taylor, *Philosophical Papers*, I, Chapter 2, "Self-Interpreting Animals."

[24] Levinas, "Philosophy and the Idea of Infinity," in *Collected Philosophical Papers*, 58.

is something one learns about oneself only when engaged by the face of the other person. It is a shame about being free that somehow lies within that very freedom. To be free and expansive, enjoying the world and all it has to offer, may seem enriching and elevating, but with the other person present, it is also and only then shameful and unsettling, disturbing. Levinas may agree with Taylor that shame is part of what distinguishes us as human beings, but his reasons differ dramatically.[25]

"Shame," "responsibility," "desire" – all these terms shed the same light on the subjective side of the face-to-face relationship. It is unsatisfied. That is why it is a continual striving, always desiring, aspiring – but for what? To relieve the unique other person's suffering, to remove her misery, provide aid and support for her. Since the scope is unlimited, I am responsible for everyone and everything, and hence my responsibility can never be fulfilled. There is always more to do. In this sense too the face is infinite, because the desire to give is never satisfied and can never be satisfied. Levinas also calls this desire "conscience," for it is a sense of one's own being held to a standard that challenges one fundamentally, a moral standard, of giving or generosity. It is a being aware of the imperative that comes with the face. Conscience, as Levinas puts it, lies beyond consciousness.

ETHICS BEYOND TOTALITY

In "Philosophy and the Idea of Infinity" Levinas contrasts his understanding of the face with the dominant impulse of Western philosophy. He finds in Descartes an especially valuable hint about infinity and the relationship with the other and about this heteronomous tendency. But this is paradoxical. Descartes, after all, is the founder of the modern epistemological turn in Western philosophy and a powerful advocate of the subject-object relation. Yet in him Levinas finds a clue about our exposure to the other person's face and command and hence about the centrality of responsibility to discursive thought, logic, and so forth. The main focus of the essay, however, is on the way in which Levinas's commitment to the primacy of the ethical stands vis-à-vis the philosophical tradition. In *Totality and Infinity* this focus is widened to include a great deal more. But before we turn to that work, I would like to consider an important essay of

[25] Jean Paul Sartre gives a famous account of shame in *Being and Nothingness* (Washington Square Press, 1966), 369. For discussion, see Kim Atkins, *Narrative Identity and Moral Identity* (Routledge, 2008), 51.

1962, "Transcendence and Height," which summarizes the early sections of the book from an epistemological point of view.

According to Levinas's own testimony, the way in which Western philosophy has been totalizing and the recognition of its limitations as forms of totality are lessons that he learned from Franz Rosenzweig.[26] With Hegel especially in mind, as Levinas puts it, Rosenzweig delivered a "radical critique of totality."[27] Rosenzweig shows that philosophical systems respond to a desire to know both what exists and why. They tend to be reductionist, on the one hand, and inadequate, on the other. They take God, world, and man and reduce two of them to the third, and they always deal with the general, never with the utterly particular. Hence, Western philosophy fails to respect the differences among God, world, and man and ultimately misses altogether the utterly particular, actual God and the utterly particular, actual I. Rosenzweig, then, finds in the call of that God to that I the ground of meaning for all that lies within the domain of thought, understanding, and action. This is why divine revelation, for him, is the ground of meaning for human existence in the world. Philosophy, like science, finds the meaning of nature, human beings, and religion in knowledge of the world, the human, and the divine. But, for Rosenzweig, the real meaning of my existence in the world is grounded in God's revelation to me, which is an event of love and generosity and not a matter of my knowledge of God or the world or human reason. In a sense, then, for Rosenzweig, knowledge of the everyday and of a scientific kind is useful but limited. Whether it is based on a kind of idealism or realism is another issue; Rosenzweig's point is that knowledge of this sort is limited in what it can show and do. It cannot tell us how to live, what is important in life, and what human beings should value and devote themselves to. Philosophers and scientists may know a great deal, but what they know is not a sufficient foundation on which to base a human life.[28]

Viewed in this way, Rosenzweig in one sense does not argue for or against epistemological realism or idealism. Both are forms or modes of cognitive life or thought as ordinarily conceived in Western philosophy

[26] Levinas, *Totality and Infinity*, 28. This acknowledgment is one of those almost "legendary" facts about Levinas's biography that is cited again and again and that is widely discussed, although not always with an accurate appreciation for what Rosenzweig himself thought.

[27] Levinas, *Ethics and Infinity*, 75–76; see also *Is It Righteous to Be?*, 94, 147; *Beyond the Verse*, 151–152, 155–160; "Franz Rosenzweig," in *Outside the Subject*, 53–59; and "Between Worlds," in *Difficult Freedom*, 187–191.

[28] See Franks and Morgan (eds. and trans.), *Franz Rosenzweig: Philosophical and Theological Writings*, Chapters 4 and 8; Rosenzweig, *Understanding the Sick and the Healthy*; and Rosenzweig, *God, Man and World*.

and culture. His concern is with the overall limits of both; each reduces the other to the same. If we think of knowledge broadly enough, as including knowledge of how we ought to live and what value or meaning human life has for us, then for Rosenzweig the problem with traditional philosophy and science is that they do not know enough. From one point of view, then, Rosenzweig's issue is independent of the debates between epistemological idealism and realism; both are limited forms of Western philosophy. From another point of view, however, Rosenzweig might be seen as a kind of realist, a moral realist or even a kind of epistemological one. That is, on the issue of the knowledge of the meaning of human existence, Rosenzweig believes that only something outside the world of traditional philosophy and science can provide it. It will be interesting and important to determine whether Levinas, in his own way, agrees with Rosenzweig in this regard. That is, do Rosenzweig and Levinas agree about the limitations of Western thought? Do revelation for Rosenzweig and the face for Levinas provide what is needed beyond those limitations, the knowledge of meaningful human life and its ground? "Transcendence and Height" is a good place to look for Levinas's attempt to confront these issues.

Levinas's essay is divided into twelve sections. In sections 1–6 he discusses Western philosophy and its characteristic feature, that as a "search for truth" it involves the attempt to suppress all multiplicity and to assimilate all difference into the Same. Levinas uses the Platonic expression "the Same" to refer to mind, spirit, or reason, to the domain of the subject – personal or absolute. Hence, he says, "the great myth of philosophy" is "the myth of a legislative consciousness of things, where difference and identity are reconciled."[29] This myth, he says, "rests upon the totalitarianism or imperialism of the Same." All philosophical thinking is some type of idealism, which extends from metaphysics and epistemology to politics and ethics. Even the traditional distinction between realism and idealism, insofar as it distinguishes types of philosophy, must bow to the *overall idealistic character* of all philosophy. That is, philosophy is rational thought; it is the activity of mind or self seeking to understand everything. Its unqualified hegemony makes it idealist. Everything is encompassed or comprehended by the self, thought, mind, or reason. The real is rational. Even Husserl and Heidegger do not overcome *this* sense of idealism; even realism, in the narrow sense, does not refute idealism, in the broad sense.[30]

[29] Levinas, "Transcendence and Height," in *Basic Philosophical Writings*, 14.
[30] Ibid., 14–15.

Levinas's first conclusion, then, is that all philosophy, whether traditionally metaphysical or epistemological or more contemporary versions of transcendental phenomenology, is idealist and acknowledges nothing transcendent to the philosophizing self, no *Other*. This conclusion applies to Heidegger too and to recent attempts to understand pre-philosophical life as it is lived, the so-called *Lebenswelt* (life-world). In short, Levinas understands all Western philosophy, whether metaphysical, epistemological, or ontological, to be totalizing or imperialistic in this way.[31] This outcome is the "triumph of the Same," of the self, spirit, mind, or reason. Against this background, then, Levinas raises the question whether there is a realism *beyond* this broad, totalizing idealism, that is, whether there is an Other that the self does not assimilate but that nonetheless *calls the self into question*.[32] In sections 7–12 he introduces this Other as the face of the other person and explores it in ways that we have already discussed.

Levinas makes these points about the engagement with the other person. First, when the Other is wholly other, when it is a human other, it calls the self or the I into question; the other person summons the self to responsibility.[33] Second, the other person is not the object of intentionality, strictly speaking; the self is not conscious of the other person as Other.[34] Third, before the other person, the I "can no longer be powerful"; the I feels shame for its "naive spontaneity" and is unsettled by this shame.[35]

[31] It is worth emphasizing two points about this conclusion and the approach in this essay. First, the essay focuses attention on philosophy, but Levinas's point is ultimately a larger, more embracing one, that the same strictures he here applies to the philosophical tradition apply too to science, religion, and everyday life, i.e., to all thinking and all living, which, he claims, are shaped by the same tradition and vocabulary and modes of thought, by the Greeks. Second, as we have claimed earlier, we should not treat this as a conclusion about the limits of philosophical thought as a kind of epistemological or metaphysical claim about the limits of our cognitive abilities or the existence of certain objects. Rather, it is a claim about the way that philosophical concepts, principles, approaches, and practices fail to catch sight of a dimension of what is part of everyday living and, in particular, of everyday social interaction. Levinas's point is that as long as we remain within the philosophical world as we have it, something fundamental and determinative about human existence remains occluded or "hidden" from us.

[32] "Transcendence and Height," in *Basic Philosophical Writings*, 16.

[33] Ibid. We have discussed this summons or plea-and-command, which Levinas frames as an imperative, taken from the biblical text "thou shalt not kill (me)."

[34] Ibid. That is, insofar as the other presents herself as face to the self, the self does not "see" the face or observe the other person, but this does not mean, of course, that the I does not see or perceive the other person along with "acknowledging" her, "accepting" her, and giving her a piece of bread to eat.

[35] "Transcendence and Height," in *Basic Philosophical Writings*, 17. That is, the self's freedom and power are compromised, in a sense, prior to their existing at all. Or, we might say, the free and powerful self is always "already" bound to respond to the other when its freedom and its power take shape. In *Time and the Other* and in *Totality and Infinity* Levinas tells his dialectical and genetic story about how the self as powerful and capable of enjoying the resources of the world it finds itself inhabiting is confronted by the other person who calls to the self. But, as we have

Fourth, the I also welcomes the other person, who both "challenges and commands" the I as a face through its "nakedness and destitution."[36] This destitution Levinas calls "humility" and this command "height." Together they and the face that expresses them "summon [the I] to respond."[37] By "destitution" Levinas means, I think, both the actual need or poverty that the other person endures because of particular historical experiences and that calls out to the I for assistance on the one hand, and, on the other, the very fact of the other person's existence as dependent and as calling for the I's acknowledgment and acceptance – prior to anything the other person endures or suffers. Before any more specific needs are to be addressed, there is the primary issue of "sharing the world with the other." Fifth, the I is not conscious of its responsibility as a duty or obligation; it is "responsibility through and through."[38] Later, especially in *Otherwise than Being*, Levinas will develop this theme, that in a deep sense responsibility is not a characteristic or feature of the self but rather is what the self is, "before" it is anything else. This responsibility is therefore inescapable; it is, in Biblical terms, an "election."[39] Sixth, this election is an elevation. It does not diminish the self; rather, by emptying it of imperialism, egoism, and power, this being chosen or elected "liberates" the self. "Such an engagement is happy; it is the austere and noncomplacent happiness that lies in the nobility of an election that does not know its own happiness...."[40] Responsibility is not a burden; it does not deflate the self. It fulfills it, or, perhaps more accurately, it makes it possible for the self to fulfill itself by responding to, accepting and serving, the other person. Seventh, in virtue of this engagement or relationship, the I is morality. Through the face, the I is lifted out of nature and consciousness; it is promoted or elevated and receives height; exercising my responsibility is an act neither of pity nor of obedience.[41] For the same person "*to* whom" I am responsible is the one "*for* whom" I am responsible; the tie of responsibility is doubly strong.[42]

already indicated, the narrative and dialectical character of the story is intended to expose levels or dimensions of human social interaction and not to be taken literally.

36 Ibid.

37 Ibid.

38 Ibid.; cf. 18.

39 Levinas uses the biblical expression for God's choice of the "children of Israel" as his *special treasure* [*am segulah*]; they are the "chosen" people, "elected" by God. By transference, what in Judaism (and of course in Calvinism and other forms of Christianity) refers to "divine election" becomes at this deep level the way each other person "elects" each subject.

40 "Transcendence and Height," in *Basic Philosophical Writings*, 18.

41 Ibid.

42 As Levinas puts it, the self is responsible for and to the other – for fulfilling the other's needs, alleviating the other's suffering, etc., and to the other for fulfilling them, i.e., accountable to the other.

The I, then, is elevated and enriched by being infinitely responsible. This is Levinas's special way of claiming that human life is more than natural existence, that it is fundamentally social and ethical.

Having described the face-to-face in these terms, Levinas asks about its relation to the idea of the infinite, to metaphysics, to idealism and realism, and to the philosophical tradition. This grounding moral relation is the idea of the infinite, but "idea" is not to be taken literally, as an intentional entity or relation. In Husserlian terms, "the I *receives* absolutely and learns absolutely … a signification that it has not itself given, a signification that precedes any *Sinngebung*."[43] That is, as Husserl has shown, the senses or meanings of all intentional objects, their *noemata*, are constituted by the self, and only insofar as these meanings are constituted are they objects of consciousness of one kind or another. The face, however, has meaning prior to all meaning constitution; its meaning is given prior to any constitution by the self. Levinas says that intentionality is overturned by an act that is both submissive and spontaneous; the other has height and the self dignity, so that the engagement is both spontaneous and critical, a kind of double movement of approaching and receiving, producing "its own critique of reflection" that involves consciousness, judgment, thought, and eventually philosophy. In this sense, "moral consciousness is primary and the source of first philosophy."[44]

Levinas contrasts his own view with the hegemony of thought or reason; he calls the latter "idealism" and his own view a kind of "realism."[45] "Only the idea of the infinite renders realism" possible. As I have said, this is not epistemological realism or moral realism as philosophical positions, of course. It is a realism prior to all philosophy and philosophical positions, prior even to ontology and to everyday life in its fullness, a realism that does not verify or justify or explain but one that makes all else possible for human existence. Moreover, as he did earlier, Levinas associates this engagement with the infinite or at least hints of it with Descartes, Plato, and Plotinus, all of whom seemed to be groping toward a conception of "thinking more than one can think." For Levinas, this thinking is never mere thinking at all; it is a responding to the other person by acknowledging, accepting, and aiding that person.

In "Transcendence and Height" Levinas notes how traditional Western philosophy sought to grasp the truth about the everyday world in various ways, some realist, some idealist, and some neither, strictly speaking.

[43] "Transcendence and Height," in *Basic Philosophical Writings*, 19.

[44] Ibid., 20; cf. 20–21.

[45] Ibid., 21.

Within the tradition, especially after Descartes, much attention was given to the role of the mind and reason in determining and verifying that truth. Modern skepticism challenged belief in the existence of the external world, in the existence of other persons, in the existence of God, and much else. God, the brute given of sensation, and things-in-themselves became points of conflict, especially in epistemological debates about knowledge and its grounds and the limits of what we can know. But, as Levinas notes, those debates and issues were subsumed in a larger one, about the character of philosophy itself and the world it sought to encompass and comprehend. At this level, he claimed, all philosophy qua thought was idealist, and the question about it was not whether it should accept a thing-in-itself or a God but rather whether it was itself as an idealism comprehensive and groundless. Was even first philosophy genuinely "first?" His answer in this essay is that no form of thought is primary for human existence, and this means not only that philosophy is not the most basic or most elevated human activity but also that the everyday world as ultimately lived in and grasped in terms of thought or reason is not all there is to everyday human life. Indeed, language, thought, and discourse are not what is most basic and determinative about human life as social and interpersonal. To say that ethics is more primary than philosophy is also to say that praxis is more primary than theory and that acting on behalf of the needs of other persons is more important, more basic, and more the point of being human than thinking about them or even following rules aimed at them or their well-being. Caring for you is the most human thing I can do, and a world in which I act toward you by acknowledging, accepting, and aiding you is best, enriched by my act and the acts of everyone who acts similarly.

TOTALITY, INFINITY, AND BEYOND

Totality and Infinity is a large and complex book, and its formulations are often difficult to grasp. By looking at the two essays, one written before the book, one after, we have been able to focus on the main features of Levinas's treatment of philosophy as totality and the role of the infinite in his own account. But now we should look at *Totality and Infinity* itself to see if anything has been omitted that it is important for us to consider at this point.

The general theme of this chapter is the relationship between the self's engagement with the face of the other person and everyday or ordinary social life. Thus far we have been discussing the concepts of totality and infinity in order to clarify how the face as the infinite is related to philosophical rationality and the way in which everyday life is permeated by and understood through philosophy. In Chapter 2 I sketched Levinas's thinking in *Time and the Other* in preparation for discussing his method. One feature of that account becomes central to his exposition in *Totality and Infinity*, and because of its relevance to the relation of the face to everyday life, we should return to it now. It concerns the order of his exposition and the relation between Levinas's accounts of interiority and exteriority. I do not propose to examine Levinas's very complex, detailed account of interiority; what I want to consider is the structure of the overall argument and, specifically, why and how it is not genetic or narrative.

Section II of *Totality and Infinity* is called "Interiority and Economy." Basically, this is Levinas's account of the *Lebenswelt* or life-world or his version of a phenomenology of human *Dasein* (existence) as being-in-the-world. Levinas calls it "economy" or "economic existence." At one point he describes his overall project this way: "we propose to describe, within the unfolding of terrestrial existence, of economic existence (as we shall call it), a relationship with the other that does not result in a divine or human totality, that is not a totalization of history but the idea of infinity," that is, an engagement with the face of the other person.[46] For the most part, this statement tells us what we already know, but for our purposes here the crucial phrase is "to describe, within the unfolding of economic existence." We might paraphrase this claim as meaning that Levinas will be describing how the encounter with the face of the other person occurs or is indicated *within* everyday experience. It does not say that the face-to-face derives from or arises out of ordinary life, nor that it takes the self outside of that life. Rather, it says that the face-to-face occurs *within* ordinary life, in some way or other. The idea of the infinite is the engagement with the face; the ordinary world is the domain of totality. The former occurs within the latter, albeit in a unique way. When I meet my friend David, I speak to him; I notice that his hair is curlier than usual, that he is wearing a T-shirt, and that he has a new backpack. But also, at the same time, as it were, and within the orbit of that same meeting, in seeing him and speaking to him, I acknowledge and accept him. I respond to him and welcome him; I make room for him and give myself to him. Moreover, this acknowledgment, acceptance, and responding is more primary, more fundamental and determinative than whatever else I do in relating to him. In a sense, the ordinary life I live is grounded in this relation.

[46] *Totality and Infinity*, 52; cf. 51.

In Section II of *Totality and Infinity* Levinas describes "economic existence" or ordinary life from one perspective, that of the individual's relation to the world. In Section III, "Exteriority and the Face," he describes the ethical, the face, *within* that life, that is, he describes that same life from the perspective of its ethical ground.[47] Put this way, Levinas's project is to show how everyday life has both of these dimensions, which correspond to our natural existence, on the one hand, and our peculiarly human existence, on the other (although this distinction does not match Levinas's exactly). I think that Levinas wants us to see that human existence has both dimensions and that they are interdependent, even though one is still more fundamental or determinative of the meaning and character of our social existence. To see this, let us look at his ideas of enjoyment, nourishment, possession, labor, and gift.

Basically, the presence of the other person asks and demands of me that what I have or possess be shared, that the private be made common, that I make of it a gift. This might lead us to think that the demand and my responsibility to fulfill it are dependent upon my private possessions, my control over things, my power, and ultimately on my freedom. Hobbes would say so, and his account of the state of nature and the social contract is organized to show this dependency of social institutions, exchange, and civil norms on basic human powers and liberty and their unlimited character in the state of nature. It is tempting to read Levinas this way, as plotting a line of dependencies, so that his account looks genetic, beginning with a sense of existence as dark, forboding, and indeterminate, leading through the emergence of selfhood as self-conscious, its finding its place in the world, enjoying what is available to it, and so on. For Hobbes, however, this kind of story reveals a firm set of dependencies that operate in one direction only. For Levinas, by contrast, this outcome is not wholly false, but neither is it wholly true. From one point of view, we have needs, seek to satisfy

[47] Alternatively put, Levinas sees that same life as ethically grounded or determined, or he describes that same life "under the description" of being ethically meaningful or as grounded in interpersonal responsibility. In *Donald Davidson*, edited by Kirk Ludwig (Cambridge, 2003), in the essay by Alfred R. Mele, "Philosophy of Action," there is a discussion on pages 66–67 of Davidson's thesis that actions can be intentional under one description and unintentional under another description. I think that it is useful to characterize Levinas's account of our relationship with others in terms of this vocabulary used by Anscombe of "under a description," so that we might say that a relationship with others is face-to-face under one description and something that supervenes on the face-to-face under another description. This characterization is an alternative vocabulary for articulating the relationship between the face-to-face and other relationships between the I and the other, making the same point as treating the face-to-face as a dimension of our interpersonal relationships or a perspective on them that is most often hidden from view or unattended to.

them, acquire nourishment, and so forth. But this is only one dimension of who we are, so to speak; our natural situatedness in the world as a locale for nourishment and enjoyment is one way of understanding or describing our existence. It is, as it were, a picture of us as wholly within totality, as the objects of naturalist explanation, for example, or as the objects of social scientific investigation and comprehension. Yet while totality is not false and systems of thought – philosophical, scientific, moral, political, and religious – do contain some truth, they do so only partially.

What makes some fruit that I have picked enjoyable and nourishing has to do with my needs, my labor, my effort, and my possession and use of it. But the fruit is also or can also be a gift, a common benefit, and a shared resource. However, it will be these things and can be described in these ways, Levinas says, only given the presence to me of the face of the other person, that is, in view of the other's needs addressed to me and my responsibility to her to confront those needs and satisfy them – to feed the hungry, clothe the naked, and relieve the suffering with which she confronts me. For the fruit to be fully what it can be in the human world, then, I must need or want it, but I also must be faced by your needs as well. Levinas wants us to see that in fact the fruit is first and foremost food-to-feed-the-hungry and only secondarily a source of nourishment and enjoyment for me; it is giveable to you before it is consumable by me.

Levinas describes this situation in the following terms. The things around us – "good soup," air, light, spectacles, sleep, and so on – are not simply objects that I examine, describe, or analyze. I "live from" them; they nourish me, and I enjoy them. These things "are lived; they feed life."[48] This enjoyment, moreover, is not one psychological state like others; it fuels life and in part constitutes the I as living.[49] What I enjoy nourishes me; things become food, consumable. As Levinas sees it, they are nourishment and enjoyable first and foremost. But that is not all they are; these objects and states also become available for inspection, description, classification, and more. "The separation accomplished as enjoyment … becomes a consciousness of objects. The things are fixed by the word which gives them, which communicates them and thematizes them.… Over and above enjoyment … a discourse about the world takes form."[50] Within enjoyment subject and object exhibit a separation, and this separation then becomes the framework in which language, discourse, description, perception, and so forth take place. Morever, as Levinas points out,

[48] *Totality and Infinity*, 110–111; cf. 109–121 generally.

[49] Ibid., 113.

[50] Ibid., 139.

other activities take place, such as labor, which transforms things, and habitation, which transforms space.[51] The upshot is that this situation makes responding to the face possible, for that response requires giving, a wholly benevolent giving, and it is only because of enjoyment, possession, labor, and habitation that I have something to give.

> The transcendence of the face is not enacted outside of the world, as though the economy by which separation is produced remained beneath a sort of beatific contemplation of the Other [person].... The 'vision' of the face as face is a certain mode of sojourning in a home, or ... a certain form of economic life.... no face can be approached with empty hands and closed home.

Levinas calls this act of responsibility to the other "hospitality."[52]

Economic existence – everyday life in the world – and responsible hospitality or kindness, then, are two points of view on the same human existence, on social and interpersonal human life. Engaging the face is not an esoteric or ecstatic experience, a "beatific contemplation" or "vision." "The relationship with the Other [person] is not produced outside of the world, but puts in question the world possessed." It is a "primordial dispossession, a donation," a giving, and it "institutes a common world." Hence, the two perspectives are interdependent and linked, contemporary, coordinate.[53] Without things or possessions to give, hospitality and donation are not possible, and without the engagement with the face of the other, all our possessions are just our things and the objects of our enjoyment; they are not gifts – or "giveables." "This *offering* of the world, this offering of contents which answers to the face of the Other [person] ... first opens the perspective of the meaningful." Here we have Levinas's own version of the joining of nature and morality, fact and value. "Transcendence is not an optics, but the first ethical gesture,"[54] but neither – that is, neither sensibility nor morality – can occur alone. The book's title after all is "Totality *and* Infinity," not "Totality *or* Infinity."

We are in a position to say something about an important criticism that is regularly made of Levinas. The criticism is that ethical relationship with the particular other cannot be expressed in moral rules or political principles. Our discussion of totality and its relation to infinity, however, provides us with a way of responding to this criticism.[55]

[51] See ibid., 146, 150, 152–174.

[52] Ibid., 172.

[53] See Michael Purcell, *Levinas and Theology*, 101, 162. This point is what Purcell means, I think, when he says "Responsibility and justice are two sides of the same coin" (162).

[54] *Totality and Infinity*, 174.

[55] See also below, "Conclusions, Puzzles, Problems."

Earlier I pointed out that there is, in Levinas's philosophy, a way up and a way down, as it were. We have been discussing, by and large, the way down, what Levinas means by "the idea of infinity" and the way the infinite or the face is a breach in totality, or, in other words, how the infinite occurs in human existence as a hidden dimension or perspective of everyday life and our thinking about it. We have also tried to show how the two are interdependent and how Levinas can be understood as reflecting on two perspectives on the everyday or the ordinary world under two descriptions. To develop that sense of interdependence, however, we need to turn to the "way up" and show how, according to Levinas, the face is the ground of judgment, language, concepts, thought, and eventually moral systems and political values. This is a project for a book, in and of itself, so what I propose is only a schematic account based on a few texts that sketch the basic features of Levinas's view. What we need to see is how Levinas shows universality and commonality to arise out of the utterly particular encounter of the individual and the other and how ethics as a primordial event leads to language, society, and politics.

This account of the emergence of society and politics is crucial for several reasons. First, ontology and all the systems of totality – our theories and our world in the everyday sense – are unavoidable. Levinas takes our task to be the employment of all of this for ethical purposes, to assist the other person, reduce suffering and misery, and act responsibly toward others. "To ensure the survival of the other we must resort to the technico-political systems of means and ends."[56] But this task is plausible only if these *means* are somehow grounded in this end – if, that is, there is a deep connection between them. The account of how the face-to-face leads to society and politics is an important vehicle for understanding this connection.

Second, we do not live in the face-to-face encounter. We live in the world. If everyday life and the face provide different perspectives on the same experience, in a sense, we need to be sure that this distinction does not harbor a rigid, exclusive dualism. Showing how language, society, and politics occur and yet how they are linked to the face-to-face encounter, we see how unified Levinas's understanding of human life really is.

Third, it also clarifies and justifies, in a sense, Levinas's assessment of Western culture, politics, and civilization. The twentieth century has witnessed a kind of degeneration or divorce or infidelity, according to which life has become estranged from its deepest origins and grounds. It might even be viewed as a kind of Oedipal rebellion, an uprising against parental

[56] Kearney, "Dialogue with Emmanuel Levinas," in *Face to Face with Levinas*, edited by Richard Cohen, 28.

love in favor of self-righteous conceit.[57] This account will make clear how Levinas's critique works and where its grounds lie.

ETHICS AND SOCIETY

Before I turn to some key texts in *Totality and Infinity* and *Otherwise than Being*, it will be helpful to look at some of Levinas's comments in interviews where the issue of society and the political arises. Levinas does seem to be facing a serious set of problems. The face-to-face is uniquely particular, yet society involves rules, principles, institutions, and in general the notion of the universal. How does the universal come from the particular? Furthermore, the encountering self and the face seem to be isolated and alone, a pair, yet society is made up of a vast plurality of people, in multiple relationships, institutions, and more. How does Levinas account for the leap from one to the other? Indeed, how does he account for human community at all?

Although we must be cautious about using Levinas's interviews to clarify his ideas, they do contain very lucid, succinct formulations that provide good access to themes addressed more technically in his written works. This is especially the case when Levinas talks about society, politics, and what in his later work he calls "justice." Let me start by recalling something I have emphasized throughout: the encounter with the face is not an experience isolated from everyday life; it is not a mystical or quasi-mystical experience that one has only when separate and detached, in exile from the ordinary. The face-to-face is not like an intuitive grasp of beauty or the good or a visionary, ecstatic experience of God. It is instead one way of being related to another person, a fundamental and determinative way to be sure, but one way along with others. It is, alternatively, one dimension of our interpersonal lives or one perspective on such lives. Hence, it makes no sense to ask where other people come from. The point is that except for extreme and unusual circumstances – that of Robinson Crusoe, for example – we always live among other people, many of them. The issue is not where the others come from; it is what their being in our world, each one *set over against us*, means to us. Levinas makes this point clearly on several occasions. In his 1986 interview with Francois Poirié, for example, he

[57] According to Joseph Frank, in his magisterial intellectual biography of Dostoevsky, this conflict between love and egoism is a major theme of Dostoevsky's writings. For Dostoevsky it is a dynamic characteristic of Russia and Europe from the 1840s through the 1870s; for Levinas it is characteristic of the twentieth century. See Joseph Frank, *Dostoevsky: A Writer in His Time* (Princeton University Press, 2010; abridgement of his five-volume work), passim.

says: "There is always a third, a fourth, because in fact we are in a multiple society where, on the fundamental relation to the other the whole knowing of justice, which is indispensable, is superimposed."[58] The third and the fourth are people, beyond myself and the other; there are *always* others, and the face-to-face always takes place in a social world where I and the other are related to a host of others, all as selves face-to-face with many particular others. No single face-to-face is an island; each takes place amid a vast ocean of others, the entire social world. This social world is "the whole" that is the venue for justice, as we shall see. It is "indispensable" and therefore not just unavoidable; it is also the totality of everyday social and political relationships, institutions, and practices that it is our task to employ in behalf of assisting others and reducing their suffering.

Levinas reiterates the same point in 1989:

> But we are never, me and the other, alone in the world. There is always a third; the men who surround me. And this third is also my neighbor. Who is nearest to me? Inevitable question of justice which arises from the depth of responsibility for the unique, in which ethics begins in the face of that which is incomparable. Here is the necessity of comparing what is incomparable – of knowing men … [the] transformation of faces into objective and plastic forms.… The other is no longer the unique person offering himself to the compassion of my responsibility, but an individual within a logical order or a citizen of a state in which institutions, general laws, and judges are both possible and necessary.[59]

Levinas regularly calls the third the "third party" and takes it to represent the people who make up the social world we live in. Each and every such person, when related to me, presents me with a face and calls forth my responsibility. Moreover, once we turn to these others and ask about our responsibilities, we must compare them, their needs, their suffering, and their relations to us; we develop concepts, principles, and policies; we assess our resources and capabilities, and we evaluate others to see how they fit or suit our norms and our resources. The unique other hence becomes for me a fellow citizen or another moral agent or a person deserving respect or a hungry person or a criminal. In order for our comparisons to occur at all, we develop conceptual resources or adopt ones to facilitate the comparisons, and in order for them to be regular, consistent, and fair, we develop principles of justice to normalize these comparisons. That is, we develop laws and practices according to a sense

[58] *Is It Righteous to Be?*, 54; see also *Entre Nous*, 106–107. In "Peace and Proximity," in *Alterity and Transcendence*, 142–143, Levinas speaks of the necessity of reason; he calls the face and peace the "origin, justification, and measure" of the structures of society.

[59] *Is It Righteous to Be?*, 115–116; cf. 193–194, 230, 246.

of fairness and impartiality that is, for each of us, grounded in our sense of responsibility.

Or, to put this point otherwise, it is only when we recognize our fundamental responsibility to each and every other person that we see what justice, moral norms, policies, and practices mean to us and to our lives, what their point is. Only people whom we can describe and classify can be evaluated and compared, and once we organize our social world politically in this way, we realize that it is as necessary as it is possible to structure our social interactions in some way or other. Ethics is fundamental; politics and political justice are necessary. This comparing of incomparables is what Levinas elsewhere calls "the Greek moment in our civilization ... [for] the importance of knowing, the importance of comparing comes from them."[60] As we shall see, the Bible teaches the centrality of the ethical and its primacy; Greek culture and philosophy teach the significance of knowledge, science, and politics.

Levinas often sketches how, in this way, the presence of multiple other persons, the fact of social life, is what gives rise to thought, rationality, judgment, and even philosophy. In 1983 he puts it this way: "But I don't live in a world in which there is but one single 'first comer'; there is always a third party in the world: he or she is also my other, my neighbor. Hence, it is important to me to know which of the two takes precedence.... Must not human beings, who are incomparable, be compared? ... Here is the birth of the theoretical; here is the birth of the concern for justice, which is the basis of the theoretical."[61] The word "birth" must be understood with the greatest sensitivity. Theory, for Levinas, involves forming concepts and categories, judgment, comparison, examination, and all that is built on these activities. This is what we associate with thinking, scientific inquiry, and explanation. It is also what we think of as organizational, normative, and functional. Levinas does not mean that all of these activities actually arise out of the face-to-face – in some temporal way – rising like a genie out of a bottle. His account may look genetic and developmental, but it is not, as I have indicated on several occasions about many of his accounts. What he means is that thinking, speaking, and so on are social phenomena and must be understood as serving social purposes and ultimately moral ones. Indeed, he seems to be making the strong claim that a society of human beings has reason to engage in these activities only because human life is fundamentally social and ethical. We shall have more to say about this

[60] Ibid., 133.

[61] "Philosophy, Justice and Love," in *Is It Righteous To Be?*, 165–166; cf. *Entre Nous*, 104.

later, but it is certainly part of what Levinas means by the primacy of ethics. Later, in the same 1983 interview, Levinas puts it as follows: "justice itself is born of charity. They can seem alien when they are presented as successive stages; in reality, they are inseparable and simultaneous, unless one is on a desert island, without humanity, without a third."[62] The central point here is that justice and charity or politics and ethics are not "successive stages" in a Hobbesian-like process; they are "inseparable and simultaneous."[63]

Finally, Levinas makes one last important point, that while our responsibility is infinite and in itself unbounded, it is justice that limits it, and because of this "I separate myself from the idea of nonresistance to evil."[64] In principle, everyone demands of me; I am responsible to and for everyone all the time in every way. But if a person or group or institution persecutes another, then my responsibility to those who are suffering outweighs any responsibility I have to the persecutor, and I must do what I can to oppose the persecution. Levinas says as much. "If there were no order of Justice, there would be no limit to my responsibility."[65] Indeed, given the encounter with the face of the other person and the existence of justice and the state, there is a kind of mutual limitation. Law, the state, and justice limit my responsibilities by subjecting them to calculation and regimentation, comparing them and determining whom I ought to serve, whom I ought to restrict. At the same time, my responsibility to each and every other person is what "legitimizes" the state and gives it a sense of purpose and value. Infinite responsibility is what gives point to the very existence of states, laws, and political systems; it is their raison d'etre. "A state in which the interpersonal relationship [i.e., the face-to-face, acts of kindness and benevolence] is impossible, in which it is directed in advance by the determinism proper to the state, is a totalitarian state."[66] In short, a sense of

62 *Is It Righteous To Be?*, 168–169; cf. 183. One could hardly want a more explicit statement from Levinas that the face-to-face is a relationship between the self and the other that occurs alongside and at the same time as other everyday relationships.

63 A nice analogue is the account of the *demiourgos* or Divine Craftsman and the formation of the cosmos in Plato's *Timaeus*; even in antiquity there was a debate about whether Plato intended this account to be genetic and creationist or, rather, an analytical representation of the rational structure of an eternal cosmos. Levinas's view is akin to the nonliteral, rational interpretation of Plato's myth. The debate about how to interpret the *Timaeus* on creation goes back to Aristotle and Xenocrates. For a classic discussion of the issue and whether the dialogue is a myth or not, see Gregory Vlastos, "The Disorderly Motion in the 'Timaeus'" (orig. 1939) and "Creation in the 'Timaeus': Is It a Fiction?" (orig. 1964), both in R. E. Allen (ed.), *Studies in Plato's Metaphysics* (Routledge & Kegan Paul, 1965), 379–399 and 401–419.

64 See "Philosophy, Justice and Love," in *Entre Nous*, 105.

65 Ibid.

66 Ibid.

humanity limits the state and determines whether a given state is admirable or perhaps even legitimate. Here, then, we see the ground for Levinas's judgments about fascism and Stalinism that we observed in Chapter 1.[67]

I have been considering the relationship between the face-to-face and the world as totality – the world of language, thought, judgment, politics, and justice – as Levinas informally discusses this theme in various interviews. It occurs in these interviews in especially clear and vivid ways, I think, but it is a theme that goes back to formulations in *Totality and Infinity* in 1961.[68] There, late in the book, Levinas uses familial, erotic, and gendered language to characterize features of the face-to-face. In introducing the idea of society he employs the term "fraternity." Speaking of the son who is "elected" by his father, who becomes an I as unique for his father, Levinas says: "because the son owes his unicity to the paternal election he can be brought up, be commanded, and can obey, and the strange conjuncture of the family is possible." But the child is both unique and not unique; fecundity yields many children, a family.

> The I engendered exists at the same time as unique in the world and as brother among brothers. I am I and chosen one, but where can I be chosen, if not from among other chosen ones, among equals? ... The human I is posited in fraternity: that all men are brothers is not added to man as a moral conquest, but constitutes his ipseity [i.e., his selfhood].... The relation with the face in fraternity, where in his turn the Other appears in solidarity with all the others, constitutes the social order, the reference of every dialogue to the third party by which the We ... encompasses the face to face opposition, opens the erotic upon a social life....[69]

Levinas's language here is more obscure and mannered than we have seen it in the later interviews, but he is making the same points that we have seen him make in those interviews: society comes with the third party, with the plurality of people who live together, each one set over against every other; but each self is the "chosen one" – summoned by the face of the other person – "chosen from among other chosen ones"; in terms of responsibility, all are equal, that is, I am equally responsible for all, and each is equally responsible for each and every other; social life is grounded in the face-to-face and also, in a sense, in the basic humanity of all, their equality, which arises out of the face of total responsibility when it occurs in a world of people.[70] Assessing what laws and rules to establish and determining what

[67] See also ibid., 108: "Politics left to itself, has its own determinism. Love must always watch over justice."
[68] See, for example, *Totality and Infinity*, 213.
[69] Ibid., 279–280.
[70] See also ibid., 214.

to do in particular situations, these judgments take place against the background of humanity and equality.

Furthermore, the face-to-face is utterly particular. Not only does its priority provide a standard against which all rules, principles, policies, and institutions should be measured, it also tells us that even when we consider what to do and how to act by employing such rules and principles, we should keep in mind that our actions are always very particular ways of responding to the needs and claims of particular other persons. Moreover, when we actually do perform an action, that performance, even if it was facilitated by a rule or principle, is always a real interpersonal encounter, a face-to-face meeting with many particular other people. Acts of generosity and justice and acts of neglect and harm – all are done by concrete individual persons to other persons. Rules, practices, and institutions are not intermediaries between persons; they do not separate a self from another, even when we might be inclined to think that they do. And rules and practices are never the direct objects of our action. In a suggestive image, Franz Rosenzweig, referring to Jewish law, says that the Jew should perform the legal requirements of the Halakhah (the law) in such a manner that he or she turns a *Gesetz* (legal statute) into a *Gebot* (commandment). His meaning is that every law is a device –indeed, an opportunity – whereby the believer, when he performs it in the right spirit, can come into a living relationship with God, the commander. Analogously, for Levinas, the face-to-face is not only a dimension of every personal relationship we have that is regularly hidden from our view; it is also the very personal interpersonal dimension of all laws, rules, practices, policies, and institutions in everyday life, a dimension that is too often obscured by the regularity and generality of those laws and institutions. The goal of our actions is never to perform a rule or to perform a duty; it is always to respond to another person in one way or another.

In this chapter I have been considering what Levinas means by totality, by the critique of totality, and by the way that the face of the other person is the idea of the infinite. I have been especially interested in showing how Levinas's critique of totality is not a disposal or rejection of it. For him, human life is a unity of totality and infinity.[71] In the course of my discussion, I have given only occasional attention to the other features of life as totality that arise out of or depend upon society and social relations – thought, conceptualization, and language. I have paid more attention

[71] As I have already pointed out, the title of Levinas's book is, after all, *Totality* and *Infinity* and not *Totality* or *Infinity*.

here to ethics, politics, and justice.[72] In Levinas's later work, especially in *Otherwise than Being*, language becomes an increasingly important subject. Suffice it to say for now that the importance of the third party and society does not wane in the later works, for there too Levinas notes that "the responsibility for the other ... is troubled and becomes a problem when a third party enters."[73] As in earlier work and in the interviews, "enters" is a metaphor; the central point is that living among people requires comparison, judgment, and all the apparatus of conceptualization, theory, and politics. "Proximity [another word for the face-to-face] takes on a new meaning in the space of contiguity [i.e., society]."[74]

[72] As I have indicated, the whole question of the relevance of Levinas's insight to moral and political life is a very contested one.

[73] *Otherwise than Being*, 157.

[74] Ibid.; cf. 157–161.

CHAPTER FIVE

Subjectivity and the Self: Passivity and Freedom

One of the most bewildering and puzzling points that Levinas makes concerns subjectivity and the self.[1] He says that primordially or originally the self or person is passive because it is responsible before anything else. First and foremost, I am summoned and called into question. In Kantian terminology, the self is heteronomous (determined by something other) before it is autonomous (self-determined). It is passive before it is active. Subjectivity is accusation, hostage, obsession, and the like. These features may seem so strange that one can hardly grasp what they mean or even what they might mean. This chapter is our opportunity to discuss them and to show that they are extreme and provocative but not at all as bizarre and unintelligible as they first appear.

Shortly we shall have to consider the story of how modern culture, at least from the seventeenth century, has come to enshrine the subject, the individual, the autonomous, free, rational self, as the fountainhead of knowledge, morality, politics, culture, and even religion. Levinas does not ignore or denigrate this self or this conception of the self as the autonomous, rational individual, but he does reconsider its most fundamental dimension, its essential character, and how that dimension reverberates throughout its existential and historical career. To be sure, he believes that this new understanding of the unique individual person as passive and responsible echoes from the ancient past, but in the modern world, it is preempted by another view, modern, individualist, and powerful. Levinas's understanding of the self, then, can be understood from both philosophical and historical points of view; we will be served best if we do not ignore either one.

Levinas's thinking about subjectivity goes back to the 1940s and 1950s, but its culmination is the account of responsibility and substitution in

[1] In this chapter I use the expressions "person," "subject," "self," and "I" interchangeably, as a matter of convenience. Such usage is fairly standard. For Levinas, of course, it is problematic, especially with regard to the word "subject," as we shall see, but I hope the issues are not confused by holding to standard usage.

Otherwise than Being. I shall say something about his early views but focus on his response, in the later work, to the antihumanist critique of the sixties.[2] By that decade it was widely appreciated that the self is not given as a matter of fact; it is constructed by institutions and people. The concept of the subject is historical, shaped and constructed by philosophers, religious thinkers, novelists, and political theorists, as well as by less theoretical agencies within cultures and societies.[3] Levinas's understanding of the subject is embedded in this debate and in the modern tradition, and without a few words about it, his innovation will hardly be intelligible.

MODERNITY AND THE SELF

When philosophers talk about modern views of subjectivity, the self, or the individual, a number of issues are run together. Obviously these notions are not modern, post-Renaissance inventions. In the philosophical tradition alone, ignoring religious, political, and legal contexts, the idea of the self or the individual person is at least as old as Heraclitus. Soul or *psyche* was a matter of importance and an object of reflection and examination for Socrates, Plato, Aristotle, the Pythagoreans, Anaxagoras, Empedocles, and virtually all of the Hellenistic schools. What happens in the sixteenth and seventeenth centuries, alongside significant political, social, and economic changes, is that the soul, the individual person, or the self becomes primary in three areas in ways that carry special weight – epistemology and science, religion and morality, and politics – and hence is distinguished by features in virtue of which it achieves its preeminence.

First, the self becomes primary in the domain of science and epistemology. Here the self is the mind, the investigator, the knower, the agent of examination and understanding. The individual person is preeminently a thinking thing – in Descartes's famous expression, a *res cogitans.* From the sixteenth century, a shift occurs; more and more responsibility for the scientific knowledge of nature falls upon the potential knower. Doubts about there being such knowledge, skeptical doubts, challenge the self to find secure grounds, and the Cartesian response, via the *cogito* and its sequel, leads to turmoil about how preeminent the thinking self is, what it grasps and how, and what it is capable of knowing outside of its

[2] See Simon Critchley, *Ethics, Politics, Subjectivity*, 62.

[3] Foucault explored the construction of the idea of the author in ways helpful to any understanding of the modern subject or individual. Authorship is a particular mode of individuality. See Michel Foucault, "What Is an Author?," in Paul Rabinow (ed.), *The Foucault Reader* (Pantheon, 1984), 101–120.

own contents. To be sure, Descartes's views are indebted to Augustine, Platonism, Montaigne, and others, but his innovation is to have privileged the thinking self as *the*, or at least *one*, starting point for the achievement of science or natural philosophy. Originally isolated epistemologically in its lonely confinement, the self or mind grasps its own contents incorrigibly and securely; all other knowledge it must struggle to earn through its own efforts and devices. To the privileged examiner, thinker, and knower, the essential characteristic is impeccable self-knowledge,[4] and it is this self-knowledge that provides the foundation on which science as knowledge of nature, other persons, and even God is grounded.

This epistemologically primary self is also ethically and politically primary. In Hobbes, for example, although each person is the individual bearer of natural capacities and desires and a dire threat to the other, he is also the vehicle by which social organization, the state, sovereignty, and law come into being, or, if one eschews a genetic reading of Hobbes, this individual, rational and the locus of desire, is the justification for these institutions. Then, in Locke, the equation of right, liberty, and power is fragmented, and rights as moral claims become the central feature of individual dignity and the raison d'etre for the state and political institutions. Science is based on self-knowledge; morality and politics are based on self-control and the capacity to determine one's choices and one's actions. Thereby, the moral and political agent comes to be characterized as worthy of respect and capable of autonomous choice, in short, free and dignified.[5] This is the second, moral-political primacy that the self achieves during the period from the sixteenth to the eighteenth century.

The self's third dimension of preeminence is religious. To be sure, Christianity, and this includes various Protestant denominations as well as the Roman Catholic Church, has always treated God as uniquely primary. But it is clear that various developments, even in Lutheranism and the many forms of Calvinism, granted remarkable new roles to the particular individual, the believer, in the arenas of ritual practice, the interpretation of Scripture, and the politics of the church. And as reason and science attracted greater and greater allegiance, rationalist revisions of Christianity – the Romanstrants in the Netherlands and the

[4] See Alexander Nehamas, Foreword to Renant, *The Era of the Individual*, xii. For important discussions of self-knowledge, see Richard Moran, *Authority and Estrangement: An Essay on Self-Knowledge* (Princeton, 2001), and David Finkelstein, *Expression and the Inner* (Harvard, 2003). For an important collection of essays, see Crispin Wright, Barry C. Smith, and Cynthia Macdonald (eds.), *Knowing Our Own Minds* (Oxford, 1998).

[5] Cf. Nehamas, in Renant, *The Era of the Individual*, xii.

Latitudinarians in England, for example – gave the individual rational believer an increasingly large part to play in the understanding and practice of faith. In place of a selfless submission to divine will, many saw human rationality as God's means for communicating His revelation and as the human way of teaching and expressing one's faith in God.

Throughout the nineteenth and early twentieth centuries, these dimensions of the primacy of the self – what came to be called "humanism" – became entrenched. It changed, was reinterpreted and qualified, and yet persisted, to such a degree that it was hardly ever questioned and even more rarely doubted. To be sure, there were challenges to those who installed the self's autonomy as its preeminent feature, to those who enshrined rationality or self-knowledge. But what was largely accepted without debate was the primacy of subjectivity itself as an all-encompassing starting point, ground, and foundation. This is the conventional story, too one-sided to be sure but sufficient for our purposes.

Simon Critchley helpfully suggests, however, that Levinas's understanding of subjectivity is not directly a response to this dominant modern tradition. Rather, as he sees it, it is a response to a later development, to the "post-structuralist and anti-humanist critique of subjectivity" that Ferry and Renaut call *La pensée 68*.[6] What was that critique, and how, for example, did Ferry and Renaut respond to it? Alexander Nehamas gives an excellent, succinct account in his Foreword to Alain Renaut's *The Era of the Individual*.[7] Ferry and Renaut are part of a defense of liberal democracy, and hence of a kind of humanism, against the anti-humanist critique, "the thought of '68," which is a legacy of Heidegger and to a certain degree of Marx.[8] To Ferry and Renaut, Heidegger's attack on modernity and democracy is politically and intellectually objectionable. They are committed to the protection of rights and opposition to domination and repression. They take the connections between Heidegger's antimodernism and his associations with Nazism to be authoritarian, reactionary, and grim.[9] While they agree with Heidegger about the alienating and oppressive results of technology and mass culture, Ferry and Renaut do not believe that democracy can be similarly indicted. In the modern technological world, the individual is the center, as the agent of control and manipulation but also as the victim of her desires and drives.

[6] Simon Critchley, *Ethics, Politics, Subjectivity*, 62; see Ferry and Renaut, *French Philosophy in the Sixties* and *Heidegger and Modernity*.

[7] See Alexander Nehamas, in Renaut, *The Era of the Individual*, vii-xviii.

[8] Ibid., vii-viii. Also structuralism and other postmodern developments.

[9] Ibid., viii.

In democratic society, the individual is also at the center, but, for them, it is as the bearer of rights and the autonomous agent of moral and political action.[10] Heidegger's attack on modernity ends up throwing out the baby with the bath, for while it is linked to the same metaphysical tradition and deplores its effects on all subject-centered thinking, rationality, and more, it is also in the end itself heir to the metaphysical tradition it attacks, with its cultivation of a poetic language of Being and its distortions of Plato, the pre-Socratics, and figures like Nietzsche – and of course with its allegiance to right-wing fascist politics.[11]

The "thought of '68," inspired by Heidegger, was indebted to thinkers such as Foucault, Lacan, Derrida, Bourdieu, and Althusser, all of whom saw the individual or human subject as incapable of the self-knowledge and autonomy once ascribed to it, most notably by the Enlightenment.[12] The human subject was not free of social codes, regimes of domination, and broad social and economic forces, even unconscious psychological ones, which exposed subjectivity as a construct, an artifact of impersonal factors. Ferry and Renaut come on the scene as critics of the critics, of their Heideggarian heritage and of their failure to respect the humanity of the subject. Levinas can be read, then, as an alternative critic, not concerned to protect the subject as the locus of rights and dignity but rather oriented to humanity in a different way. What we need to clarify is the nature of Levinas's alternative humanism.

But if Levinas is a critic of attacks on the primacy of the individual, he can also be seen as a critic of the tendency to treat the human as one would treat any other natural being. In the analytic tradition, the main challenge to the centrality of the subject has come from a certain form of naturalism.[13] This suggestion should not be misunderstood. It is not my intention to claim that analytic philosophy has not primarily been occupied with human-centered matters. It has. Analytic philosophers have been centrally concerned to explore and understand language, moral conduct, epistemological issues, art, science, and similar human activities, primarily by starting with the subject and the subject-object dualism. My point is rather that certain types of philosophical, reductive naturalism deal with these issues by placing human beings within the order of nature as understood by the natural and social sciences, but fundamentally by biology and physics. In this

[10] They owe a significant debt to Fichte and his *Grundlage der Naturrechts*.

[11] Alexander Nehamas, in Renaut, *The Era of the Individual*, x–xiv.

[12] See Simon Critchley and Peter Dews (eds.), *Deconstructive Subjectivities* (SUNY, 1996) and Eduardo Cadava, Peter Connor, and Jean-Luc Nancy (eds.), *Who Comes After the Subject?* (Routledge, 1991).

[13] A helpful set of essays is Mario De Caro and David Macarthur (eds.), *Naturalism in Question* (Harvard, 2004).

sense, then, the human subject no longer is treated as unique and privileged but rather as similar to other natural beings and ultimately comprehensible like any other natural being. This perspective on human affairs was canonized in the seventeenth century by Spinoza when, in the Preface to Part Three of the *Ethics*, he pointed out that human emotions should be analyzed and understood just like any other natural phenomena.[14] Materialists like Hobbes were even more thoroughgoing than Spinoza in carrying out this project, analyzing desire, emotions, deliberation, and indeed all mental events in terms of motion. Such reductive naturalism may still concede the primacy of the human in various ways but only by stripping it of many of its essential features, most notably (then) free will and immortality, and yet its defense of the significance of morality is controversial, and we can see Levinas as a critic of the whole naturalist enterprise, together with its inadequate defense of the individual as a subject of rights, a victim of injustice, and a self distinguished by generosity and mutual concern.

I have been trying to paint in broad strokes where Levinas stands in relation to twentieth-century views about the self and its roles in our thinking, society, culture, and life overall. In the century, as I have suggested, the primacy of the subject has been challenged from a number of quarters – political, religious, philosophical, and scientific. My emphasis here has been on two philosophical critiques – the Heideggarian and postmodernist critique and the scientific, naturalist one. These are expressions of totalization in the arena of the individual, ways in which the idealism of totality is compromised in anti-humanistic ways or in ways that qualify unconditional anthropocentrism. Levinas, in his unique manner, wants to recover that anthropocentrism. It is tempting to take him to be rejecting anthropocentrism in favor of the primacy of the other. I want to show that this interpretation is a mistake. Levinas's humanism does refer to the role of the face of the other for the subject or self, but it is clearly an effort to rethink anthropocentrism and not to replace it.[15]

THE EARLY STAGE

In order to simplify matters, let me look at Levinas's treatment of the self in two stages, first in *Time and the Other*, *Totality and Infinity*, and early essays, and then in more developed form in *Otherwise than Being*. What

[14] Baruch Spinoza, *Ethics*, Part III, Preface.

[15] Critchley agrees. See *Ethics, Politics, Subjectivity*, 67. Levinas himself entitles one of his collections of essays *Humanism of the Other*; he regularly refers to his view as a form of humanism and to Judaism as an "austere humanism."

are the essential features of human subjectivity? What gives human subjectivity its basic character? What distinguishes the self from other individual entities?

Earlier we discussed Levinas's genetic account in *Time and the Other* that traces the emergence of the subject, its situation in the world, and its engagement with the human other.[16] I explained that this account should not be interpreted literally, as if the subject does in fact emerge in stages; rather, it should be read as an examination of those features that distinguish human subjectivity from natural existence. Here we will look at those features in order to give some shape to Levinas's early conception of the self or human existence.[17]

A schematic picture of conceptions of the self in modern Western philosophy will provide us with a map on which to locate Levinas's thinking.[18] In Descartes the self is the I of the *cogito*; it is essentially a container for ideas or a center of consciousness, and consciousness is an awareness or representation of something. Primarily the self's consciousness or its ideas are cognitive; the I is an observer and investigator. It is an enclosed mental container that seeks to direct itself to what is outside – the world – in order to see it clearly and understand it; to see it means, of course, first of all to receive contents that come to it from the world. The self, during this period, then, is predominantly the theoretical subject. In Spinoza and others, this theoretical self is enriched by adding emotional states, desires, and a variety of noncognitive features that link the self to the world and issue in action.[19] And in Hume, the character of the subject is questioned but still on the basis of this same model, of a theoretical and practical container of ideas or impressions that represent and reach out to a world independent of that self. It is a picture deepened but not basically altered by Kant and the German Idealists who follow him.

With Husserl, this intellectualist picture is modified insofar as intentionality ties consciousness to objects in a variety of ways but always in an integrated nexus rather than as a relationship between an isolated, enclosed self and an external, separated world. In Heidegger and Wittgenstein, this embeddedness of self in the world is emphasized, and the modes of this

[16] See Chapter 2 of this volume.

[17] Not what makes it an I, but what makes it *human*.

[18] There are many places to go for such a picture, e.g., books by Renaut and Carr. A clear and convenient sketch can be found in a paper by Aron Gurwitsch reprinted in his collection *Studies in Phenomenology and Psychology* (Northwestern University Press, 1966).

[19] This is not to say that Descartes ignored the affective dimensions of subjectivity; they were his focus of attention in the late work *The Passions of the Soul*. And such states were also of great interest to someone like Hobbes. But for Descartes the self is primarily a theoretical subject.

embeddedness are practical, emotional, and more, embracing all the ways in which human beings exist in the public world. It is at this point that we can locate Levinas. For him, the self is not simply embedded or situated in the world. Nor is its life in the social, public world simply various and multifaceted. For Levinas, each of us is a subject in the world encountered by another person. In his early works, like *Time and the Other*, then, his account of how the subject is in the world *prior* to its encounter with the face of the other person is tailored to expose those features of the self's relation to the world without which the face-to-face encounter could not occur and make sense. As presented in these early accounts, it would seem that the self exists *prior* to the face-to-face; it lives in the world, enjoys its resources, and fulfills itself through work and appropriation. But in another sense, of course, there is no self prior to the encounter with the other. Levinas calls this self "ipseity," but in fact, in reality, the self never exists as ipseity.[20] The world we live in is social before it is a world at all. But what does this mean? In what sense is the self, as Levinas sees it, an ethical, responsible, and responsive self before it is anything at all? It is time to turn to Levinas's own discussion, to see how he approaches these themes in his own words and to see exactly how he stakes out new territory in this conception of the self.

Levinas gives a summary of the first stages of his account of the self, prior to its encounter with other persons, at the beginning of Part III of *Time and the Other*. "I have dealt," he says, "with the subject alone, alone due to the very fact that it is an existent."[21] Levinas calls this aloneness "solitude" and describes it as "the indissoluble unity between the existent and its work of existing."[22] This sounds very obscure indeed, and what follows no less so. This solitude or unity, between a being and what it is for it to be, is overcome when consciousness arises, and the existent "is put in touch with its existing." The "I" arises and with it freedom, the freedom of beginning, "starting out from something now." This is "the freedom of the existent in its very grip of existing."[23] The I can now exercise the "work of existing," and this *work* is the subject's "mastery over existing," its "power of beginning, of starting out from itself, starting out from itself neither to act nor to think, but to be."[24]

Let me try to paraphrase Levinas's account to this point. In everyday life, each of us is related to things around us, classified, compared, and

[20] See Robert Gibbs, *Correlations*, 28, 181–182.
[21] *Time and the Other*, 67.
[22] Ibid., 43.
[23] Ibid., 53, 54.
[24] Ibid., 67.

contrasted, but at the same time, each of us is fundamentally unique as an existing thing. Levinas calls this existing or being, which each of us manifests or realizes uniquely, prior to the emergence of unique existents from it, the *there-is* [*il y a*].[25] I will here ignore his treatment of it; for us the important point is that when a person distinguishes herself by taking a grip on her process of existing and by facing up to this frightening, foreboding background, Levinas associates this unique event with consciousness and becoming an I or, since he denies that the I is a substance or entity, becoming a subjective mode of existing. This means that existing for a person occurs as a unique center or locus for beginning or starting out.[26] Levinas calls this "freedom," prior to free will. It is akin to what Kant calls spontaneity or metaphysical freedom. In our everyday lives, then, we are many things; we act, think, and choose, and what makes this possible for us as the person each of us is is our being an I, which is a center of spontaneous origin. This is, he says, to have "something in its power."[27] It is "first freedom." The basic feature of subjectivity, then, is this metaphysical or existential freedom, the capacity to initiate action, in a broad sense.

The I frees itself from anonymous being and yet becomes bound to itself. It cares about itself; it is "mired in itself." Identity, Levinas says, is a "return to self"; it is "occupied with itself," and the way this occurs is called "materiality." Freed from the anonymity of existing, I am chained to myself and "responsible" for myself, for my body as my way of being in the world. I am "encumbered." "Matter is the misfortune of hypostasis," that is, of the self or the I, and "everyday life is a preoccupation with salvation."[28] Hence, if the self starts out in freedom, it then finds itself in need and with the task of satisfying those needs. Here is its second fundamental feature.

How is the self related to the world? Through its body (broadly speaking), its needs, Levinas says, and then by finding sustenance for that body and satisfying those needs in the world. With an obvious critical nod to Heidegger, he says that "prior to being a system of tools, the world is an ensemble of nourishments."[29] Moreover, living in the world and being

[25] Ibid., 46; the *there-is* is the central theme of his book *Existence and Existents* (1947). The *there-is* expresses itself in our everyday lives as the natural dimension of such lives, a kind of natural dred, whereas *illeity*, which manifests itself in religious language about God and theological vocabulary, expresses itself as the evaluative and ethical dimension of our lives. The *there-is*, then, is *Ur-Natur*, as it were.

[26] One might compare Arendt on natality.

[27] *Time and the Other*, 54.

[28] Ibid., 55–57; 67.

[29] Ibid., 63.

nourished by it involves a variety of fulfillments, satisfying our hunger, our sense of smell and touch. All of this Levinas calls "enjoyment,"[30] a posture of assimilating the world and yet remaining separate from it, of being hindered by oneself and fulfilled by the world. It is, he says, "first morality," for while it involves absorbing the world, it also requires a kind of self-abnegation: "the subject is absorbed in the object it absorbs."[31] This is morality as self-forgetfulness.

In Levinas's early work, to this point, the self is characterized as being free, needful, and enjoying the world; it is the locus of self-initiating engagement with a world that it needs and that nourishes it. These three features or dimensions of human existence, however, are only a kind of preparation for what makes that existence distinctively human. We might say that these dimensions are true of other natural beings and their modes of existing, just as they are true of human beings. Human beings, as natural and embodied beings, are not alone in needing the world to live, in being nourished by that world, and in being capable of some kind of action in behalf of gaining that nourishment. Animals, for example, also live this way. Of course, for animals, that capacity for gaining nourishment is not the same kind of capacity that human beings have, the capacity to initiate, to be an origin, and the satisfaction gained is not enjoyment per se but nonetheless a kind of fulfillment. Still, if we take Levinas's account of these three features to be "tailored" to his primary interest, which is the character of human existence, there is a sense in which these three focus on what we might see as the "natural" aspects of human existence and not the distinctively human dimension. They do not, by themselves, shed light on the humanity Levinas is seeking to disclose. So far, in a sense, the I, like other natural beings, is enclosed in the world; it has emerged from a pre-conceptual and pre-cognitive domain and has settled into everyday life, into the ordinary and natural world, into totality, into a life and a world structured and organized by culture, thought, rules, and principles.

I do not want to belabor Levinas's argument as it proceeds from here, but it is important to appreciate that he does in fact have one. Its basic structure is this: the self and its materiality need the world's nourishment and sustenance, but this – enjoyment – requires appropriation and work. The world, in other words, needs to be "conquered." But work is an expression of effort and brings with it pain, sorrow, and suffering.[32] "In suffering

[30] Ibid.
[31] Ibid., 67.
[32] Ibid., 68.

there is the absence of refuge. It is the fact of being directly exposed to being. It is made up of the impossibility of fleeing or retreating … of being backed up against life and being." Hence, suffering brings with it the "proximity of death."[33] Levinas then argues that death is a mystery, and yet when death is introduced through suffering, the subject experiences passivity; death presents itself as "an event in relation to which the subject is no longer a subject."[34] It is the "end of mastery" and "indicates that we are in relation with something that is absolutely other."[35] Existence is plural. Outside of me and my world is some other, which in this case is the other as a mystery.[36]

To this point, then, Levinas has argued that the self must confront suffering and death and that death brings with it an encounter with the other, alterity, something that transcends the totality of natural everyday life and theorizing about it.[37] Levinas's next step is to show that the self must encounter not only the *other as mystery* but also the other as other persons. But the death in question here, which first introduces the reality of otherness, so to speak, is my death, and it seems paradoxical to speak of an encounter with it. I may anticipate it or expect it or fear it, but to encounter it seems self-defeating, for death crushes the self and its freedom; it is a negation of the very subject that we might take to be experiencing it. In view of this apparent paradox about the encounter with the other, Levinas thus asks: "How can a being enter into relation with the other without allowing its very self to be crushed by the other?"[38] How can there be an other to which the self can be related without being destroyed by it? Levinas's answer to this problem of transcendence is: when the relationship with the other is the "face-to-face" where the face "at once gives and conceals the other."[39] That is, to confront my own death is to encounter negation by the other; to confront the other's death is to encounter an

[33] Ibid., 68–69.

[34] Ibid., 70.

[35] Ibid., 74.

[36] Ibid., 76. Note that, as Levinas proceeds, the experience that gives us a model of the relation with the other is *erotic*. Death is the mystery that first "introduces" the other and the notion of the other, but it is not the "mode of otherness," so to speak, that proves to be fundamental and determinative. It is not one's own death that matters most to the self but rather the death of the other person.

[37] Later, in "Transcendence and Evil" and "Useless Suffering," Levinas gives an account of suffering that takes suffering to be an experience of an other. Indeed, even in his early period, the *there-is* is already an experience of an other, which occurs in our lives in the experiences of insomnia and nausea. Such a focus on limit-experiences as evidence of access to the other is already found in *On Escape* and *Existence and Existents*.

[38] *Time and the Other*, 77.

[39] Ibid., 78–79.

other that threatens me and yet does not negate me but rather calls me to fulfillment. Here, then, we find a determination or feature of the self that lies in its passivity and yet in which the self is not "crushed" or destroyed.[40] Insofar as the self must confront the other in order to be a self, the other it must confront is the face of the other person, which both maintains its otherness and yet imposes itself on the self as other. The self in the face-to-face is wholly passive and yet not negated or destroyed; it is burdened, called into question, and yet summoned.

Levinas, then, has tried to show that work, suffering, and death are not contingent; they are part of human life – undeniably, he argues. Similarly, he must show that the face-to-face is essential to our lives, or, in other words, that interpersonal existence or social life is natural and unremarkable, even if too often we forget its character and its significance for us. Even if we lived a life of total isolation, stranded on a desert island, alone and without actual companions, still human life is essentially social.[41] This is what Levinas must show. He puts it this way: "If the relationship with the other involves more than relationships with mystery, it is because one has accosted the other in everyday life where the solitude and fundamental alterity of the other are already veiled by decency."[42] Basically, the other person faces us in everyday life as a free subject with needs. In ordinary experience, "decency" hides the unique character of the other person; I treat her according to rules or expectations, manners, politeness, and so forth. But alongside all of this formality is the brute otherness that she bears to me, and in this unique state of confronting me she is "the weak, the poor, 'the widow and the orphan', whereas I am the rich or the powerful."[43] In the most primary sense, each and every other person confronts me as one who has not to one who has.

In *Time and the Other* Levinas proceeds to clarify this encounter with the face of the other person as an asymmetrical relationship. This clarification takes the form of a quasi-phenomenological account of the erotic relationship.[44] Here he employs and develops a gendered vocabulary – eros,

[40] Ibid., 81–82.

[41] Heidegger makes just this sort of point in his account of *Mitsein* in *Being and Time*, section 26, 156–157. For Heidegger, that is, being-with is an ontological and not an ontic point about human existence. For Levinas, the face-to-face and responsibility are pre-ontological.

[42] *Time and the Other*, 82.

[43] Ibid., 83.

[44] By "quasi-phenomenological" I mean that it is like a phenomenological description even though it is pre-experiential and so, technically speaking, an account of a dimension of interpersonal experience that cannot be experienced, that does not "appear" or present itself and cannot present itself just as it is. Phenomenological description occurs at the level of what Levinas calls "ontology" or at the level of concrete everyday experience, whereas the face-to-face "interrupts"

the feminine, modesty, the caress, fecundity, and paternity. It is a vocabulary and an account extensively elaborated in *Totality and Infinity* and one that has been widely discussed (and criticized).[45] Given our earlier discussion in Chapter 2, however, we need go no further.[46]

RESPONSIBILITY AND PASSIVITY

I have taken the time to outline and paraphrase Levinas's early conception of subjectivity in order to highlight two problems. Levinas sees the self or the subject as free, needful, and immersed joyfully in the world;[47] he also sees it as passive before the face of the other person. To be sure, the self suffers, anticipates death, and bears children, but these activities and attitudes are in addition to the fundamental ones. There are two central questions, then, that this account must confront and answer. The first is how Levinas's view of the totalized subject, as I shall call it – free, needful, and joyous – should be understood, especially when compared to other contemporary views. The second is how we should understand the passivity of the subject in virtue of the face-to-face and the role of that passivity. In what sense is it a passivity prior to activity and prior to freedom? But before we consider these issues, we should turn to *Otherwise than Being*, where Levinas's conception of the subject is most fully developed.

In *Time and the Other* and *Totality and Infinity*, Levinas uses a dialectical narrative to display the basic features of subjectivity, as I have just reviewed them, and he then carries out a quasi-phenomenological description of *eros* in order to clarify the face-to-face and the subject's passivity before the other person. In the essay "Substitution" (1968) and then in *Otherwise than Being* (1974), Levinas focuses on the nature of subjectivity with a new set of terms and new interests, elaborating the earlier view by clarifying and deepening the understanding of the self's passivity, especially as part of a treatment of language. Levinas uses a number of new expressions and develops old ones – *responsibility*, *substitution*, *obsession*, *hostage*, *accusation*, *persecution*,

ontology and is of a different order or status. But Levinas's description of the erotic experience seeks to use phenomenological method to clarify, articulate, and disclose the features of the face-to-face in a way that is similar to the way such a method aims at the directly grasped sense or meaning of various modes of everyday experience.

45 *Totality and Infinity*, Section IV, 251–285.

46 It is worthwhile to look at Levinas's discussion of paternity and fecundity, where he answers the question he had raised about enduring the encounter with the other. This would provide the last ingredient in his early conception of subjectivity; see *Time and the Other*, 91. One's offspring, one's child, is an other who is independent and yet who commands responsibility and devotion unqualifiedly.

47 Cf. *Totality and Infinity*, 110–151.

subjection, *saying*, *proximity*, and more. Many of these terms intensify the sense of passivity of the self's relation to the other person and emphasize precisely what seems so paradoxical, that the self is passive, obligated, and burdened, prior to being free and active – that, in a sense, the self is object before it is subject. Before we can consider why Levinas says such things and whether they can be justified, we need to ask what they mean and how they add to our understanding of human social existence.

Subjectivity, the self, or the human individual is beyond freedom; it is "responsibility for the faults or the misfortunes of others" and "cannot have begun in my commitment, in my decision." It is the "null-site" where the Good "has chosen me before I have chosen it."[48] I am commanded to and by the other, who "provokes this responsibility against my will … by substituting me for the other as a hostage.… I am ordered toward the face of the other."[49] The self, then, is responsibility in response to a trauma, before understanding, "for a debt contracted before any freedom and before any consciousness." Subjectivity is the point where "essence is exceeded by the infinite." Levinas calls this point a "breakup of identity" and a "subjection to everything," a vulnerability. He summarizes these descriptions in a passage that reveals how developed his conception of the human subject has become:

> Vulnerability, exposure to outrage, to wounding, passivity more passive than all patience, passivity of the accusative form, trauma of accusation suffered by a hostage to the point of persecution, implicating the identity of the hostage who substitutes himself for the others: all this is the self, a defecting or defeat of the ego's identity. [50]

The central idea here, which we need to examine and clarify, is substitution. Fundamentally, the self should not be characterized as the subject of theory and thought[51] or as the subject of action and *praxis*.[52] The self is not first of all an actor or agent. From the first, the self is animated by responsibility; it is, in Levinas's words, saying and substitution. In *Otherwise than Being* Levinas does not ignore the other features of the self – its freedom and uniqueness, needfulness, and enjoyment.[53] He calls this unified self the "subjectivity of flesh and blood in matter."[54] But his attention is ultimately

[48] *Otherwise than Being*, 8, 10, 57, 102.
[49] Ibid., 11.
[50] Ibid., 15; cf. 54.
[51] Cf. ibid., 23–26.
[52] Cf. ibid., 53.
[53] See ibid., 65–81.
[54] Ibid., 78.

on the prior or more fundamental subjectivity that he characterizes as responsibility, saying, and substitution. These other features – freedom, needfulness, and enjoyment, which ground, in a sense, any account of the theoretical and practical agent, are not as important to him, for they do not show, as responsibility and substitution do, the point and purpose of human existence and its essentially social nature.

Having said this much about the subject or subjectivity in *Otherwise than Being*, I now need to provide some clarification. Commentators regularly cite passages like the ones I have quoted and repeat what Levinas has said, most commonly his unusual vocabulary. But his intent was in part to show the limitations of prior discussions, from Descartes to Heidegger, and to shock his readers into seeing things differently. That can hardly be the goal of commentators. Even the best of these readers formulate important problems about the idea of the subject, only to lapse into citation or paraphrase of Levinas's unusual and surprising expressions when it comes to introducing his own thoughts. But this strategy is even less satisfying than providing a traveler with a guidebook and then leaving her at the border of a foreign country without an entry visa.

Many of the terms for this basic level of subjectivity or primary dimension of the self are terms that dramatize the self's passivity vis-à-vis the face of the other person: the self is accused, obsessed, persecuted, and subjected. The self is made the hostage of the other person; it substitutes for the other person. By itself, such vocabulary is vivid and colorful, but in everyday use it seems unproblematic. We have no trouble understanding what it means to be accused by another person of a fault or injury, to be persecuted by someone who mistreats or dominates us, or to be subjected to questioning or even demands by one who confronts us. But while Levinas draws on the normal uses of these words, he does so in order to place them in a wholly unique context. In some sense, that is, the self's being persecuted or subjected or accused is primary, first, "an-archic" insofar as it is prior to all beginnings, and so prior to freedom and agency. This vocabulary, then, aside from the drama and intensity it wants to suggest, is intended to point to a truly radical passivity; as Levinas says, it is a passivity that is prior to the passive-active distinction altogether. What, however, does this mean? What could it mean? It is one thing to be persecuted before one has done anything, even to be accused prior to any action, but it is wholly inconceivable how one can be subjected in these ways, from the outside, when one cannot be said to be or to have identity or to be an object of conscious experience. The former conduct might be challenged, as unwarranted or unfair; the latter is intended to precede the very distinction between justified and unjustified persecution or accusation. It is intended to call attention to a fundamental, primary, and unique kind of passivity.

Levinas also says that the subject is substitution, responsibility, and a hostage – all with respect to the other person. If the earlier set of terms looked at the self from the other person's point of view, so to speak, these look at it from the self's own perspective. Of course, Levinas would never put it this way, but it is helpful to notice that he ramifies his terminology in part in order to describe the face-to-face and the subject from all possible perspectives. Moreover, when he is being precise, he does not say that the self is responsible or substitutes for the other; more precisely, he says that subjectivity – what it means for the self to be a subject – *is responsibility*; it *is substitution*; it *is being a hostage*. But in all these cases, the self is these things before it acts, before it thinks, before it chooses, before it does anything, and before it is free, that is, before it is capable of originating or initiating anything. Once again, then, we find Levinas saying things that seem to make no sense; he asks us to grasp that the self is capable of and required to respond and that it stands in for the other, before the self is or is free or is capable of acting at all.

Levinas himself appreciates that we might in fact be confused by all this. At a crucial point, in the central chapter of *Otherwise than Being*, he asks: "But how does the passivity of the self become a 'hold on oneself'? If that is not just a play on words, does it not presuppose an activity behind the absolutely anarchical passivity of obsession, a clandestine and dissimulated freedom?" The question has been answered, he says, with the notion of substitution.[55] In the remaining sections of the chapter he explains how this is so.

What does Levinas mean by this account of subjectivity? How does substitution solve the problem of how passivity can also be a kind of activity, of how it can be prior to both ordinary activity and ordinary passivity and yet be what it is – responsibility?

If we take the notion of priority temporally, we are surely in trouble. Either the notion of passivity and its surrogates are wholly equivocal and mean nothing like what they normally do, in which case responsibility and the related concepts are obscure and mysterious, or we are asked to understand and accept that such a capacity or state is coherent even if without a subject or agent. Alternatively, however, suppose that the priority is conceptual. What could this mean? What sense does it make to say that being responsible or accused or obsessed is conceptually prior to

[55] Ibid., 113.

being free? I think that we can dispense with these and similar attempts to read Levinas's conception of subjectivity as passivity; all lead to obvious incoherence and impenetrability.

We get closer to Levinas's meaning, as I have suggested, when we think of the self as passivity as a transcendental condition, and this suggestion is akin to thinking about the priority as conceptual, for it directs us to ask: a transcendental condition for what? And how is it such a condition? Indeed, here we seem to be on familiar ground; this reading might be understood as Levinas's version of Husserl's transcendental idealism, with the responsible self replacing Husserl's transcendental ego and the Kantian unity of apperception as a transcendental condition of human existence.[56] On this reading, the responsible, passive self is the transcendental condition for the possibility of everyday experience, not precisely insofar as it is experience but rather insofar as it is meaningful, social human existence. The face-to-face and the responsible self – they are one thing characterized from two perspectives – are what give language, thought, communication, and social life point and purpose. Hence, everyday human life is meaningful and significant as human (and social) only because of the responsible self. The self as responsibility and substitution is the transcendental condition for meaningful human life, for the ordinary and the everyday as the fabric of social, intersubjective, and interactive human experience. Ethics is the metaphysics of meaningful human existence.

This proposal, however, can be developed by realizing, as we have done before, that such a condition is not a postulated entity or a theoretical discovery or construct. Rather, it is a *dimension* or *cluster of dimensions* of everyday experience that may rarely – or all too rarely – be in view or that are obscured by contemporary life and culture. Alternatively, we might say that Levinas wants us to see everyday life from a different perspective, one that is determinative of what meaning that life has as social and ethical. On this reading, the transcendental condition of the responsible self is not an *object* of theoretical, philosophical insight; it is a *feature* of our lives that we regularly fail to grasp and hence a mode of existence that we fail to live or act on. If, on the one hand, we ask about our identities or egos, about our character as cognitive agents, practical actors, and free agents, and about what it is for us to be such selves, the answers to these questions can be given by looking at the self or subject in various ways. But if we seek, on

[56] John Drabinski has suggested such a reading, and it is hinted at in the work of Theodor DeBoer. See John Drabinski, *Sensibility and Singularity*, and Theodor DeBoer, *The Rationality of Transcendence*.

the other hand, to understand what the *point* of our theoretical selfhood is or what the *significance* is of our practical agency, the answer to *that* question drives us ultimately to the self's responsibility, to its character as substitution, hostage, and so forth.

If we ask, then, what the agency or selfhood is to which responsibility or substitution is ascribed, the answer is: our normal everyday selves. The priority of responsibility does not mean that we should reject our normal understanding that there must be some person to whom we ascribe responsibility; what it means is that my being responsible is what ultimately gives point to my being me at all. There is no time when I am responsible and not yet an I, although there certainly are times when I am I, in any number of ways, and yet am not responsible or, perhaps better, do not act responsibly.

When Levinas says that the subject is responsibility before it does anything, then, this should not be read temporally. It is puzzling but in the end not obscure. For what it means is that whenever I am engaged with another person or persons, whatever I am doing, my relationships and my actions are ultimately of significance, in a sense, before I am who I am and before my capacity to think or act, precisely because of the capacity I have and the necessity that falls on me to respond to that other person's needs and very existence. I may be blind to this capacity and necessity to respond – my responsibility as responsivity[57]– but it is always there, an aspect of me and my relationship with each and every other person, whether I realize it or not. Hence, in a sense, I am always, in whatever I do, satisfying its directions or failing to do so, unavoidably. I am responsible for and to the other person "before" I am a person, but now we can see that this shocking statement is no contradiction; it is not as paradoxical as it seems. Rather, it is Levinas's attempt to unsettle us into seeing our ordinary everyday life in a different way.[58]

Let me suggest that we read Levinas's most extreme terminology in this way. Rather than say that the self is accused before it is free, or persecuted before it acts, I suggest that what Levinas means is that the free agent is always already accused by the other; his actions are always under indictment, and his freedom is always being judged. He is persecuted, held hostage, but not prior to being a free agent with an identity. There is no temporal *before*. As we have argued, the face-to-face is a structural, real,

[57] See Critchley, *Ethics, Politics, Subjectivity*, 62; cf. Buber as well, in "Dialogue" in *Between Man and Man*.

[58] These paragraphs are my reading of *Otherwise than Being*, 113–118.

and normative dimension of all human relationships. Similarly, the self is free, active, and yet at the same time that freedom and its actions are always "under indictment" by each and every other, whose claim on the self is never adequately met and certainly never fully met. Why? Precisely because the self always limits its help and generosity; its responsibility is always partial, imperfect, and distributed among all those who call it into question. From its point of view, the self is always persecuted or accused, traumatized and held hostage. In a sense, the self is irredeemably on trial.

THE SELF AND CONTEMPORARY PHILOSOPHY

In this chapter I have tried to show that Levinas's conception of the self and of what it means to be a person is not as strange as it might first seem. The primary reason that Levinas's conception might seem strange is that we are inclined to think that it is basic or fundamental to being a self to be free or autonomous, rational and active. But Levinas emphasizes that as selves, we are passive before we are active, responsible before we are free. I have argued that the word "before" does not mean temporally prior. There is never a time when we are not free and rationally capable at the same time that we are responsible. We are not as beings the objects of the actions or impact of other things prior, in time, to when we are agents, subjects of various forms of conduct, which might seem incoherent. "Before" means something like "prior in importance" or "prior in the order of what makes life meaningful or significant." In this sense, we, as persons, find that what gives our lives point and purpose is our relationships with other persons, for in such relationships we are responsible first of all.

Levinas's point is that being free to act does not make us persons. To put this in other terms, Levinas is not interested in the question, what is it to be a self, or what is it to be a person, insofar as this question is a metaphysical one about the kind of thing a self is.[59] Nor is he interested in

[59] That is, Levinas is not interested in the metaphysical question: what makes a person at a particular time T1 the same person as a person at another time T2? He is not interested in the problem of continuity in this sense. There is a large literature that has grown up around this question, historically about John Locke's views about memory and personal identity, and systematically, frequently responding to various imaginative examples of brain transplants, fission, and such. Two older anthologies collect a number of important contributions: A. Rorty (ed.), *The Identities of Persons* (University of California Press, 1976), and John Perry (ed.), *Personal Identity* (University of California Press, 1976). See also Harold W. Noonan, *Personal Identity*, 2nd ed. (Routledge, 2003). These issues are relevant or have been thought to be relevant to questions about self-interest and justice; a crucial work is Derek Parfit, *Reasons and Persons* (Oxford University Press, 1984). Parfit's work has generated an enormous literature in and of itself. For an interesting critique of Parfit and the whole enterprise of showing that the metaphysical issues of personal identity are

persons or selfhood in other ways that have been most important to many philosophers.

In twentieth-century philosophy, thinking about the concept of personhood has moved from metaphysical issues, such as personal identity over time, to practical matters, treating the person as an agent and asking what agency requires, and finally to ethical considerations, when it is argued that to be a person one must be capable of acting on moral reasons.[60] These three approaches have developed in response to different, often overlapping, problems and issues. The metaphysical approaches have worried about the role of the body and spatio-temporal continuity in guaranteeing personal identity into the future; they have asked whether a psychological rather than a physical account can better account for the kind of survival we take to be required for someone's being a continuous, self-identical person. They have asked whether the self is a thing or a person, and if it is a thing, whether it is a physical or immaterial one. The practical approaches have argued that a person must be capable of rational action, of being an agent who acts on reasons, and this approach has required freedom, to some, while to others what is required is a will that incorporates rationality and desire, coordinated in a specific way. Finally, the moral approaches, and there have been many adherents with a variety of strategies, have held that a person must be capable of moral conduct and susceptible to moral judgment, both of which require being responsible or accountable for what one does, being reflective and capable of the evaluation of one's desires and reasons, of committing oneself to act in behalf of one or the other, and of asking what respect for human life requires of them to do. What all of these approaches share, no matter how close or how far they are from taking ethics seriously as distinctive of what a person is, is that they begin with capacities or features of the subject or agent and work outward, so to speak. And this is precisely where Levinas differs from them. He does not deny that persons – metaphysically or as agents or as moral beings in an everyday sense – must have these subject-centered features. What he

required for drawing ethical implications about self-interest, justice, and so forth, see Marya Schechtman, *The Constitution of Selves* (Cornell University Press, 1996), especially Part I. I think that one could show how Levinas's claim about the priority of responsibility is related to these metaphysical questions, but there is no need to do so here.

60 See Marya Schechtman, "Experience, Agency, and Personal Identity." For an important discussion that takes seriously the special contributions of P. F. Strawson and Derek Parfit, among a host of others, see Quassim Cassam, *Self and World* (Oxford University Press, 1997). Also, on more recent narrative approaches, see Marya Schechtman, *The Constitution of Selves* (Cornell University Press, 1996); Galen Strawson, "The Self," in Shaun Gallagher and Jonathan Shear (eds.), *Models of the Self* (Academic, 1999); and John Christman, "Narrative Unity as a Condition of Personhood," *Metaphilosophy* 35:5 (October 2004), 696–713.

denies is that these can be understood as distinctive of persons, insofar as they live in the world with other persons, without grounding them or their significance in a deeper relational fact about interpersonal encounter, that is, the summons of the other, as we might call it.[61]

Levinas is concerned with the question of who we are as persons, what kind of lives we live, what makes our lives as persons the kind of lives they are. In this sense, he claims that our responsibility to other persons is what makes our lives good ones. It is not our capacity to act freely and rationally that does so. Neither does being the subject of thinking and speaking, nor being rational agents who can deliberate and form intentions to act, nor being selves that are unified in virtue of having a narrative or temporally organized understanding of what we have experienced and done and what we hope or plan to do.[62] Levinas does not deny that there may be some value and some truth in conceiving of ourselves in these various ways. His concern, as I have tried to show, is that alongside all these features of our selfhood, some of them arguably essential features, such as rationality and freedom and linguistic capability and occupying a first-person perspective, there is a feature or dimension that characterizes human existence most deeply and determines it most importantly. That feature is our relationship with other persons, conceived as a face-to-face event that constitutes our responsibility to her and to all others, one by one. It is the feature of being summoned by the other to respond to her by acknowledging her and doing more, providing for her in every way.

In order to clarify Levinas's point, even if I cannot here argue for it in a conclusive fashion, let me propose an analogy. When dealing with what it is to be a person, the context for understanding what it is for us to be persons, let us say, is agency and especially moral agency. The issues concern human freedom and rationality and whether these are primary or fundamental for our personhood. Consider, however, a different but

[61] Although she does not treat intersubjectivity as a transcendental dimension of human existence and hence as primary in the way Levinas does, Kim Atkins does express the way in which intersubjectivity in the form of the face-to-face and moral value are related: "The second-personal processes of primary and pragmatic intersubjectivity articulate not just one's physical body but also the existential and moral dimensions of one's embodied existence. Through my second-personal relations, I come to regard aspects of myself as desirable and shameful, powerful or feeble, even worthy or unworthy, or any contradictory combination of these. As a result, my third-personal perspective of myself takes on specific content, style, and value." See Kim Atkins, *Narrative Identity and Moral Identity* (Routledge, 2008), 52.

[62] For a very helpful discussion of personhood and personal identity, see Marya Schechtman, "Experience, Agency, and Personal Identity," *Social Philosophy and Policy* 22:2 (July 2005), 1–24. See also J. David Velleman, *Self to Self* (Cambridge University Press, 2006), especially the Introduction, and Catriona Mackenzie, "Bare Personhood? Velleman on Selfhood," *Philosophical Explorations* 10:3 (September 2007), 263–281.

analogous context, that of language. There are surely those who claim that what distinguishes us as human beings is the capacity to develop and use language to communicate with one another. Levinas does not deny that we do have this capability, that we use language to communicate with each other and that this depends upon our personal abilities – to create symbols and symbolic systems, to employ metaphors, to generalize, to follow linguistic rules and to adapt them creatively, and so forth. But all of this involves the construction of languages and their implementation in particular cases; language in this sense concerns what Levinas calls the *said*, the form and content of linguistic systems, of systems of symbols. Levinas proposes, however, that language is not simply the creation and grasping of such systems. Language is communication; it is a vehicle that allows us to respond and to call out to one another, to share information, to acknowledge and command, to persuade and to promise, and much else. That is, the point and purpose of language is to facilitate in various ways our responses to one another as a vehicle for acknowledgment and acceptance. Levinas calls this the *saying*; it is the ethical matrix in which language as communication takes place. Without it, there would be no ultimate reason to have language or languages and no point in their employment. The social, concrete context for language is the interpersonal setting in which it is employed, and the ethical core of that interpersonal setting is the call of the other person to the self to accept and acknowledge it, to respond with a linguistic "piece of bread," so to speak, to share a word with it.

Unlike contemporary philosophers such as Charles Taylor, then, and unlike Christine Korsgaard and David Velleman, for whom our personhood is tied to the unity of ourselves as practical agents and ultimately to our role as moral agents, for Levinas this ethical character is grounded in the other's call to us.[63] Hence the core of personhood is its ethical character, but only in this sense, that we are passive before we are active, accused before we have done anything. As substitution or hostage for the other person, we are subjects prior to being persons with our own identities and independence.

[63] See Christine M. Korsgaard, *The Sources of Normativity* (Cambridge University Press, 1996); "Personal Identity and the Unity of Agency: A Kantian Response to Parfit," *Philosophy & Public Affairs* 18 (Spring 1989), 101–132; "Self-Constitution in the Ethics of Plato and Kant," in *The Constitution of Agency: Essays on Practical Reason and Moral Psychology* (Oxford University Press, 2008), 100–126; and *Self-Constitution: Agency, Identity, and Integrity* (Oxford University Press, 2009).

CHAPTER SIX

God, Philosophy, and the Ground of the Ethical

Our appreciation of what philosophy is at any given historical moment, how it is understood by its practitioners and derided by its critics, is helped by examining its relationships with what are commonly called theology and religion.[1] The stories of the relation between philosophy and religion and between philosophy and theology are complex and lengthy. Frankly, the more we understand of these tales, the better would be our grasp of Levinas's references to religion and God and his penchant for using theological and religious expressions to refer to the face and the ethical.[2] Both topics are present early in Levinas's writings. Long before *Totality and Infinity*, he could say: "The absolute which supports justice is the absolute status of the interlocutor. His modality of being and of manifesting himself consist in turning his face to me, in being a face. … This is not at all a theological thesis; yet God could not be God without first having been this interlocutor."[3] These words come from 1954. They raise the question: how is God related to the face-to-face and its ethical import if their relationship is not a theological matter, if, that is, God is not a divine commander and ethics is not constituted by His commandments? Even at this early stage Levinas struggled to articulate how his insight about the central importance of the face-to-face and responsibility is related to God and religion. His views, I believe, certainly developed and changed, but at the same time they retained a common core. Ethics and religion are intimately related, but we need to understand exactly how. In this chapter I want to look at what he says about God, how he should be understood,

[1] Religion is the collective experience of religious believers, a complex network of practices, beliefs, and institutions. Theology is the reflective understanding of religion, especially dealing with divinity and its various relationships with history and the natural order.

[2] An excellent treatment of these themes can be found in Jeffrey Kosky, *Levinas and the Philosophy of Religion*; see also the essays in Jeffrey Bloechl (ed.), *The Face of the Other and the Trace of God* (Fordham University Press, 2000), and Jeffrey Bloechl, *Levinas the Liturgy of the Neighbor*. See also Wyschogrod, Gibbs, Cohen, Wright, Purcell, and Peperzak.

[3] Emmanuel Levinas, "The Ego and the Totality," in *Collected Philosophical Papers*, 33.

and why he says it. In view of recently renewed philosophical interest in God, theology, and religion, these matters – so important to Levinas – are also important to us.[4]

GOD AND THE PHILOSOPHICAL TRADITION

In his *Theological-Political Treatise* (1670), Baruch Spinoza explains that the word "miracle" is used to refer to events or facts that we have yet to understand.[5] One might extrapolate: God or the divine or the transcendent refers to a cause or agency for events and facts that we cannot (yet) explain satisfactorily based on our everyday (and then scientific) understanding of how things occur in the natural world and why. There is an element of truth in this account; it is certainly not true of all theological belief at all times and in all places, but in the West it is partially true that as science and the social sciences grew and developed, many found their belief in and commitment to God or divinity waning, and especially their belief in divine providence or in divine agency directly operative in nature and history. The history of Western philosophy, to a degree, reflects these changes. One can take Aristotle's treatment of the divine in *Metaphysics*, Book Lambda, and in the *Physics*, for example, as part of a strategy to make room for natural explanation, to maintain a link to transcendence, and to tie the two together. Many of Aristotle's descendants and heirs, in the Middle Ages and the early modern period, appropriated his model and adapted it to changes in science.[6] Moreover, when the need for God or the divine in theoretical matters waned and then disappeared completely, philosophers could either find another role still necessary or dispense with theology altogether. Kant and Hegel, for example, took the former route, albeit in very different ways, as did Kierkegaard, while, one could argue, the "masters of suspicion" – Marx, Nietzsche, and Freud – famously took the latter route.

Philosophy in the twentieth century moved away from religion and the theological and then, more recently, has made room for movements to return to them.[7] Early twentieth-century responses to historicism and the

[4] For a recent account, see Michael Purcell, *Levinas and Theology* (Cambridge, 2006).

[5] Spinoza, *Theological-Political Treatise*, 2nd ed. (Hackett, 2001), Chapter 5.

[6] If we are liberal about whom we consider such heirs of Aristotle, we could include Descartes, Hobbes, Spinoza, Locke, Leibniz, and Newton among them.

[7] I am thinking of the critique of religion, theology, and metaphysics we associate with Logical Postivism and scientistic forms of analytic philosophy, largely naturalist of one kind or another, perhaps best exemplified by A. J. Ayer's *Language, Truth, and Logic*. Then, in the postwar period, we have the return to an interest in the philosophy of religion and philosophical theology – early

relativism that was associated with certain accounts of the social sciences included philosophical ones that navigated from religion or near to it, such as some versions of Neo-Kantianism, *Lebensphilosophie*, and even phenomenological developments like those of Karl Jaspers and Rudolf Bultmann. Some might even argue that the early Wittgenstein left room for religious and theological experience,[8] and if one considers figures like Karl Barth, Rudolph Bultmann, Paul Tillich, Martin Buber, Franz Rosenzweig, Georg Lukács, and Walter Benjamin philosophical, then the age of high modernism can be read as a moment of special rapport between philosophy and religious impulses. In one way or another, all of these figures found in God or transcendence a ground of meaning in and for human life. But with the rise of logical positivism and its influence in England and the United States, religion was marginalized and largely excluded from serious philosophical discussion until late in the twentieth century. In the fifties and subsequent decades, with the influence of the later Wittgenstein and ordinary language philosophy, various religious phenomena were sanitized and examined, especially issues of language and the proofs for God's existence, but outside of this almost "experimental" approach to the rationality of religious belief, such matters were of only incidental philosophical interest. In the late decades of the century, this began to change, and even in the circles of Anglo-American philosophy, there has been a revival of sorts in which religion and theology have become interesting in new ways. Levinas might best be viewed, in this venue, as contributing to this revival or at least, once he is made accessible and available, as a potentially significant and interesting contributor.

Part of the story to be told about Levinas and his role is that he is responding to Neitzsche's slogan "the death of God" and to the challenge put to twentieth-century philosophy, by Nietzsche and others, to address the question of the meaningfulness of human existence and the challenge to the sources and foundations of value. This kind of story is so well known it is hardly necessary to retell it.[9] The point is that if Levinas increasingly seeks to clarify the character of religion and the role of God, the sacred, and holiness in human existence, the avenue he chooses is largely an ethical one. In

in figures like Antony Flew, Alasdair MacIntyre, and Basil Mitchell; more recently in philosophers like Alvin Plantinga, Nicholas Wolterstorff, William Rowe, and Richard Swinburne. All of this activity occurred within the Anglo-American, so-called analytic circle; a quite different but significant shift occurred in the world of continental philosophy with figures such as Derrida, Henry, Marion, and Levinas himself. See Kevin Hart, *The Trespass of the Sign*.

[8] An important contribution is Fergus Kerr, *Theology after Wittgenstein* (Blackwell, 1986).

[9] For a recent telling, see Julian Young, *The Death of God and the Meaning of Life* (Routledge, 2003).

this sense, Levinas is structurally like Kant insofar as Kant too, once he had banished God and religion from the domain of science and the life of theory and explanation, sought to recover them by showing how moral agency required a belief in God and a revised interpretation of religion as a moral faith. There is indeed something like this going on in Levinas: that God is, in some sense, present in the face of the other person does have something to do with the ethical, and to say that this is not a theological thesis is to deny that God has a theoretical or cognitive role to play. But as it is, this is much too simple and inaccurate to be helpful. We need first to look much more carefully at what Levinas says and then to place him within recent philosophical discussion of the grounds and sources of normativity in ethics. This metaethical setting may not turn out to be the only venue for understanding what Levinas says about God and religion; it may not even turn out to be the best venue. But it is a natural starting place, especially, I think, given his proximity to someone like Charles Taylor, who himself increasingly has shown an affinity for religious sources of the good.[10]

EARLY WORKS

Throughout Levinas's career, religion and the sacred provide a vocabulary for the ethical that he finds seductive and compelling. And yet, in his early works, Levinas stays within the bounds of philosophical analysis and philosophical exploration. These are not confessional discussions, and the outcomes are not parochial. Dealing with the God of everyday life and discourse requires a philosophical understanding of what the language about God means for ethics.

As we begin to look at Levinas's writings, we should keep in mind some features of his thinking that we have already seen in operation and their relevance to the issue at hand. For Levinas, traditional theological beliefs and theological language occur within the domain of totality. They employ concepts and discursive argument, make general claims, and so forth. Theology is theoretical, and it is continuous, to one degree or another, with philosophy, metaphysics, and science, as well as with ethical theory and even political thought. In addition, religious practices, texts, and religious life in general occur within the ordinary everyday experience of many people. Whatever the explicit intentions and attitudes of religious practitioners, religious life can be and has been examined by the social

[10] In addition to *Sources of the Self*, one should look at *Varieties of Religion Today*, *Modern Social Imaginaries*, and *A Catholic Modernity?* See also *A Secular Age*.

sciences and given explanations rooted in psychology, sociology, and even economics. Theology and religion, then, are manifest in historical life and contemporary experience, and existing accounts of religion and theology examine the meaning of their beliefs and practices in scientific terms.

Religious life may be taken to reflect or express beliefs about God and the world or to express attitudes and feelings or to indicate principles of behavior and hopes for the future. Theological statements may be understood to be descriptive of God, and religious statements may be interpreted as petitions or eulogies or reprimands. But as we might expect, Levinas, we shall see, associates our language and practices concerning the sacred and the divine with the primary ethical dimension of our lives, as he has characterized it. After all, human existence is wholly ethical, and religious life is one aspect of human existence. Therefore, we can ask, with respect to the idea of God that we think about and the word "God" that we use in our ordinary lives, what is the relationship between these thoughts and utterances and the ethical relation? In everyday thinking and speech and in theoretical experience – from ontology and metaphysics to theology and the sciences – words mean what they do and refer to things in ways that philosophers have examined and debated. But the face of the other person, while it may shed light on our lives and have significance, is not connected directly to thought and speech as everyday experience is. What Levinas needs to do, then, if he takes the face-to-face and the presence of the other person to have a primary and elevated status for us, is to clarify how it, as a dimension of our everyday lives, albeit often hidden from view or occluded, is related to the way we think and talk about God in those lives.

It cannot be the case that the word "God" simply refers to the face of the other person or to the other person herself. In a sense, that face is "unreferable" and "meaningless." But if "God" does not describe or point to something *in* the ethical relation, how is it related to that relation, if it is at all? Levinas begins, one might say, with an insight from Schelling, Kierkegaard, Buber, and Rosenzweig, among a host of others, that God in reality is never captured by thought or concepts; no matter how complete and articulate the system of thought may be, it can never comprehend God. The unique fact of God always remains outside of that system. Nonetheless, that reality is one we, as distinct individuals, can encounter. As Buber puts it, God is the Eternal Thou, the Divine Presence, one who can only be addressed and never expressed.[11] We can speak to God but

[11] See Martin Buber, *I and Thou*, passim. Levinas would not articulate the relation to the divine in this way, as we shall see, but there is a sense that his understanding of our relation to transcendence does have an origin common to this tradition.

never about God. In his own way, Levinas begins with this thought only to push it further: if this is so, then at their own level, theological thinking and theological statements should not be interpreted as descriptive; it is not that they are descriptive and false but rather they are not descriptive at all. They should be understood to have a different kind of significance altogether.

Moreover, we need to ask: when we address God, what are we doing? We are not escaping the everyday world in order to engage in an extraordinary encounter with an otherworldly being. We are not having some kind of religious or mystical experience. But if not, what then does it mean to say that I am addressing God? What kind of an experience am I having? If the idea of God signals our acknowledgment of transcendence, and if to grasp that idea is not part of a descriptive or referential act, then what does it mean to acknowledge transcendence in our lives, to receive the call of the genuinely other?[12]

If we imagine Levinas raising these questions for himself, we can see how his thinking about God might have struggled to attain some kind of clarity. For these lines of thinking suggest that the idea of God and theological language overall are associated with what is deepest and most significant for our lives as human lives, for what he calls the ethical and also the religious.[13] In a sense, God is very close to us indeed, and yet exceedingly difficult to grasp. Levinas's lifelong wrestling with the expression "God" and the idea of God shows how firm is his commitment to both the proximity and the distance of the idea. As we read what he says, we want to understand the steps that he takes as he seeks greater and greater precision and clarity about God and the ethical, at the same time that he revises and deepens his approach to the ethical itself.

There is one relationship between God and the ethical that Levinas will have to reject. That is the traditional view, what is often called "divine command theory," a divine voluntarism that takes God to be the source of moral rules or principles. Levinas may not be disturbed by narratives of divine command or theological reflections about God as a God of revealed laws, as long as these forms of discourse are not interpreted descriptively, literally, or theoretically. He may find such narratives or statements or

[12] It is a central theme of Samuel Moyn's *Origins of the Other: Emmanuel Levinas between Revelation and Ethics* (Cornell, 2006) that Levinas is importantly indebted to theological and religious debates of the Weimar period and especially to figures like Barth, Rosenzweig, and others on the notion of revelation.

[13] See "Transcendence and Height," in *Basic Philosophical Writings*, 29–30 (the discussion after the talk, which occurred in 1962).

theories valuable, if properly understood, or he may find them disturbing and confusing. What he cannot do is to attach such a notion, of God as a moral commander, to his understanding of the ethical dimension that is the orienting feature of human experience. Levinas realizes that in our lives, people hold moral views; they accept moral principles and respect them; some may even have well-developed moral theories. Moreover, God may be thought to play some moral role in such theories, or God may be replaced by natural sentiments or rational agency. But everyday moralizing and moral theorizing, even theological moral thinking, these are one thing; the encounter with the face of the other person and the burden of responsibility that accompanies that encounter are another. God cannot enter Levinas's thinking as a divine commander, no more than he could enter Kant's moral thinking in that role. The thought of a commanding God may be important, but like any thought of God, it would be one thought too many.

In 1954 Levinas said that God has something to do with the encounter with the other, but that this is no theological thesis, even if it is true that "God could not be God without first having been this interlocutor."[14] This suggests that Levinas, at one stage in his career, identified God with the other person; I am inclined, however, not to take this sentence literally but rather to see it as a rhetorical device meant to exaggerate what seems paradoxical, that God must be something else before being God – indeed, that God must be *human* before He is God. To understand what this means, however, we are better served by turning to some pages on the sacred in *Totality and Infinity.*

Levinas's affection for apparent paradox is evident when he says, "To relate to the absolute as an atheist is to welcome the absolute purified of the violence of the sacred."[15] Strange thing to say, that one draws near to God, the absolute, only when one becomes an atheist and rejects the traditional theistic God with its tendency to violence.[16] Theism and the domain of the sacred are the province of everyday religious life and traditional Western theology. What Levinas will advocate is a new sense of religion and of God, where the weight falls on the face-to-face and its ethical character. This is one meaning of atheism, an acknowledgment of God that is not, strictly speaking, theistic, an acknowledgment of God that is not a belief in the existence of a transcendent God. The theistic God is a "myth,"

[14] Levinas, "The Ego and the Totality," in *Collected Philosophical Papers*, 33.
[15] Levinas, *Totality and Infinity*, 77.
[16] Cf. Richard Cohen, *Elevations*, 180–182.

Levinas says, whereas the God who "speaks" to us does so through the other person, the *real* transcendent, who engages me as the stranger, the widow, and the orphan, out of her destitution and yet, as he puts it, with her "eminence, height, and lordship."[17] The idea of infinity, transcendence, and the face of the other are "the dawn of a humanity without myths."

In these pages, then, Levinas rearticulates what occurs in the encounter with the face but this time in religious, theological language: revelation, epiphany, and the comprehension of God. The encounter with the face is the relation with God. "There can be no 'knowledge' of God separated from the relationship with man."[18] But what does this mean? Is God the human other? Or is God somehow associated with what he calls the "height" of the face? And if so, what does *this* mean? How are we to understand such a reformulation of the face-to-face in religious language?

First Levinas tells us that "the Other is ... indispensable for my relation with God. He does not play the role of a mediator. The Other is not the incarnation of God, but precisely by his face, in which he is disincarnate, is the manifestation of the height in which God is revealed."[19] The relation with God, then, makes sense only insofar as the self is engaged by the other, but that other – the other person – is not a "mediator" or bridge between the self and God, as in Christianity; nor is the other identical to God. Rather, the face reveals a *height* that is the locus of the divine revelation. In a moment we will have to ask what "height" means, but even without an interpretation, we can say this much. "Theological concepts," Levinas says, possess the "signification they admit of" only in virtue of "our relations with men." And these relations, between "the being here below" and "transcendent being," that is, the face of the other person, he calls "religion."[20]

In *Totality and Infinity*, then, God, as a theological concept, is a myth, which means that it does not refer to a real being but rather expresses something – a relationship or a feature of a relationship – that, given its honorific and elevated tonality, is especially significant for human existence. Moreover, divine revelation is not the epiphany (or revelation) of the face of the other, nor is it mediated by the other, as if God were a distant being, beyond direct encounter. For Levinas, God is *revealed in* the *height* of the face. God is not revealed by that height; it is revealed in it. God is

[17] Levinas, *Totality and Infinity*, 76–78. Elsewhere Levinas takes such a God to be the product of "childish" imagination rather than "adult" understanding.

[18] Levinas, *Totality and Infinity*, 78.

[19] Ibid., 78–79.

[20] Ibid., 80; cf. 81.

not the face or its height, but the language of God – of the divine, the sacred, and the holy – is a theological way of expressing something about that height, of calling attention to it and acknowledging it. But what does "height" – itself a metaphorical expression – signify? Adriaan Peperzak notes that "height," as a metaphor, underscores the asymmetrical character of the face-to-face; the other addresses the self, supplicates, and commands; the self is passive to all of this but especially to the command. The other person commands like a ruler. "Height" calls to mind the status of such a monarch or ruler. The self is called upon to respond and, in a sense, made to respond.[21]

Richard Cohen, commenting on this sentence in *Totality and Infinity*, emphasizes that the divine is *a* dimension or that height is *the* dimension of the divine, and he identifies this dimension as "a *moral* dimension, the dimension of moral height, goodness."[22] He also associates the notion of height with the *asymmetry* of the relation between the self and the other. Cohen's best formulation is this: "By 'height' Levinas means the *moral* force encountered in the *other's* face *as* the *subject's* obligation to and responsibility for that other person."[23] If Cohen is right, then for Levinas in *Totality and Infinity* God is not the other but rather the moral force in virtue of which the other commands the self, the fact that the face engages the self's responsibility and calls for goodness rather than, say, presents itself as a certain kind of person, with a precise role, or calls for a judgment of aesthetic commendation, or is wholly petitionary.

But even this seems to outstrip Levinas's cautious formulations and transgresses what is possible, as he sees it. The problem comes from asking in too literal a sense what the word "God" refers to.[24] Levinas's starting point is to acknowledge the widespread use of religious language and theological concepts, and his most decisive claim – like Buber's, Tillich's, and others' – is that such language is not referential or descriptive; the term "God" does not pick out or describe any reality or fact. Levinas has nothing to say about God as a reality, so to speak. But as a myth, the word "God" does perform some functions; it is, after all, a linguistic expression, and its use is a matter of linguistic behavior. It expresses human aspirations, obligations, attitudes, or hopes. It is a response to some dimension or aspect of human experience, and it is Levinas's view that there are more

[21] Adriaan Peperzak, *Beyond*, 125, 133, 137, 208.
[22] Richard Cohen, *Elevations*, 183; cf. 183–188.
[23] Ibid., 185.
[24] There is a very good discussion of this issue in Tamra Wright, *The Twilight of Jewish Philosophy*, 71–73.

and less accurate accounts of what that dimension is and hence more or less genuine ways of responding to it. Generally speaking, he contends that such concepts as "divine revelation" or "relationship with God" are responses to the moral determination that, he claims, is central to human life. Cohen is right to associate the height of the other's face with this moral determination or force; he is wrong, however, to think that this is God. For what this might lead one to think is that God reveals Himself to us in the moral force of the other's face. But this is to distort Levinas's thinking dramatically. It is more correct to say that in uttering statements about God's revealing Himself, if we accept Levinas's view that our lives are significant first and foremost as responsive to the needs and the suffering of others, our utterances are in part a response, as an acknowledgment, to that insight. To say "God reveals Himself to me" is one way of expressing one's acknowledgment of the primacy of the ethical and our responsibility to and for others. To say that human beings are created "in the image of God" is to say that human beings present themselves to us, each to each, as valuable, worthy of care and generosity and help. The language of God and the divine image are not about God and His image; they express the sense of value, significance, and worth other people have for us. In *Totality and Infinity*, I believe, this is the significance of Levinas's appropriation of religious and theological language.[25]

Furthermore, theological language expresses one's recognition of a particular aspect of the ethical relationship and responsibility, what Levinas calls "height." The metaphor points to a number of features of the encounter with the face of the other: that the other person stands at a distance, that it addresses the self from above or from a higher status, that the other has a priority or eminence and is elevated with respect to the self, that the other has authority over the self and perhaps power over it as well, that they are not equals in every way, and that they are related asymmetrically in at least one respect. All of this and perhaps more is contained in the metaphor, and I am inclined to think that Levinas wants us to think of the

[25] In "A Religion for Adults" (1957), Levinas makes this point and clarifies it with a reference to Maimonides's treatment of divine attributes: "The moral relation therefore reunites both self-consciousness and consciousness of God. Ethics is not the corollary of the vision of God, it is that very vision. Ethics is an optic, such that everything I know of God and everything I can hear of His word and reasonably say to Him must find an ethical expression. In the Holy Ark from which the voice of God is heard by Moses, there are only the tablets of the Law. The knowledge of God which we can have and which is expressed, according to Maimonides, in the form of negative attributes, receives a positive meaning from the moral 'God is merciful', which means: 'Be merciful like Him.' The attributes of God are given not in the indicative, but in the imperative. … To know God is to know what must be done." (*Difficult Freedom*, 17).

metaphor broadly and suggestively, rather than narrowly. Just as "face" is novel as a philosophical term, so is "height," and its association with divinity and the sacred is meant to call attention to the traditional nomenclature of divinity as royal and paternal and yet to represent a declension away from that terminology, both like it and unlike it, just as face is like appearance and yet unlike it. The primordial or originary encounter with the other person presents us with a face that means something other than and more than how the other person looks; so the height of the face presents us with a status that is other than and more than the status of God as King or as Father. The face has an authority beyond all authority, more basic than the difference between authority and its lack, for it is authority that both pleads and commands. It singles us out and calls us into question at once and so "speaks to us" or "addresses us" from a height that is as low as it is high, so to speak. The suggestiveness of the metaphor of height, like so much of Levinas's vocabulary, is meant to perplex and to redirect our thinking and attention; it is not meant to clarify and make precise what begins as vague and unclear but rather to change our perspective altogether.[26]

The motif of the height of the face, then, calls attention to the moral force or ought-to-be-doneness that comes with the address of the self by the other person. But that is all that the metaphor of height does; it calls attention to what we might now call the face's moral authority. It does not, however, clarify it or explain it. Only after *Totality and Infinity* does Levinas turn to this task.

LATER STAGE: THE TRACE AND *ILLEITY*

In *Otherwise than Being* and in the essay "God and Philosophy," Levinas develops his understanding of the relationship between the ethical relationships of the face-to-face and theological language.[27] He discontinues the use of "height" as the chief metaphor that points to the locus of their relationship. But does his thinking change in significant ways? Does he continue to understand religious language as an expression of the moral responsibility that orients human life?

[26] Here and throughout this chapter I focus on the relation between "God" and moral force, and the key early notion is height. For Levinas, however, God also expresses the universality of the ethical, especially through the idea of monotheism. See *Totality and Infinity*, 212–214.

[27] See Tamra Wright, *The Twilight of Jewish Philosophy*, 80–94; Richard Cohen, *Elevations*, 190–194.

Let me begin with the neologism "*illeity*," which Levinas uses in "Meaning and Sense" (1964) and in "Enigma and Phenomena" (1965), drawing on an earlier essay, "The Trace of the Other" (1963).[28] In the years after the publication of *Totality and Infinity*, it is clear, Levinas seems to have thought hard about the relationship between ethics and religion, between the face of the other person and God. It is a line of thinking that begins in these essays, continues in *Otherwise than Being*, and culminates for all practical purposes in "God and Philosophy" (1975; 1986). The key terms that mark this route, I think, are "trace" and "*illeity*," and I want to begin with the latter. Levinas tries to pry the terms away from this referential dimension or referential role and yet at the same time to draw attention to the sense that the present is not really present at all. By employing a religious or theological vocabulary, then, if the moral force of the face is what conveys the face *as* a command, one might assume that what is not present and yet is present, as a trace, is God or an epiphany of God. But Levinas wants to draw transcendence, the infinite, and the absolute into the picture while steering us away from such a conclusion, and the term "*illeity*" is part of his warning, an indirect but recognizable directive to avoid the belief that God is a being who authorizes through command the obligation to care for the suffering of others.

Levinas draws on his essay "The Trace of the Other" in the last section of "Meaning and Sense," which is entitled "The Trace." In this early paper, Levinas describes the face-to-face and its significance as a "return to Platonism in a new way."[29] This remark is illuminating, for throughout the essay Levinas keeps both Platonism and Neo-Platonism in mind. The question of its last section, "The Trace," is whether the absolute or the One, from which the face comes, is not another philosophical idea or principle, like a Platonic Form or Idea. In other words, perhaps there is no transcendence here at all; perhaps the One or God is just another element in the idealist system. To avoid this, Levinas must clarify how the face does not point beyond itself to something transcendent or absolute that it signifies. In a sense, there is nothing beyond the face. And yet in order for the face to carry the force it does, there must be such a beyond or absolute ground; either each face must be such a ground, or each must point beyond itself

[28] It is generally believed, at least by many commentators, that in these years following the publication of *Totality and Infinity* Levinas's thinking is directed in part by issues provoked by Jacques Derrida's long and influential review of that book, "Violence and Metaphysics." This is an issue that I largely ignore in this book. Among the best comments on the Derridian influence can be found in several essays by Robert Bernasconi and also in the work of Simon Critchley.

[29] Levinas, "Meaning and Sense," in *Basic Philosophical Writings*, 58.

to a ground.[30] Perhaps, Levinas suggests, Plato and Plotinus can help us to see how to solve this problem, how to see the Good or the One as a ground and also as genuinely transcendent, beyond Being.[31]

The face of the other person, Levinas says, "proceeds from the absolutely Absent," but its relationship "*does not indicate, does not reveal*, this *Absent*; and yet the *Absent* has a meaning in the face."[32] The language of relationship is no more apposite here than it is for the link between the self and the face, but it may be unavoidable. The face is not a thing or an appearance of a thing, the Absent not an entity, and the relationship is not one of signifying, referring, pointing, revealing, or representing, in one direction, nor is it one of explaining, justifying, or demonstrating, in the other. For the Absent is no "world behind our world."[33] Levinas uses the word "trace" for this relationship; "the beyond from which the face comes signifies as a trace. The face is in the trace of the utterly bygone, utterly past Absent." We will discuss the temporal aspect of this relationship in the next chapter, the sense in which the face itself is a past that is never present and the Absent or *illeity* an utterly bygone past. Here I want to ask what this Absent or beyond *means* for the face. What function does the Absent or *illeity* serve? What does it do? And particularly what is its ethical role? Levinas approaches these questions in stages.

First, Levinas gives it a name. Since it is not encountered, nor does it encounter the self, it is neither in the first nor the second person. This *beyond* is neither I nor you. It is there, in the third person: something distant, separate, and always so. Not I or you, it is *that*. It can never be a *you*; it is always detached, out of the line of meeting; it is what Levinas calls "*illeity*" ("that-ness" or "he-ness").[34] Second, the relationship with the face as it proceeds from *illeity* is ethical; it is a relationship that bears on responsibility and obligation. *Illeity* is the otherness of the other that is present in that other as a trace. But since that other person, as other, is the stranger, the widow, and the orphan, whose otherness from me pleads for help and commands aid, its otherness is constitutive of its ethical force, its

[30] See ibid., 59.

[31] For Levinas, Plato and Plotinus are like Descartes in this respect, i.e., in identifying a true or genuine infinite or transcendent, which is beyond Being and yet to which we have access; cf. "Meaning and Sense," 59. The notion that I use here, of a ground, is of course a metaphor, in a sense, since the relation between what is genuinely transcendent and what is within the circle of being is not, strictly speaking, one of ground to grounded, or explanans to explanandum, but rather a relation analogous to such relationships, at best.

[32] Levinas, "Meaning and Sense," in *Basic Philosophical Writings*, 60.

[33] Ibid.

[34] Ibid., 61; cf. 64.

obligating me to respond to it, its compellingness and *gravitas*, as it were. In this sense, then, as a trace – as in the everyday phenomenon of traces – *illeity* "disturbs the order of the world." A trace is what is left by what seeks to escape but fails; it "obliges."[35] Finally, Levinas calls *illeity*, with its "height," "divinity," and he quotes Plotinus's account of the One when he says that "the trace of the One gives birth to essence, and being is only the trace of the One."[36] As a footprint in the sand is a trace of a step that has passed by and is gone, so *illeity* or divinity is in the face of the other person as a trace of what is forever absent – and never present. The divine is only present in the face; it is never present in itself, and it is the *obliging character* of the face that is this trace of divinity.[37]

Clearly the main point of Levinas's analysis and account in "The Trace of the Other" is that *illeity* is not an entity and its trace in the face not a sign. In addition to relying upon Plotinus to help him make these points, Levinas also calls upon a contrast with Martin Buber and Gabriel Marcel, who prefer the Thou to the It. Levinas's face is not exactly a Thou, and certainly *illeity* is no It. Levinas also turns to the biblical text. He interprets "being in the image of God" as meaning "to find oneself in his trace." The trace of God is in the face of the other person; hence, to find oneself, to find who one is, is to respond to that face. Then, Levinas turns to Exodus 33: the God who has passed by is forever absent, never present.[38] He always has passed by, and the trace God leaves behind is in the face of the other person. To draw close to God, then, is to respond to the face of the other person. This is the meaning of human existence. Levinas calls it "the illuminated site of being [which] is but the passage of God."[39] When we speak

[35] This point is underscored in "Enigma and Phenomenon," 75–77.

[36] Levinas, "Meaning and Sense," in *Basic Philosophical Writings*, 63; see Plotinus, *Enneads* V, 5, 5. On *illeity*, see "The Name of God according to a Few Talmudic Texts," in *Beyond the Verse*, 122, 126–128.

[37] In contemporary analytic metaethics, this weight might be called "normative force," although the notion of a norm or rule would not apply to Levinas's conception of the ethical character of the face; it would, however, apply to the rules or principles that one finds in moral theories and that are employed in everyday moral reasoning in various ways. As we shall see shortly, Levinas also, in discussing these matters, calls attention to Moses's encounter with God in Exodus 33. It is interesting to compare Levinas's interpretation of this passage with Buber's in *Moses*.

[38] Exodus 33:18–23: "And [Moses] said: 'Show me, I pray Thee, Thy glory.' And He said: 'I will make all My goodness pass before thee, and will proclaim the name of the Lord before thee; and I will be gracious to whom I will be gracious, and will show mercy on whom I will show mercy.' And He said: 'Thou canst not see My face, for man shall not see Me and live.' And the Lord said: 'Behold, there is a place by Me, and thou shalt stand upon the rock. And it shall come to pass, while My glory passeth by, that I will put thee in a cleft of the rock, and will cover thee with My hand until I have passed by. And I will take away My hand, and thou shalt see My back; but My face shall not be seen.' "

[39] Levinas, "Enigma and Phenomenon," in *Basic Philosophical Writings*, 77.

of encountering God or of God revealing Himself to me, this is an expression of my desire to respond to the other person with kindness and generosity, my sense of being called by the other and being obligated to her. Indeed, doing the latter is the only way one can experience the former. One cannot know God or encounter God directly; all religious experience is ethical action.[40]

In *Otherwise than Being* Levinas makes the same point: "The Infinite passes in saying."[41] In the face-to-face and responsibility God has passed by, and His trace remains. Insofar as "saying" or the encounter with the face of the other person is witness, it testifies to this fact, as it were; the glory of the face occurs as the self's responsibility, and this is witness – to the face, to God, to itself. God is present only in His glory; He shines forth. And His glory is always reflected, as it were, in the face. And the face is always how I encounter the other and my responsibility to and for her. Hence, my responsibility is witness. But to witness is not to talk about or refer to or represent; it is to be responsible, to receive the order from the other, to accept it, and to obey it.[42]

Here in *Otherwise than Being*, then, as in his earlier works, Levinas claims that the face-to-face is the way God is present or effective in human existence, although words like "present" and "effective" are themselves to be taken only figuratively. We have argued, however, that this is not intended as an extraordinary, isolated event, as if the encounter with the other person is Levinas's substitute for religious or mystical experience or indeed a leap of faith. Rather, we have argued that Levinas takes all human existence to be social and interpersonal and that his examination of the face-to-face is meant to call attention to that dimension of social existence that gives point and purpose to human life. Here, in *Otherwise than Being*, he elaborates the link between society and the face-to-face in the light of his discussion of God, the trace, and *illeity*.[43] This is not the place for a detailed reading of these pages; rather, here we want to focus on this last set of themes – how God, the trace, and *illeity* figure into his account. What role does God play in the way responsibility is related to social justice? If, in his earlier works, God as *illeity* was present in the face as a trace and as its ethical force, does this role still dominate this later treatment? Does God have any different or special role to play in social justice, above and beyond His role in the self's responsibility?

40 See Levinas, *Otherwise than Being*, 147.
41 Ibid.
42 Ibid., 149.
43 Ibid., 140–162.

I think that these questions confuse Levinas's approach and his goals. He is not seeking to find the way in which God as *illeity* contributes uniquely or directly to social justice. Rather, his task should be conceived differently. We find ourselves, in everyday life, in society, engaged in institutions, policies, and roles. Our lives are just or seek to be. And religious vocabulary is regularly used by some to articulate our goals, for justice and peace, for religion is a significant aspect of our lives and has been historically. If, as Levinas has argued, theological language expresses our sense of personal responsibility for each unique other, how then can it also express our commitments to justice and peace? Why do we say that God commands us to seek peace and to pursue justice, to create and sustain just institutions, to feed the hungry, clothe the naked, and care for the stranger, the widow, and the orphan? How is God associated with social and political goals, if indeed His infinite, absolute absence is present as the trace in the face of the poor and destitute other? This, I think, is Levinas's question: what justifies our *extending* theological vocabulary into the domain of social and political life?

Levinas distinguishes the "third person" character of *illeity* from the "third party" that is the source of society, justice, language and more: "This 'thirdness' [of *illeity*] is different from that of the third man; it is the third party that interrupts the face to face of a welcome of the other man, interrupts the proximity or approach of the neighbor; it is the third man with which justice begins."[44] What exactly does Levinas mean? First, that God as *illeity* is present in the face, but that the third party has a different relation to the face of the other. In society, God is related to the other but not as a third party; God is the other's ethical force. The third party is other to my other; there is a third, a fourth, and more; society is complex and multiple and is always with us. God as *illeity* is other but not as an other. Secondly, God is what calls to me from the face, whereas the third party compels me to stand back and to judge and assess how I am to execute my responsibility to all others. The third party pushes me to judgment, deliberation, and the formulation of principles and rules. God pushes me to responsibility without any of these. Finally, God is the author of responsibility and a kind of identity through substitution for the other; "God" is the term that comes to mind when we seek to express the weight or burden that we feel toward the other. It is the term that in ordinary parlance comes to mind when the authority of moral responsibility comes to mind, while the third party is the author of justice through detachment and evaluation and separation.

[44] Ibid., 150; cf. 156–162.

But while the third party or third man brings on justice and is not identical to the third-person character of *illeity*, the two are related. For in every social interaction, which is potentially or actually just, responsibility is felt. That is, *illeity* is what accounts for the ethical force not just of one face but of every face, that is, of *all* others. Hence, it accounts for the universality as well as the normative force of responsibility. In other words, the face of my neighbor orders me; "the order [is] in my response itself," and *illeity* is "this way for the order to come from I know not where." "It is the coming of the order to which I am subjected before hearing it."[45] Moreover, all this is present in society and gives society the urgency of justice and hence its purpose, its significance. Levinas calls this social condition and striving for justice "a betrayal of my anarchic relation with illeity" that is also "a new relationship with it." That is, God is involved in my being "a member of society," but this involvement is a betrayal of and also the establishment of a new relationship with God as *illeity*.[46] It is a betrayal of the infinity of each particular insofar as it is a commitment to the demands of all.

I think that it is clear what Levinas means. There is a sense in which the reciprocal relationships of social life "betray" (or compromise) the utter particularity of the face-to-face and its asymmetry. The infinite responsibility to the other person is now qualified, restricted, and directed; it enters into a kind of calculation and a distribution process. We have moved from personal kindness to a welfare system, as it were. Moreover, we shift from being wholly passive – accused and traumatized – to being active. Hence, the purity and infinitude of our original responsibility is "betrayed." But at the same time that this shift is a betrayal of God, of the divine trace in this particular face, it is also true that "it is only thanks to God that, as a subject incomparable with the other, I am approached as an other by the others." That is, I am put in a position, with everyone else, of developing institutions and principles of justice – as Rawls argues, for example – only insofar as I am encountered by others, and this means if God is present in her face. It is only because the other is valuable to me by being someone I care about and sense a need to help and assist that I then, in the social situation with many others, indeed vast numbers, feel bound to set about developing principles, institutions, and policies concerning just and benevolent distributions. As Levinas puts it, "the reciprocal relationship binds me to the other man in the trace of transcendence, in illeity. The

[45] Ibid., 150.
[46] Ibid., 158.

passing of God ... in precisely the reverting to the incomparable subject into a member of society." Society and the responsibility that underlies it, so to speak, are both grounded in the ethical force of God.[47]

We can conceive of that force and its relation to *illeity* in the following way. In traditional theology and philosophical thinking about God, God is conceived as infinite, omnipotent, and overwhelming. Such thinking can seem to be confronted with a paradox, that the human can confront the divine, the finite the Infinite, and still survive – indeed, that the finite can encounter the divine and respond to it. The reason for the paradox is that if divine power is unlimited and infinite, it leaves no room for finite freedom, and yet the latter exists. A traditional response is that in the very encounter the divine exhibits its infinite power both by commanding and by conferring upon the human the freedom to respond to the command. On the one hand, then, in order to cope with the relation to the infinite God, traditional religion must somehow reconcile divine power and human freedom or, on the other, God would be taken to withdraw completely from such relationships and become a hidden God, *deus absconditus*. But Levinas sees things differently. It is as if there are moments in human existence when the divine encounters the human and yet "departs" at the same instant, and in departing, the divine leaves behind a "trace" of itself. That trace resides in the face of the other person to whom we are related; it is a trace of a divine presence that is in fact a divine absence, an *illeity*, and its effect is to leave behind a residue of its overwhelming power, of its infinity, a residue that is manifest in the other person's face, her vulnerability which in virtue of being the site of the divine trace is also her demandingness. It is God's "having passed by via the other's face" that gives the other person's presence to me its obligatoriness, its ethical force. And with that, together with the fact that the divine is not present other than in this way, the self is free, to respond in one way or another. In this sense, as Levinas says, "I am obliged without this obligation having begun in me, as though an order slipped into my consciousness like a thief, smuggled itself in. ..." (OB, 13).

Levinas takes it that the normative force of the ethical resides in the way the other person, in all his or her particularity, is present to me and calls to me. Here, in his account of *illeity*, he depicts what lies behind that force, so to speak, where it comes from, what grounds it. After all, it cannot come from the other person, who is just another person like me. It must come from transcendence, not a transcendence that is present but

[47] Ibid. For Levinas's fullest account of society and justice, see 158–162.

rather a transcendence that always "has passed by" and leaves its residue or "trace" – the way the other person's very existence matters to me, concerns me, obligates me. Later in *Otherwise than Being*, Levinas says that "the Infinite orders to me the neighbor as a face. ... This way for the order to come from I know not where, this coming that is not a recalling, ... we have called *illeity*. It is the coming of the order to which I am subjected before hearing it, or which I hear in my own saying. It is an august command, but one that does not constrain or dominate. ..." (OB, 150) This latter – this elevated order that does not overwhelm – I have said is the residue left behind by an awesome transcendence that has passed by, so to speak. It is the normative force left behind in the face of the other person who confronts me; it is what makes that face not only vulnerable to me but also binding for me. Indeed, there is *no other way* in which ethics could be binding, for Levinas.

Otherwise than Being elaborates and develops what we found earlier in *Totality and Infinity* and the essays written shortly after it. Levinas adds a rich temporal analysis that we will look at in the next chapter along with the role of theological language for expressing the meaning of social and political justice. But *illeity* remains the term he uses for pointing to the trace of divinity in the face, its ethical force or ethical character, as I have called it.[48] In a sense, *illeity* is what accounts for the normativity, the compellingness, or the obligatoriness – what in ordinary terms we might call the authority – of the other person's face. It is what makes it the case that when we encounter the other person, it is with this sense of moral burden, of having to respond to her and to do so with care and concern. He adds explicitly comments on God and politics, not because God contributes *directly* to political justice but rather because he wants to show how the political and social is grounded in responsibility and the face-to-face, how our responsibility to others is social and universal, and hence how theological language is appropriate to both. This discussion is Levinas's opportunity to comment on the relationship between church and state or, better, on the relationship between religion and politics; it is his way of engaging with the Hegelian commitment to the primacy of the state and the objection of those who take religious institutions to be the primary vehicle of history. In his own way, Levinas returns to the Kantian synthesis of the religious, the ethical, and the political. We might put it this way: we can now understand why God wants us not only to love one another, to be kind and generous, every one of us to each other, but also to

[48] Cohen uses the phrase "*moral* force" in *Elevations*, 185.

make the world just.[49] We can appreciate why religious Jews, for example, acknowledge God and God's role in social and political affairs as well as in personal ones, but, on Levinas's view, only if they take the religious to be the locus of the ethical.

How does this groundedness of moral obligation express itself in religious life and in religious language? In the language of divine command. That is, what Levinas shows us is that the trace or residue of the absolute absence of *illeity* occurs, in the terminology of Judaism especially, as the vocabulary of God's commands, what in Hebrew are called *mitzvot*. In other words, the Bible's terminology of God's commanding Moses and the Israelites to perform the laws and statutes is one of the ways religious sensibility indicates its appreciation of the *moral force* that manifests itself in the face-to-face with other persons, in their pain and suffering, in their expression of need. Such moral force is *in* the face but only insofar as that face itself is the trace of an unbounded, overwhelming power that no individual could confront and survive.

In this chapter I have examined Levinas's way of understanding the word "God" and the associated terminology of divinity, the sacred, and such. He takes this terminology and these ideas to arise for humankind in thinking and in practice as one way of acknowledging and articulating what responsibility means in our lives. The word "God," that is, comes to mind when we are drawn to the moral force of responsibility and justice, when we recognize that the obligations to care for others and to live just and humane lives have a weight or gravity for us that makes them paramount over other interests we have, and when we take responsibility and justice to be social and even universal in scope. In short, "God" and our images of God and divinity are ways of expressing the authority or power of the ethical and its universality.

We have also clarified the language of trace and *illeity* that Levinas comes to use as he uncovers the way in which the authority of the ethical occurs in the face of the other person. This language is difficult and obscure. It may not even be clear why Levinas introduces it. Having already employed the notion of the face, why is this new terminology necessary? What does it add? What is going on here?

It is helpful to remember that the word "trace" does not mean "evidence." An object or fact is evidence for a certain conclusion when it counts in favor of that conclusion. But Levinas is not involved in the project of

[49] See Wright, *The Twilight of Jewish Philosophy*, 89–93, on theological language in *Otherwise than Being*. My account has similarities but also significant differences.

proving God's existence. Traditional proofs for God's existence use premises about motion or the orderliness of natural objects or the nature of causal relationships in order to conclude that God – as a first cause or as an intelligent designer – exists. In using the expression "trace," Levinas is saying, in part, that he is not drawing our attention to a fact or principle that can function as a premise in such an argument. Furthermore, in pointing to something with the expression "*illeity*" Levinas is not identifying the conclusion of an argument for the existence of anything.

Levinas's account is more like Martin Buber's and other existential theologians' than it is like traditional theists'. For such religious thinkers, God is beyond our normal everyday epistemological and emotional attitudes; one does not experience God, or one is not related to God in the same way that one has beliefs about the weather or about natural facts or that one fears someone or hates him. The encounter with God is distinctive. God is met or encountered as a presence, and that presence has an impact or force about it. It is orienting or directive; it moves us and changes us. This is Buber's view. Levinas's point is that one meets God, insofar as one uses that language to express a kind of human experience, when one responds to another person with a sense of concern and accountability. What the word "God" picks out is that aspect of this human social encounter that involves a sense of compulsion or authority or force for each and every human relationship. Moreover, the term "*illeity*" is used in order to say first that the origin of that authority or force is not the face itself; it is not this particular person in all her uniqueness. Second, it is used to indicate that there is nonetheless in that face the residue or a "trace" of an absolute power; the face is not wholly weakness or need, what Levinas calls "nudity" or "vulnerability." Third, the term, since it is not in the second-person but in the third-person mode, tells us that the source of the force or authority has always passed by; the face is never without this authority; it always has been deposited, so to speak. The face of the other person always addresses us and makes its claim upon us. It never is without this normative force, and without it the face is nothing but the need that pleads and demands to be satisfied.

Levinas's account of *illeity*, then, bears a certain similarity to Immanuel Kant's argument for what he calls "postulating the existence of God" and also to William James's conception of the ethics of belief. I do not want to go into the details of Kant's account in the *Critique of Practical Reason* or James's famous analysis of the decision to believe in "The Will to Believe." But we can say this. If postulating is a kind of deciding to believe, then what Kant and James share is the idea that when it comes to God, even if we do not or cannot have evidence or arguments for God's existence, we still may have strong reasons to believe that God exists. Levinas does not think that the word "God" picks out anything in our totalitizing schemes or ways of thinking; hence the experience of God cannot be a matter of seeing or hearing or believing with regard to some existing thing, and our knowledge of God cannot be a matter of knowing that God exists in virtue of having some argument or proof to that effect. If the word "God" means anything, it calls attention to something that has an important effect on our lives but something that is somehow beyond our normal cognitive, affective, and experiential grasp. If we are going to acknowledge it and its impact, we will need some reasons for believing or acknowledging it that are not simply proofs or evidence for its existence. Levinas finds that reason in the face of the other person and in the way in which the face speaks to us with authority and with force and speaks to us from every other. His point, one might say, is that only if something like his account is accurate does it make sense to go on talking about God, the divine, the sacred, and such things, when talking about these things is one way of acknowledging the force of the ethical in our everyday social experiences. Or, to put it in other words, for Levinas, our social existence and our moral sensibility are good reasons to use the language of God and divinity and to continue to use theological language and to engage in religious life. If we take various forms of rationalism and naturalism to exclude the notion of transcendence, then Levinas is opposed to them in their traditional forms.

Consider this picture of thinking about the ground of ethics: in Western thinking, in antiquity, ethical matters are part of a seamless whole of life, together with what we now would call custom, politics, culture, and religion. The authority for this melange was frequently enough given to the gods; it was they who provided the mandate for the practices of religion, politics, communal life, and ethics. In Plato, Aristotle, and then in later philosophical schools, this authority was also associated with divinity, but in their view such divinity was associated with reason, rational order, and even natural order. With the growth and development of Judaism and Christianity and then Islam, different views of divinity flourished and then were enriched and modified by conjunction with forms of Platonism and Aristotelianism, but in one way or another the authority of ethics was still tied to divinity, whether as a divine product or grounded in a divine mandate or associated with divine reason.

One hallmark of modern philosophy, beginning with the seventeenth century and the impact of the scientific revolution, was that ethics, in one way or another, as a central dimension of human experience, required a new account of its character and authority. The process took time, and each and every important philosophical contributor had his own view about the matter. Until the nineteenth century, there is no unanimity about where God finds a role. Descartes, Spinoza, Malebranche, Arnauld, Hobbes, Locke, Leibniz, and others do not dismiss God altogether, although the role of the divine differs for each. If, for Spinoza, for example, ethics is grounded in human psychology and social conduct, and if the ultimate ground for human thought and action is self-preservation within the natural order, then insofar as that order is divine, we might still say that the authority of ethics in Spinoza's worldview is religious. But the virtual identity of God and nature certainly attenuate what such a theological account really means; in the end, for Spinoza, as for Hobbes and others, we are on the way to a naturalist account of ethics and the grounds of its normative force. One of Kant's great innovations, then, is to segregate everyday experience and scientific inquiry from practical and moral action, and to give an account of how knowledge of the world is possible and then of how action in it is possible. Given the claims that scientific inquiry makes for itself, God plays no role in the world as an object of experience and inquiry; nor does he play a role in the world as a venue for practical everyday conduct. It is only in the world of moral deliberation and action that God retains a place, and that place is unlike the role of divine legislator or ideal so common in the tradition. In effect, for Kant, the authority of the ethical lies within the human and not outside of it – in particular, in that aspect of the human that tradition had often enough since Plato taken to be the very presence of the divine in the human or at least the primary gift of divine grace, human rationality. Kant's sequestering of the ethical and then of the religious, however, made it easy indeed, via a kind of Ockham's razor, to lop off the divine altogether and to leave the authority of ethics solely up to reason.

That is, prior to the emergence, in the nineteenth and early twentieth centuries, of various widely influential critiques of religion and the reality of the divine, the effort in Western philosophy and religious thought to understand the authority of the ethical took the form of turning within the human to find that source. To some it was a tendency or disposition, to others a sentiment or feeling, to still others it was the human capacity for rational understanding, but in one way or another, the search for the ground of the authority of the ethical sought its ultimate foundation within the individual person or within human nature. At the same time, of course, there were those who continued to find the source outside individual persons but not outside human beings altogether. They turned to society or community, the communal life of persons living together, in order to locate that source of authority, even if such a claim did carry risks. After all, one advantage of God's being the course of the authority of the ethical had been that God was absolute and ultimate; His status was unconditional. Moreover, human rationality and even features of human nature could also be taken to be, in one form or another, unconditional and ultimate. But one could not say the same thing about societies, groups, and communities; they were clearly historical, mutable, and fragile. A shelter built on them was built on sand. They could help to explain, in a certain sense, why ethical practices and ideals held people in their grip, but the way they did so might have seemed to many to be too transient and too impermanent to serve the purpose well. Or, as we might say today, such communal or social accounts could explain what motivated people to ethical conduct, but they could not justify that conduct as worthy of human commitment and respect. They could explain why people would find ethics compelling but not why they ought to find it valuable.

Viewed against this background, Levinas's thinking about the primacy of the ethical and about the relationship between ethical authority and human thinking about the sacred and the divine can be seen to combine what might seem to be incommensurables. On the one hand, he believes that the authority of the ethical does not lie within us; the normative authority we need in order to understand the compelling character of the ethical cannot be a matter of self-determination. Rousseau and Kant have misled us. On the other hand, if we turn outside the human, to society or beyond, what we need is a source of authority that is permanent and unconditional. And yet, the critiques of older pictures of the divine, of God or the gods, are compelling. We neither can nor should believe in those pictures. At best, they are attractive artifices that fascinate and move but that do not present us with a true picture of what ethics is and what the divine dimension of the ethical involves. In principle, then, Levinas, in order to find a solution to this grand problem, must turn to what lies beyond us and yet must do so in a way that we can believe and understand, in a way that we can live with and that nonetheless serves the purpose of locating in human experience that which gives to ethics its primacy and its power, its universality and its importance, its value or worth.

As I have argued, when we talk about God's commanding his people to act with justice, humanity, and integrity, we are using an everyday religious motif to express this inexpressible, deep feature of all social relationships. And the philosophical interpretation of this religious and theological language employs, for Levinas, the vocabulary of "*illeity*" and "trace" in order to express it. We might put it this way: Levinas's account of *illeity* and trace provide the tools for a philosophical interpretation that links our everyday conviction that ethics is obligatory or has normative force, on the one hand, with biblical imagery about God and theological claims about God as the source of moral imperatives and the source of moral ideals, on the other.

Does this mean, then, that Levinas's ethics is theological? In one sense, obviously not. Moral authority is intrinsic to human relationships, and all the objects of our moral interests and concern occur within the context of such relationships and hence have an ethical dimension to them. In another sense, it certainly is, for Levinas's understanding of the normative dimension of human existence acknowledges a transcendence that is the occasion for religious thought and that is signified, broadly speaking, by religious texts and theological claims. All of this, then, is very different from a literally theological account of moral authority; it is also different from rationalism, noncognitivism, or some form of naturalism. Nor does it ground ethics in our social or communal lives, if that means that the authority and content of ethics is conventional and derived from practices and institutions. Levinas's metaethics, if one wants to call it that, is social in a different way altogether.

CHAPTER SEVEN

Time, History, and Messianism

Levinas's interest in time, temporality, and history was lifelong. He wrote about these themes early and throughout his career. They are one of the most difficult aspects of his thought to grasp, yet they are central to his philosophy. Especially given his orientation to these issues – against the background of European philosophical and theological treatments of time, history, messianism, and death – what he says may sound strange to the ears of Anglo-American philosophers. But these are important matters. In this chapter I will situate his treatment in the context of thinking about time during the period from the turn of the century through Weimar, follow the basic stages of his views about time, and then place the latter in the context of contemporary philosophical discussions of time and history. Without understanding Levinas's discussion of time, we would fail to appreciate fully what he says about ethics, religion, and politics.

THINKING ABOUT TIME

It is helpful to see the interest in time, at the turn of the century, as part of the debate concerning the *Naturwissenschaften* (natural sciences) and the *Geisteswissenschaften* (social sciences). In this context, time entered into questions of scientific method, of the nature of philosophy, of history and historical method, and of ethics, especially relativism and historicism. In his own way, Levinas reflects on issues in several of these areas; his thinking is part of the revival of Kantian philosophy.[1]

[1] It is post-Kantian insofar as the debate was, and indebted especially to Bergson, Husserl, Heidegger, and Rosenzweig. For an overview of the historical and cultural role of changing views of time at the turn of the century, see Stephen Kern, *The Culture of Time and Space, 1880–1918* (Harvard University Press, 1983). Mary Ann Doane reflects on the relationships among time, photography, and early cinema in *The Emergence of Cinematic Time: Modernity, Contingency, the Archive* (Harvard University Press, 2002).

The natural sciences examine and attempt to explain empirical phenomena, and they do so from a detached, impersonal perspective. Their objects are viewed from the outside, as it were, and their interactions are comprehended according to causal laws, laws of probability, and mathematically formulated relationships. The social or cultural sciences analyze and examine human actions and interactions. Hence, as Wilhelm Dilthey and others – including philosophers like Windelband and Rickert of the Southwest or Baden school of Neo-Kantianism – would argue, they treat human beings as agents who from their individual and collective point of view value objects, institutions, and actions, who communicate linguistically in speech and writing, and for whom acts, events, and objects mean something. There is a continuity, that is, between the way human beings as agents, thinkers, and speakers are studied by the cultural sciences and the way they live in the world. Human beings live as subjects with values and as both providers and consumers of meaning; insofar as they are biological or physical entities governed by natural laws and understood like any natural entity, they are not subjects but rather objects. As subjects, they are centers of significance and experiencing selves.

Experience, however, has its own temporal character; it flows into the future and recedes into the past. It goes on. To be sure, there is the time that exists objectively, that is divided into past, present, and future, and that is measurable, an analogue of spatial, linear magnitude. There is, that is, time measured and chopped into bits – years and months, weeks and days, hours, minutes, and seconds – astronomical time, clock time, public time. But this is not our sense of temporal passing, of flowing experience, what Henri Bergson, in a famous expression, called "duration." When, in 1981, Levinas was asked to clarify Bergson's "principal contribution to philosophy," he answered: "The theory of duration. The destruction of the primacy of clock time; the idea that the time of physics is merely derived. … [Bergson] liberated philosophy from the prestigious model of scientific time."[2] And with this liberation, Levinas points out, comes a dispelling of the fear of mechanism or fatalism, of lack of purpose, of living without hope and future – a lived future. It is no wonder that Levinas would consider Bergson's *Time and Free Will* to be one of the four or five finest books in the history of philosophy.[3]

[2] Levinas, *Ethics and Infinity*, 27. Bergson introduces the idea of duration in Chapter 2 of *Time and Free Will: An Essay on the Immediate Data of Consciousness* (Harper, 1960; originally in English, 1910; originally 1888).

[3] Levinas, *Ethics and Infinity*, 37–38.

When history and the other cultural or social sciences study human beings, then, they (should) study agents who experience their lives temporally in this first-person or subjective sense and for whom the world and everything in it mean something. In the language of turn-of-the-century neo-Kantianism and much of the German philosophy of the day, human agents take the world and its contents, including items, facts, actions, and institutions, to have worth or value. Historically, these insights flowed into various philosophical streams and into the study of knowledge, experience, metaphysics, social and psychological phenomena, and more. In their own ways, Dilthey and Bergson are lone voices, but alongside them there emerged schools and traditions that adopted and modified their insights – *Lebensphilosophie* (Life-philosophy), Southwest Neo-Kantianism, and Husserlian phenomenology among them.[4] One of the outcomes of these developments was a tendency toward relativism and historicism; another was the movement to a philosophical anthropology grounded in the subjectivity of human existence and its temporality, its embodiment, and historical situatedness. There were some who took routes along this way that led to hermeneutical accounts of human existence and to the brink of relativism; others stayed with the temporality of human experience but sought some kind of unconditional orientation for human life, for ethics and existence, by linking time to "eternity," as it was often called. It was left to Levinas – and perhaps not to him alone – to find that unconditional orientation in a strange transcendence that is immanent to human life and transcendent as well, or, perhaps more accurately, that is beyond immanence and transcendence.

One dimension of Levinas's account of time, then, is an attempt to follow Bergson – and Husserl and others – away from the forelornness of scientific time to a commitment to subjective temporal experience, only to realize its risks and to find in the relationship with the other person a way out of relativism. Another dimension involves a new account of subjective temporal experience. As we trace the development of his discussion of time, we need to keep our attention on both dimensions of his thought.

[4] To a certain degree, as well, the perspective of the engaged, historically and culturally embedded agent was taken up by students of society and the founders of modern sociology, from Georg Simmel to Max Weber. See Wolf Lepenies, *Between Literature and Science: The Rise of Sociology* (Cambridge, 1988).

EARLY REFLECTIONS ON TIME

The earliest version of Levinas's philosophy, as we have seen, is entitled *Time and the Other*, the very title of which signals that time figured centrally in Levinas's thinking from the outset. It continued to do so throughout his career. There are obvious reasons for this centrality, among them his indebtedness to Bergson, Husserl, and Heidegger, all of whom focused attention on our experience of time and on the fundamental temporality of human experience and existence. But Levinas adds something important, an account of why the encounter with the face of the other person is associated with our experience of time and how it gives to our temporal existence its human significance. This insight is already present in his account of time and death in *Time and the Other*.

The path to time leads through suffering. Levinas introduces suffering and death in Part III of *Time and the Other*. Suffering, he explains, is pain and hence an engagement with one's own existing, as a physical being, that is beyond escaping. It is "the impossibility of fleeing or retreating" from being, "the fact of being backed up against life and being" and "the impossibility of nothingness."[5] At the same time, suffering points to death and even hints at death as an unknown, a mystery. Death presents itself as something that we cannot master, in the face of which we are utterly passive. It is, Levinas says, the "limit of idealism."[6] If suffering is the impossibility of nothingness, then death is the impossibility of possibility. With it, he says, I am confronted by what is wholly beyond my experience and beyond me, even though it happens to me. Calling upon Epicurus, Levinas notes the temporal character of death: since death is beyond experience, it never occurs in the present.[7] Our relationship with death is a "unique relationship with the future." Levinas uses a language of agency and control to clarify what is not present in the relationship with death. There is no "mastery," "heroism," or freedom. With suffering and hence with the hint of death, my activity becomes passivity, and I lose my capacity to grasp, master, and control.

In *Time and the Other* Levinas draws several conclusions from this account of death. First, the approach of death is an end of activity and mastery. Second, this means that death is "the impossibility of having a project."[8] Third, "the approach of death indicates that we are in relation

[5] Levinas, *Time and the Other*, 69.
[6] Ibid., 70–71.
[7] Ibid., 71.
[8] Ibid., 74.

with something that is absolutely other"; it is absolute alterity, since it is outside experience and marks the "impossibility of possibility," not an anticipation of nothingness but the presence of what is outside of experience. Fourth, this means that "existence" is plural; there is, in my very being, an other as well as myself, and yet this other is a mystery to me. Death presents me with what is other-than-me, even if that other, in this case, is a negation of me. Levinas then proposes that *eros*, in life, is a "prototype" of this relationship with the other as death. That is, if death presents me with an other but an other that is beyond me or negates me, *eros* or love presents me with an other that is beyond me but does not negate me and does so *in life* and not *beyond life*. Finally – and this is the central point for us here – this analysis of death shows us that the future, as ungraspable, is the other. What Husserl calls the "protention" of the future in the present and what Bergson notes is our present anticipation of the future are *not* the future; they are "the present of the future and not the authentic future."[9]

What does Levinas mean when he associates the future with otherness? Clearly he means more than the obvious point that in the present we experience the future as an anticipation or as a projection, that is, that in the present we experience a flowing into what is not-yet but which we expect will-be. How is our relationship to the future to be understood in relation to the relationship to the other? To begin, Levinas claims that there is an other, unlike death, that we are related to that does not crush us or destroy us but rather in a sense affirms us. Levinas takes the face-to-face encounter with such an other, the other person, to be this relationship. So the question becomes: how is our relation to the future associated with our relation to the other person in the face-to-face? I can make some sense of the idea that for me death is the future, but what sense is there in saying that the face of the other person is the future? Frankly, this new proposal seems to be nonsense.

I think that Levinas gives us some clues regarding his meaning. He says, "It seems to me impossible to speak of time in a subject alone, or to speak of a purely personal duration."[10] This doubt is expressed immediately after Levinas concludes that the "relationship with the other" is the "relationship with the future." Here he seems to be claiming that in idealism there is no genuine sense of temporality, and, in the second clause just quoted, he denies that "a purely personal duration,"or what Bergson thought of

[9] Ibid., 75–76.

[10] Ibid., 77.

as subjective time, is really time. Indeed, insofar as objective, measurable time is also conceived as a human structure, even it is not really time. Somehow, real time requires transcendence, something genuinely other, and death will not do. Levinas actually says precisely this: "The future that death gives the future of the event, is not yet time."[11] What is it, then, that ties the future to the present in a way that constitutes real time? This relationship is accomplished, he says, "in the face-to-face with the other." As he puts it in the last sentence of Part III, "the condition of time lies in the relationship between humans or in history."[12]

We can make sense of these statements by contrasting Levinas's view with two others, what I have earlier called objective and subjective time. These can be taken to be two ways in which we conceive of temporality or two ways in which we experience time. According to the objective view, time is measured change, and it is experienced in terms of the categories of past, present, and future that are imposed by our cognitive capacities and measured by objective means, – for example, astronomical events or clocks. According to the subjective view, time is the flow of our experiences, which are experienced by me from my I's point of view as here and now, with a sense of flowing from what has been in view and what will be, as anticipated, expected, and projected. In this sense, the past is before what I now experience, and the future is after or what is yet-to-be. In one way, then, time is objective, and in another it is subjective. We might call the first "natural" time, or time as science understands it and as we understand it – measured and in measurable units – in everyday life. The second is personal time, from each of our personal or first-person perspectives. Now, to be sure, Levinas does not deny that in our lives we experience temporality in both of these ways. He acknowledges the special significance of Bergson's distinction between the two ways of understanding time and accepts it, to a degree. What he does deny, however, is that the distinction captures everything that is important about our experience of time.

Indeed, this distinction does not capture what Levinas thinks is the deepest and most profound dimension of our temporal existence. It is not enough to experience time in these ways, nor is it enough to live with the sense that time and history are going nowhere and have no purpose or that their only purpose is what each of us gives to them. In other words, Levinas's concern with time is that it is meaningful in a way that we do not usually realize. Bald naturalism and subjective relativism or idealism

[11] Ibid., 79.
[12] Ibid.

do not tell the whole story about time. Our temporal experiences mean more than either the objective view or the subjective view suggests, and it is the ethical character of our social existence that gives them their meaning. Moreover, to turn our attention to the meaningfulness or significance of our existence as temporal is not to change the subject. For our experience of time, as flowing or as measurable and an object of calculation, is shaped as well by our sense of its being the modality in which our living occurs.

ROSENZWEIG AND LEVINAS ON ESCHATOLOGY

Franz Rosenzweig has a similar concern about time and history. What he thinks is provided by divine revelation and what he conceives as a link to eternity, Levinas thinks is provided by the encounter with the face of the other person. Both believe that time and history have an absolute direction and significance only if our lives are tied to transcendence. In his famous letter to Rudolf Ehrenberg in 1917, Rosenzweig attributes the idea that "revelation is orientation" to Eugen Rosenstock. He says "in 'natural' space and in natural time the middle is the point where I simply *am* …; in the revealed space-time world the middle is an immovably fixed point, which I do not displace if I change or move myself."[13] For Rosenzweig, revelation is the divine command to redeem the world through love; for Levinas, a similar sense of obligation to accept and help others and to alleviate their suffering is the content of the face-to-face. Just as revelation, then, gives time and history an absolute structure and direction – and a determinate future and goal, so does the face-to-face. Or, in other words, for Levinas our experience of time takes on meaning and purpose only when understood in terms of the face-to-face with the other person, when understood as the temporal setting of social existence in its deepest sense.

For Rosenzweig, revelation is the event of divine grace, of the divine coming to manifest itself to the human in an act of love that is also an act of command; God says to each person that her life is valuable and with purpose. In other terms, as an act that orients or places each person in a certain position, posture, or attitude, revelation calls the human to a life of love and concern that seeks the creation of genuine community and solidarity with others. Levinas too believes that revelation is an event that places each of us in a certain position, posture, or attitude, prior to anything that we do or any act we perform; for Levinas too revelation is an

[13] Paul Franks and Michael Morgan (trans.andeds.), *Franz Rosenzweig: Philosophical and Theological Writings*, 49–50; cf. 63–65.

event of election or summons and command, and for him too the call is to create communities of love and concern. But the difference between them is about the setting for that call, that summons, and the way in which that revelation or election occurs. For Levinas, as we have seen, the location of revelation is the *face* of the other person; the needfulness, the destitution, the suffering of the other person, these call to each of us and place us under a burden and under the umbrella of an expectation for the future, for every future, that we respond and realize that each act we perform is a response to others and that prior to every decision and every act, we are so bound. For Levinas as for Rosenzweig, then, without revelation, time and history have no meaning, and that meaning is in one sense a gift and in another a duty.

It is for this reason that Levinas can appropriate the religious vocabulary of messianism and eschatology for the face-to-face and its relation to history.[14] Of course, what it means for him differs from what it means in traditional religious thinking, Jewish and Christian. But to understand that meaning, we need to look at *Totality and Infinity.*

Levinas does not delay introducing the notion of eschatology in *Totality and Infinity*; it occurs in the Preface. The early pages of the Preface use a language of war, politics, morality, eschatology, and violence. Levinas also introduces here the terminology of totality and infinity or transcendence that is central to the book. Prima facie this seems obscure and confusing. Why begin a book about metaphysics and ethics by talking about war and violence? And what does eschatology, doctrines or beliefs about the end of history or the end of time, have to do with any of these matters?

The early pages of *Totality and Infinity* anticipate what Levinas will discuss more fully later. For now let me consider first the relation of war, totality, and politics. Then I will turn to the expressions "eschatology" and "prophetic eschatology." To begin with, war, Levinas says, threatens morality. "The state of war suspends morality." If politics refers to the rational strategies for foreseeing war and winning it, and if war is essential to politics, then, like war, "politics is opposed to morality" as well.[15] Levinas of course is being literal here, but he is also anticipating larger issues, for he takes war to be a feature of what he calls "totality." War is everything that forces people to play roles and to betray themselves through institutions, practices, and public life. It is whatever impedes our being

[14] See Levinas, *Totality and Infinity*, 22–26, and the Talmudic readings on Messianism in *Difficult Freedom*. See also Robert Bernasconi, "Different Styles of Eschatology: Derrida's Take on Levinas's Political Messianism," *Research in Phenomenology* 28 (1998), 3–19.

[15] Levinas, *Totality and Infinity*, 21.

ourselves uniquely by forcing us into roles and types. War is egoism writ large. Morality, on the other hand, is our expression of our unique selfhood and hence something that system cannot capture. It is love, justice, and a humane concern for others. Yet, we live in both worlds, in a sense, in the world of politics and war and in the world of morality, but only if we are attentive to morality and this means to peace, as Levinas calls it.[16] "The moral consciousness can sustain the mocking gaze of the political man only if the certitude of peace dominates the evidence of war."[17]

From one point of view, then, war and politics are opposed to peace and morality. A life lived in society, without any appreciation for our obligation to others in all its depth and pervasiveness, is war or susceptible to war. The antidote is to be aware of peace and strive for it, to seek to realize it. Levinas then glosses this picture with a religious terminology: what needs to be done is to graft "the eschatology of messianic peace" onto the "ontology of war." That is, war is the ultimate form of totalizing thinking and ways of life, of idealism, and Heidegger's ontology is its most recent avatar. We need more than the threat of war so central to ontology; we need to live according to the goal of messianic peace; instead of ontology, we need to orient our lives by eschatology, that is, by a sense of purpose, obligation, and direction. Levinas calls this "prophetic eschatology" or "eschatology" by itself. But it is not an old-fashioned, traditional eschatology; it does not provide a goal or orientation *within* ontology and history. What it does provide – through its link with the infinite, the other – is a significance *for* our lives and hence *for* history. Prophetic eschatology tells us that our lives are invested with goodness insofar as they are ruled by a sense of compassion and concern for others.

This kind of messianic eschatology, then, is not a doctrine about the end of history; it is unlike views even about the wars that some think will occur at history's culmination. "The eschatological, as the 'beyond' of history, draws beings out of the jurisdiction of history and the future; it arouses them in and calls them forth to their full responsibility."[18] That is, it is outside the wars of history's end, outside politics and such. "It restores to each instant its full signification in that very instant." As Levinas puts it, this is not a last judgment but rather "the judgment of all the instants in time."[19] In other words, history or time is lived day to day. Religions, some sacred in spirit, some secular, confer on the years, months, days, and

[16] For peace and the face, see "Peace and Proximity," in *Alterity and Transcendence*, 139–141.
[17] Levinas, *Totality and Infinity*, 22.
[18] Ibid., 23.
[19] Ibid.

hours purpose through the expectations of an end to historical development. Not so for true or genuine eschatology, which is not about an end of days. It is not about a conclusion or resolution to history as a measurable sequence of temporal units; it is about living every instant with a sense of what one owes to each and every other person, and hence about living each moment, with suffering and need and with a devotion to alleviating the one and caring for the other. Life becomes meaningful not because of what will ultimately occur but because of how we live and act at each and every moment.[20]

Later in *Totality and Infinity* Levinas elaborates these themes by developing the account of *Time and the Other*.[21] I do not think that it is necessary to survey the details of these pages, but it is worth noting some points that underscore what we have been saying. First, Levinas calls "time" a "space" that is opened up when, through our acts and experiences, death is "postponed."[22] It is in "this space of time" that a "meaningful life" is "enacted," not in virtue of a "measure of eternity" but rather through the relation with the other person.[23] Religion would typically associate this shaping of a meaningful life with eschatology; earlier Levinas reinterpreted the term to suit himself, but ultimately, I think, he eschews it for the expression "messianism."[24] But the central idea is that this meaningful life is *not* something realized only after history, time, and human experience have run their course. Rather, it involves a "perpetual duty of vigilance and effort that can never slumber … the incessant watching over the other."[25] Eschatology or messianism is a matter of living every moment of life in a certain way, with compassion and concern for others.

Clearly Levinas has a very episodic view about what makes human life meaningful. His conception is distinctive in this respect. For Rosenzweig, for example, as for traditional eschatologies that view history as a kind of *Heilsgeschichte* (salvation-history), it is primarily the totality of history or the sum total of all human experience and all human action that has meaning, and this meaning is developmental.[26] The significance of the linear route comes with its ultimate resolution, its goal or *telos*. Given such a picture, individual and discrete actions or events are significant as

[20] See ibid., 22–26.
[21] See especially ibid., 220–247 and 281–285.
[22] Cf. ibid., 236–239.
[23] Ibid., 232.
[24] See ibid., 285; see also Kearney interview in Cohen (ed.), *Face to Face with Levinas*, 30–31.
[25] Kearney interview, 30.
[26] A classic discussion of such philosophies of history can be found in Karl Löwith, *Meaning in History*.

means to that end or as stages along the way to it. Levinas's view differs. To him, such a view totalizes human experience; either it conceives of all of each person's life as a whole, or, more often, it conceives of all human experience or history as a whole, and then takes discrete actions as instrumental and derivative. But for Levinas the significance of our lives arises for us as particular, unique individuals, and that particularity is tied to our responsibility in each and every situation, with respect to each and every other person. Hence, human life is meaningful insofar as each of us responds out of kindness and generosity at each and every instant. It is for this reason that I said Levinas's view is episodic. The very temporality of each experience we have is conferred by its relationship to the messianic, by its potential for itself being messianic. Like Walter Benjamin, but in a quite different spirit and with a different sense, Levinas would say that "every second of time [is] the strait gate through which the Messiah might come."[27] Neither life as a whole nor history as a whole is meaningful; rather, it is each instant, one by one.[28]

This way of living meaningfully is about living with a sense of responsibility to and for others. One religious expression for this way of living is to say that one lives under "the judgment of God." That is, if we think of history as having some standard or as being measured by some ideals or principles, this expression means that the real standard for understanding and assessing what goes on in history is not *in* history; it must be somehow a measure for history and not a mere apology. Levinas says that this standard of judgment is "the invisible [which] must manifest itself if history is to lose its right to the last word, necessarily unjust for the subjectivity, inevitably cruel." Ultimately, then, this standard is what in religious terms is called "the judgment of God." It "is produced as judgment itself when it looks at me and accuses me in the face of the other – whose very epiphany is brought about by this offense suffered, by this status of being stranger, widow, and orphan. The will is under the judgment of God when its fear of death is inverted into fear of committing murder."[29] This marks a crucial shift, from a view of human existence as living toward death to a view

[27] Cf. Walter Benjamin, "Theses on the Philosophy of History," in *Illuminations*, 266, and "On the Concept of History," in *Walter Benjamin: Selected Writings, Vol. 4, 1938–1940*, 397: "For every second was the small gateway in time through which the Messiah might come." Also: "The historian [of the new kind] establishes a conception of the present as now-time [*Jetztzeit*] shot through with splinters of messianic time." These texts and Benjamin's late reflections on history have been the subject of extensive discussion. Cf. Michael Morgan, *Interim Judaism*, 104–108.

[28] See Levinas, *Difficult Freedom*, 89–90: "Messianism is therefore not the certainty of the coming of a man who stops History. It is my power to bear the suffering of all. It is the *moment* when I recognize this power and my universal responsibility" (italics mine).

[29] Levinas, *Totality and Infinity*, 243–244, especially 244.

that sees it as living for the other person at every moment or, to put it otherwise, as living against the other's death at every moment. It marks a shift from living for oneself to living for the other person, from struggling with one's own finitude to being burdened by the threat of the other person's finitude, from self-concern to concern for others.

Moreover, Levinas sees added significance in the notion of *judgment*. It signifies that history and time are being measured and hence that they have meaning in virtue of that process of measurement and of aspiring to realize an ideal. But there is more to the idea of our being judged. "Judgment is pronounced upon me in the measure that it summons me to respond. Truth takes form in this response to a summons."[30] The expression "judgment of God," then, means that what gives human experience, time, and history their significance is the fact that each and every unique person is under this judgment; each is summoned, called, elected. This is justice (in *Totality and Infinity*; later justice arises only with the social and the third party) and goodness; it is a summons "to go beyond the straight line of the law," to become a unique I.[31] It is to "dread murder more than death"; it is a "deepening of the inner life."[32] This understanding of the judgment of God is not eschatological in the ordinary sense; it looks forward to no peculiar perfect age, no end of history. It transforms the ordinary and the everyday and renders us subjects or agents of a different kind.[33] This "judgment of God" confirms me as it judges me; I am who I am insofar as I am being judged and am called to responsibility.

In view of the reflections in *Totality and Infinity* that we have been discussing, then, one might think of Levinas's early thoughts about time and historical experience as his account of how we should understand the way we experience the future. Such experience is not an anticipation of death, nor simply a projection or imaginative expectation based on current experiences – "protention," in Husserl's vocabulary. When Levinas tells us that we should fear murder more than death, he is not recommending that we replace one mode of anticipation or expectation with another. Rather, he is asking us to reconceive dramatically our sense of what is ultimate about the self and what its deepest concern ought to be, of what makes human life valuable and significant. Our experience of the future, then, is not a hope for a perfect age for us individually or collectively. Rather, the future is about what we should do in the present and for the future; it involves

[30] Ibid., 244.
[31] Ibid., 245.
[32] Ibid., 246; "beyond the judgment of history" and under the judgment of truth.
[33] Ibid.

what is expected of us, demanded of us, and what we should expect of ourselves. In this way, the central issue about the future is what it does for the present as meaningful life and how it does it.

DIACHRONY AND RESPONSIBILITY

If Levinas's early concern with time and temporality is about the future, in his later work he turns to the past and how our experience of the past is significant for the present. In fact, he comes more and more to reflect on time – in *Otherwise than Being* and in later essays, such as "God and Philosophy" and "Diachrony and Representation."[34] And at least part of the reason for this preoccupation concerns the face-to-face itself and the role of God and the way in which their relationship articulates how our sense of the past is determinative for the present.[35] Responsibility is about what is still yet to be done and ought to be done, but it also involves a sense of obligatoriness that is given to us from the past. This past-orientation of our experience is what we now have to understand.

Probably Levinas's most advanced statement of these later interests and what he means by focusing on the diachrony of the face-to-face, is the essay "Diachrony and Representation." It is also explicitly about cognition, concepts, and philosophy; in a sense, the essay does for the issue of diachrony and time what "God and Philosophy" (1975) did for God and theological language. So let us turn to this late essay first and, if necessary, we can fill in any gaps between it and *Totality and Infinity* thereafter.

In an interview in 1983, Levinas summarizes what this essay seeks to accomplish:

> … there is the time that one can understand in terms of presence and the present, and in which the past is only a retained present and the future a present to come. Re-presentation would be the fundamental modality of mental life. But starting from the ethical relation with the other, I glimpse a temporality in which the dimensions of the past and the future have their own signification. In my responsibility for the other, the past of the other, which has never been my present, 'concerns me': it is not a re-presentation for me. The past of the other and, somehow, the history of humanity in which I have never participated, in which I have never been present, are my past. As for the future – it is not my anticipation of a present which is already waiting for me, … 'as if it had already arrived.' …

[34] See Levinas, *Entre Nous* (1985), 159–177; see also *Is It Righteous to Be?*, 176, 268–269; and "Transcendence and Intelligibility," in *Basic Philosophical Writings*.

[35] See *Is It Righteous to Be?*, 204–210, and *Entre Nous*, 232–233; see also the courses found in *God, Death, and Time*.

The future is the time of pro-phecy, which is also an imperative, a moral order, herald of an inspiration. ...[36]

Here Levinas points to his plan in "Diachrony and Representation." Even for someone like Husserl, our internal time consciousness involves a present that contains, as it were, a present experience of a past that was once present and a present experience of a future that is yet to be present. In short, our retentions and protentions – and then our memories and our anticipations, hopes, and expectations – are derivative of present experience, which is shaped by the subject and which tolerates no genuine transcendence or what Levinas also calls "exteriority." What Levinas calls to our attention is a sense of the past and a sense of the future that are radically different. These are a real past and a real future, that are not just recalled or projected or expected *presents*. The past and the future are not, as it were, states of affairs or facts. The past "concerns me," and the future is an "imperative." But in order to see what this means, we need to turn to the essay of 1985.

In 1988, in an interview, when asked about the "major preoccupation" in his current work, Levinas said that the "essential theme" in his research was "the deformalization of the notion of time."[37] He gives a nice, if brief, sketch of the problem of time, as he sees it, and the roles played by Kant, Hegel, Husserl, Heidegger, and Rosenzweig in dealing with it. Basically, as Levinas sees it, Kant, Hegel, and Husserl all saw time as the form of human experience, but none felt that time requires as a *condition* any "meaningful content somehow prior to form."[38] In other words, the flowing of the past and the imminence of the future are not seen as "attached" to a "privileged empirical situation" that gives these temporal experiences meaning. Certainly, we might think, Kant and Hegel had philosophies of history, and they saw human experience as oriented to goals, individual but also, more importantly, social and collective. But neither they nor Husserl understood actual temporal experience as itself oriented in terms of specific features of our human existence, past and future. Levinas takes Heidegger and Rosenzweig to have added just this, and that accounts for their novelty.

In Heidegger's case, he asks: what are "the situations or circumstances" characteristic of human existence that are associated with the experience of past, present, and future? Schematically, Levinas describes Heidegger's

[36] *Is It Righteous to Be?*, 176.

[37] Levinas, "The Other, Utopia, and Justice," in *Entre Nous*, 232.

[38] Ibid.

answers: *experiencing the past* involves "the fact of being, without having chosen to do so" and "of dealing with possibles *always already* begun"; *experiencing the present* involves "the fact of control over things" and "being near them"; and *experiencing the future* involves "the fact of existing-toward-death."[39]

Rosenzweig, on Levinas's reading, sought to answer the same question, to add content to the formal character of temporal experience. To him, our experience of the past refers to "the religious consciousness of creation"; our experience of the present refers to our "listening to and receiving revelation"; and our experience of the future refers to our "hope of redemption." The three religious ideas become "conditions of temporality itself."[40] Each of these ideas, we realize, concerns the human situation vis-à-vis God or transcendence as an orienting ground beyond our metaphysics and beyond our conceptual schemes. Hence, for Rosenzweig, the very temporality of human existence and human experience is somehow tied to our relationship with God, to revelation, in the broad sense, of our relationship to God. What are *immanent centers* of meaning for Heidegger become *transcendent centers* for Rosenzweig. Levinas's own contribution, in a way, is to realize how immanent that transcendence really is.

There is of course much more we could say about Heidegger, Rosenzweig, and their predecessors. Temporality is not just a matter of our experience of time for them. It is, at least for Heidegger and Rosenzweig, a central feature – perhaps *the* central feature – of the existence of human beings. Their very existence or being is temporal and hence, as tied to their relation to the world, to customs, traditions, and death, it is meaningful or not, or, to use Heidegger's terms, authentic or inauthentic. Levinas's argument that human existence occurs in relation to an immemorial past of ethical responsibility to the other person and in anticipation of a realization of that responsibility is his attempt to advance beyond both Heidegger and Rosenzweig and to give a more accurate account of what constitutes authentic, meaningful human existence in which the social and ethical are primary.

It is now time to turn to Levinas's essay "Diachrony and Representation" (1985). Suppose you and I are having a conversation. As we speak to one another, we may express beliefs and attitudes, share information, and do much else. Levinas asks whether, in such an encounter, what is *said* is

[39] *Entre Nous*, 232–233; cf. Robert J. Dostal, "Time and Phenomenology in Husserl and Heidegger," in Charles Guignon (ed.), *The Cambridge Companion to Heidegger* (Cambridge, 1993), 141–169; Richard Polt, *Heidegger: An Introduction* (Cornell, 1999), 96–109.

[40] *Entre Nous*, 233.

primary. Is it "the unique, original, and ultimate rationality of thought and discourse? ... Is language meaningful only in its *said*, in its propositions in the indicative, ... in the theoretical content of affirmed or virtual judgments, in pure communication of information ... ?"[41] The terminology of the *saying* and the *said* is one that Levinas had introduced in *Otherwise than Being.* The *said* refers to all our everyday language, in all its practical and theoretical uses, with its grammar and meanings. The *saying* is another expression for the face-to-face dimension of social interaction that is the basic context in which all language is employed. Hence, the question he asks about our conversational encounter is: what is primary? Levinas's answer is that what is more deeply meaningful than this discourse-as-content or the *said* is the *saying*, the responsibility to the other person that underlies it and that it actually enacts. That is, what is most deeply meaningful and what gives such conversation its point and purpose as a social encounter is the fact that in conversing each of us acknowledges and accepts the other, is responsive to the other, and is responding to the other's call or summons. Here, Levinas adds the notion of temporality. The conversation as communication of content takes place now, in the present, but is this mode of temporal activity – the present – "the primordial intrigue of time?" Is there not a temporality associated with the "from-me-to-the-other," of the face-to-face, that is deeper and more determinative of such social engagements?[42]

Levinas characterizes the temporality of our conversation, of your remarks and mine, given their content, our thinking, hearing, speaking, and responding, as "synchronous."[43] Occurring in the present, all of these things occur together, at the same time, at least roughly so, and they are grasped, when we think about them, together, as located within a temporal whole. But if all of this is experienced roughly as synchronous, the *saying* – our individual responsibility one to the other – is experienced, as it were, as *always already given*; "the face of the other obligat[es] the *I*, which, from the first – without deliberation – is responsive to the other. ... [T]he response of responsibility ... already lies dormant in a salutation, in

[41] Levinas, "Diachrony and Representation," in *Entre Nous*, 164.

[42] Ibid., 164–165.

[43] More accurately, each act, such as this conversation, is synchronous and diachronous, both relatively. That is, the act occurs at the same time as certain other events and actions and at a different time than certain other events and actions. Our conversation, for example, occurs at the same time as a meeting of the city planning commission and as a coffee break for workers at a local office; it even can be said to occur at the same time as the other event descriptions under which it falls, e.g., its being a discussion of a joint philosophical project. It also occurs at a different time from my eating lunch today at my favorite restaurant with my wife.

the *hello*, in the *goodbye*."[44] This *already* indicates that the relation between our conversation, which is a social act and which occurs in the everyday, and this original responsibility is not synchronous; they do not, as it were, occur at the same time. They are, as Levinas says, diachronous. Justice, society, and more – these place "the nakedness of the face" in the world, "destitution, passivity, and pure vulnerability," and yet it is always past, always already how you and I are related.[45] At any moment, whenever and however any two of us are related and act toward one another, it has always already been the case that we are responsible to and for one another; each of us, prior to saying anything, deciding to do something, or doing anything, is under the summons from the other and is called to respond to the other. We always *already have been* responsible; we *never are coming to be* responsible. Levinas calls responsibility "the secret of sociality"; it is "a voice that commands: an order addressed to me, not to remain indifferent to that death, not to let the other die alone."[46]

Thus, as Levinas sees it, the temporality or temporal modality that is primary to human existence as social existence is that of *the past*. It is a diachronous past, an always-past. But what does this mean? Two events are synchronous when they occur at the same time or together and hence when they occur both as past or both as present. Two events are diachronous when they occur along a temporal spectrum, when there is a temporal continuity between them. A particular event that occurs in the world and as an event in time is synchronous with some other event or events and diachronous with other events. Empirically, every event is both synchronous and diachronous relative to some other events. But responsibility, as a kind of state or attitude of the self toward each and every other person, is *only diachronous*. There are no other events or states or whatever with which it is synchronous. It is thoroughly and unqualifiedly, absolutely diachronous. As an attitude or posture or state of the self toward the other person, it is always diachronous with respect to all properties, beliefs, states, actions, and attitudes of that self.

For Levinas, then, my existing now has a dimension that points to the past, but the past in question was never a present, so that the diachronous link between that past and my present existence is unique. It is not retentive, nor is it memory, nor the past-relatedness of a reference or symbol or piece of evidence or indication.[47] In a section of the essay called

[44] Levinas, "Diachrony and Representation," in *Entre Nous*, 166.
[45] Ibid., 166–168.
[46] Ibid., 169.
[47] Levinas, *Entre Nous*, 71: "a past that is articulated ... without recourse to memory."

"Immemorial Past," Levinas calls this dimension "the ethical anteriority of responsibility." This is the face-to-face and my always already being responsible; in terms of its temporal relation to my present existence, it is "a past irreducible to a hypothetical present that it once was."[48] Levinas uses the expression "throws back toward" to describe how I am with respect to this responsibility and obligation. That is, at any moment, I experience what I do, converse, act in subjective and objective time; I recall earlier actions, anticipate what I will do, and so forth. But, if I am aware of and appreciate my responsibility to others, I realize that the impact of the other person's needs and the obligation I bear have always been with me; I enter every moment with them; unlike the lived past, they do not fade, and unlike the objective past, they never were a present themselves, so that I could say, "Before this, I was not responsible and now I am." Of responsibility, I have never recognized it for the first time or accepted it; it was never in my power or control. It came upon me, or, from my present point of view, I was "thrown back toward" what matters for me and commands me. This responsibility, then, in relation to what I am now and what I do, is an "immemorial past."[49] All the actions that I take now or at any time – noticing, accepting, rejecting, choosing, deliberating – whenever I engage in them, I do so as *already* responsible; my obligations toward others come with me. There is no action that makes me responsible. I always already am responsible. That is diachrony, pure and unqualified, not relative or conditional. However "old" is any act, responsibility is "older."[50] Or, to put it in other terms, in the face-to-face relation with a particular other person, I experience a trace of *illeity* that always has passed by and is never present.

This is the "past" of human existence; there is also a "future." What Levinas says in these later works builds on the account we gave earlier. We live out of the past and into the future, what Levinas calls a "pure future."[51] I live with an obligation to the other, one that signifies "*after and despite my death*," calling to attention "a meaningful order signifying beyond this death … an obligation that death does not absolve. …"[52] This is the content of a future that is beyond any yet-to-be, beyond "my anticipations or pro-tentions." Moreover, as in infinite obligation that is not limited even by my death, this is an *imperative* that "concerns me"

[48] Ibid., 170.

[49] Ibid., 171, 172; cf. *Otherwise than Being*, 10, 30–31, 52; *Basic Philosophical Writings*, 116–119.

[50] Note Levinas's use of "already" in *Entre Nous*, 172.

[51] Levinas, *Entre Nous*, 172–174.

[52] Ibid., 172–173.

and matters to me. Levinas notes that as an order or imperative, with no limit to its realizability, what comes to my mind is the expression "word of God" and the entire theological vocabulary of revelation. He calls this future-orientation of responsibility as an imperative to be fulfilled "the fall of God into meaning." "Time," he says, "[is] the to-God of theology."[53] The significance of our sense of the future is captured in our *obligation* to care for the other, our responsibility for the other's death, for a future that is beyond me.[54] Dying may mark the end of my life, but the meaning of my existence reaches beyond my death. Just as my natural existence is future-oriented toward my death and hence is in the grip of my own finitude, so my meaningful, social existence is future-oriented toward the death of the other by means of the imperative upon me to prevent it, an infinite and unfulfillable imperative that nonetheless has me in its grip.[55]

In the past, the meaning of my existence recovers a responsibility that is original, and in the future, it grasps a *commanding* that grounds it and expects its realization but is more than I can ever accomplish.[56] These orientations are not historical time, objective time, or even Husserlian experienced time; they are diachrony, the absolute difference between what gives my existence meaning and that existence, and at the same time the interpenetration of my existence by this temporality. Levinas draws closer and closer to religious vocabulary to express the way these modes of temporality characterize our lives. He calls it "holiness"[57] and calls reflection on it "a theology without theodicy" and a "difficult piety … of the twentieth century, after the horrors of its genocides and its Holocaust." It is the "deformalization of time."[58] For here time is conceived as more than the form of our experience; it also is its content, its ethical and religious content.

This account of responsibility as diachrony mirrors the account of the idea of the infinite and the transcendence of totality. In our everyday lives, as we experience people and things, as we live and act, our living does have temporal features. We experience others at certain times; we make plans to meet; we spend hours together and celebrate anniversaries. Also, we see, hear, walk, talk, and work, recalling the past, remembering

53 Ibid., 173.
54 Ibid., 174; cf. 174–175.
55 There is a provocative comparison to be made here to Kant's argument, in the second *Critique*, for the postulate of the immortality of the soul and the hope for the realization of ethics in a purely good will.
56 Levinas, *Entre Nous*, 175.
57 Ibid.
58 Ibid., 177, 176–177.

episodes, anticipating a vacation, looking forward to seeing a film, hoping for a brighter day. And at each moment our experiences and actions flow into the past and future like a stream – as Bergson, James, and Husserl have shown us. But – and this is Levinas's central theme – the temporal dimensions of our lives include other ones, which are unlike a measured or dated past or a remembered one and which differ radically from a date set for a fixed time in the future or a hoped-for future. Our lives recall a past that was never present and anticipate a future that will never occur. They are pure past and pure future – purely diachronous, never contemporaneous with any present. In other words, they disclose to us what it means for us to have everyday presents, pasts, and futures. They disclose why it matters to us that our existence is temporally arranged, why recollection and anticipation have point and purpose. Living in the world with other persons, and living historically and temporally, means what it does to us because of our obligations to serve the needs of others. When we respond to these obligations, individually in episodes of kindness and concern and collectively in practices of justice and generosity, we give our personal and collective temporal and historical lives what meaning they have. We can live in history and in time without attention to such responsibility, but when we do, we allow life and history to be hollow and mechanical.

As we have examined some of the things Levinas says about time, it has become clear that he is not concerned with time as an objective feature of our public lives. He is not concerned with past, present, and future as modes of time or years, months, days, and hours as units of time, or even with before, now, and after, as perspectives on time. Nor is he interested in developing a phenomenology of time consciousness or in correcting Husserl's efforts along these lines. He is responding to Heidegger's account of the temporal modalities of human existing, which are about the ways we are involved in all that is given to us, all that we now are doing, and all that we expect in the future.[59] In a sense, for Levinas, as we live each and every moment, we do so with a sense of the past and a sense of the future. But our sense of the past is *deeper* than our awareness of being situated amid things, resources, and traditions already there when we come on the scene, and our sense of the future is *deeper* than our anticipation of our own death and the realization of our finitude. Authentic living, for Levinas, is more than resolute decision; it involves acknowledging and acting upon our sense of obligation toward every other person. In the end, then, Levinas's interest in time and history are about the meaningfulness

[59] See Richard Polt, *Heidegger*, 96–98.

of human existence, individually and collectively; he is concerned with how we live each and every moment of our lives. The temporality of our existence and hence of how we live, act, and work is tied to what makes that living, acting, and working meaningful for us as human beings, and that amounts to having a sense of generosity and devotion to others, a sense of responsibility that points to a past and a future that are present in every experience we have and in every act we perform.

A crucial expression, I believe, that helps us understand Levinas's point here is the expression "always already." This is my terminology and not his – although one does find him using something like it on occasion. But I think it can help us to see why he thinks that our sense of our unique past is what is determinative for us and why that past is a "past that was never present." As I have tried to emphasize, responsibility is past in a way unlike the way any state or feature or fact is past, present, or future. At any given moment, in our interaction with others, we find ourselves in a situation already there. In a theater, watching a film, I realize that prior to my entrance, the theater was there, the chairs, the screen, the walls, and so on. But everything was, at one time or another, for us or for someone else, something new, created or shaped or built or made in the present and bequeathed to the future. There was always for these things – the theater, the chairs, the film – a time when they were not. Even the persons with whom I sit and talk and laugh and cry were, at one time or another, born, the objects of adoration, love, nurturing, and more. This fact is part of what makes the background conditions of our experience contingent. But, as we have seen, for every particular person to whom we are related in this present, not only was she already there but also our turning to her, our acknowledging her, our responding to her presence or look or her saying "hello" was, in a sense, already there. There is, however, a difference in these cases of *being-already-there.* The difference is that once she was in the present for others and for me, but my responsibility to and for her was never in the present, in the sense that there was a time when it first came into being. This means that I never chose it, created it, or acquired it – originally; it *always was already there.* And this is true for every relationship between persons; this responsibility comes first, so to speak. It is that dimension of or perspective on our social relationships that I easily forget or that is hidden from me but that is *always already there.* In my social existence, your death (your vulnerability and dependency) is more orienting for me now than my own death is – or, as Levinas puts it, I should fear murder more than death, and the future that matters most to me is yours, not mine.

Moreover, to return to the themes with which we began this chapter, this prominence of the past, when I am aware of it, can give my life meaning, and it can give history meaning, not by promising a final end to history or a personal salvation but rather by determining how I live and act at each and every moment and thereby by giving my acts and experiences their deepest significance. This is no traditional eschatology and no traditional, speculative philosophy of history. But it is a vision of peace and justice, of kindness and generosity.[60] It is a messianism of the moment in which you and I are the agents of its realization.

60 See Robert Bernasconi, "Different Styles of Eschatology."

CHAPTER EIGHT

Greek and Hebrew: Religion, Ethics, and Judaism

Throughout his career Levinas understood Western culture and society as a combination of two worlds, the Biblical and the Greek – what others have called Hebraism and Hellenism or Athens and Jerusalem. Levinas, of course, has his own special way of interpreting this trope, as we shall see, and his own way of envisioning it in order to estimate the value of Jews and Judaism for Western culture (and world culture). In part, it is a philosopher's perspective on that culture and the themes and tendencies that constitute it. At the same time, it is a Jew's perspective on what Jewish life means, both to Jews and to others. In this chapter, I want to look at this conglomeration of issues. We will cover a number of themes, for Levinas's relationship to Judaism is multifaceted.[1]

Let us first step back and place this task within the context of Levinas's philosophy. Recall that for Levinas the face-to-face encounter or the self's infinite responsibility is a structural feature of all social existence; all human experience is grounded, that is, in the ethical. Every human relationship is an ethical relationship. But, as we have seen, this interpretation of Levinas's claim that ethics is primary to human experience implies that responsibility occurs alongside a myriad of human social and cultural relationships and is concurrent with all our everyday experiences. Hence, it is possible to focus on any set of human practices or institutions in order to consider in what ways and to what degree these practices or institutions facilitate, organize, modify, and perhaps impede the realization of the ethical. To put this point succinctly, we can always examine a given cultural or social form to ask how effectively it facilitates or encourages acts of justice and benevolence. Levinas often explores particular artists, poets, and authors with just this point in mind: how and to what degree does a particular poet or novelist, say, disclose the ethical in his or her

[1] For a basic overview, see Richard Cohen, *Elevations*, 126–132. See also Adriaan Peperzak, *Beyond*, Chapter 3, and especially Tamra Wright, *The Twilight of Jewish Philosophy*, and Michael Fagenblat, A covenant of creatures.

poetry or fiction? We can ask the same sort of question about particular cultural traditions and indeed of particular religious traditions. In a sense, then, as we turn to Levinas's engagement with Judaism, Jewish texts, and the life of the Jewish people, we are asking how he evaluates Judaism in just these terms. What is the Jewish role in the task of realizing justice in human existence? In part, such an evaluation should continually focus on the ways in which Jewish life and Jewish thought disclose the obligation to be just, and it should also turn to various features of the Jewish experience – ritual practice, ideas, texts, historical memory, and moral values – to see how they are related to social existence as grounded in responsibility, in the claim of justice. This task, as I have indicated, is complex, precisely because Judaism is a complex phenomenon.

One theme that Levinas addresses is the historical reality of the Jewish people as a persecuted, suffering group, the target of anti-Jewish and anti-Semitic attacks.[2] What does the historical plight of the Jewish people reveal about justice and human responsibility to others? In this regard, the Jews are a kind of historical barometer. The level of suffering they have endured is an indication of the degree to which others have neglected or refused their responsibility to justice and goodness. Jews and their situation, then, reflect the character of Western culture. This is one of their roles, to demonstrate the ethical character of European and Western society.[3] In a sense, of course, this is true of all national, cultural, ethnic, and religious groups that have played some role or other in Western history; the history of every group discloses something about justice and injustice. What is distinctive of the Jewsh people, however, is its continuous existence and its long history of persecution.[4]

Connected to this theme is a second, the special relationship of Jews and Judaism to the Holocaust and Nazism. Levinas famously said that his life and career were "dominated by the presentiment and the memory of the Nazi horror."[5] We need to evaluate what this claim means or might mean

[2] Anti-Semitism as a central feature of Western culture and history has been a central theme for various thinkers, e.g., Arendt, Adorno, and Horkheimer. One might argue that it is characteristic of post-Enlightenment and post-Hegelian historicisms that vilify technology and urbanization and the rise of fascisms and totalitarianism as the mechanisms and outcomes of xenophobia and intolerance, of nationalisms and assault on the other.

[3] See Steven Smith's book on Spinoza and the Jewish Question; also Hilary Putnam, "Levinas and Judaism," in *The Cambridge Companion to Levinas*, 34: all people are victims of anti-Semitism.

[4] In a sense, for Levinas, the Jews are a "figure" for the paradigmatic persecuted and oppressed people. See Sarah Hammerschlag, *The Figural Jew: Politics and Identity in Postwar French Thought* (Chicago, 2010). Given the history of slavery in America and of the dispossession of Native Americans, Afro-Americans and Native Americans are the "Jews" of America. It is their histories that best reflect the level of injustice and abandonment in America.

[5] Levinas, "Signature," in *Difficult Freedom*, 291.

and especially the sense in which Levinas's work might be understood as a response to the atrocities of Auschwitz and the twentieth century.[6]

A third theme concerns Levinas's interpretation of Jewish learning, and the relation between the study of texts – primarily the Talmud – and the central ethical teaching of responsibility before the face of the other. Levinas emphasizes the tenacity and perspicacity with which the Bible and the Talmud teach the primacy of ethics, justice, and generosity. We shall discuss his Talmudic teachings, his writings about Jewish life and ritual, and how he conceives the teaching of the ethical as Judaism's central mission. This is part – indeed, a large part – of what Levinas means when he says that Jews should teach the Greek West to speak Hebrew.[7] Levinas's interpretations of the Jewish people as a persecuted minority, of the Holocaust, and of ethics as the central Jewish teaching are all then related to a fourth theme, his understanding of Zionism and the State of Israel. Levinas wrote several essays on this topic during the postwar period and then again in the 1970s and early 1980s.[8] But the core of Levinas's understanding of the significance of Judaism and the Jewish people is the primacy of the ethical, for all human life and certainly for Jewish life. In this respect, Levinas is a follower of Kant and then Hermann Cohen, but a follower of a very special kind.

Levinas's ethical view, the central and primordial character of responsibility to and for the other person, concerns all human existence insofar as it is social or interpersonal. It is, that is, universal, and if such an ethical view is the core of Jewish existence and teaching, then, in a sense, Jewish existence too is universal. To teach Greek culture to speak Hebrew is to remind everyone – if all people are by extension members of "Greek" culture – of something they already are but of which they are too little aware or wholly unaware. It is to see a special historical role for Jews and the Jewish tradition but to see such a role – as it was for Rosenzweig – as restricted to history. It dissolves in eternity. We will want to think about this tension,

[6] This will lead us to Levinas's essays "Transcendence and Evil" and "Useless Suffering," his consideration of suffering, and his views about the so-called end of theodicy. Of special interest will be recent work on these issues by Richard Cohen, Susan Neiman, and Richard Bernstein: Susan Neiman, *Evil in Modern Thought*; Richard Bernstein, *Radical Evil*; Richard Cohen, *Ethics, Exegesis and Philosophy*, Chapter 8. See also Joshua James Shaw, *Emmanuel Levinas on the Priority of Ethics: Putting Ethics First* (Cambria, 2008).

[7] In addition to the work of Robert Gibbs and Richard Cohen, one should look at the book *The Twilight of Jewish Philosophy* by Tamra Wright. A relatively early account can be found in Susan Handelman, *Fragments of Redemption*.

[8] Howard Caygill has recently discussed this literature in *Levinas and the Political*, and we shall want to see how Levinas's Zionist thinking is related both to his moral and political ideas and to his conception of Jewish destiny.

so prominent a feature of all Jewish life in the modern world, the tension between universality and particularity, from Levinas's point of view.[9]

ATHENS AND JERUSALEM

As we saw in Chapter 1, Levinas was fond of referring, in the 1980s, to the epic novel of Vasily Grossman, largely in interviews, but also occasionally in popular essays. One of these essays, published in February 1986, is called "The Bible and the Greeks."[10] In that essay Levinas describes European, Western culture as a unity of "the Bible and the Greeks," where "Greek," he says, is "the manner in which the universality of the West is expressed." Greek, that is, is the root of our ordinary everyday language, of our scientific, theoretical, and overall cultural discourse. It is Levinas's word for an attitude or posture that underlies our thought, talk, and action. Greek is the language of totality, grounded in the correlations of subject and object, of self and world, actor and action, knower and known. The Bible teaches a different lesson; it is the source of another dimension of our lives, not Greek in character. It is the lesson of ethics and responsibility, as we have explored it in earlier chapters. Hence, since all our language is Greek, the latter "intends to translate – ever anew – the Bible itself," which teaches about a "justice hidden behind justice … more faithful to its original imperative in the face of the other." This framework is the context for Levinas's primary goal in the essay, to call attention to a crisis in this European culture, a moment of threat and urgency, and to ask whether the crisis can be endured and overcome. He puts it this way:

> The history of modern Europe is the permanent temptation of an ideological rationalism, and of experiments carried out through the rigor of deduction, administration, and violence. A philosophy of history, a dialectic leading to peace among men – is such a thing possible after the Gulag and Auschwitz?

Rationalism, on Levinas's reading, is beset with the possibility and the risk of rigorous, organized oppression, dehumanization, and destruction. After these have been realized in Stalinism and Hitlerism, however, can we hope for recovery? Can peace arise after such horrors and such violence?

Levinas calls on Grossman's testimony or affirmation and associates it with the teaching he finds at the core of the Bible:

[9] This is a central theme of Levinas's essay on Mendelssohn, "Moses Mendelssohn's Thought," in *In the Time of the Nations*, 136–145.

[10] Levinas, "The Bible and the Greeks," in *In the Time of the Nations*, 133–135.

The testimony of a fundamental book of our time such as Vasily Grossman's *Life and Fate*, in which all the systematic safeguards of justice are invalidated and the human dehumanized, sees hope only in the goodness of one person toward another, the 'little kindness' I have called mercy, the *rahamim* of the Bible. An invincible goodness, even under Stalin, even under Hitler. It validates no government, but rather bears witness, in the mode of being of our Europe, to a new awareness of a strange (or very old) mode of spirituality or a piety without promises, which would not render human responsibility – always my responsibility – a senseless notion. A spirituality whose future is unknown.[11]

Levinas is referring to the incident of the Russian woman inexplicably handing the piece of bread to the hated German soldier and to Ikonnikov's commitment to the resilience of isolated, senseless acts of kindness. He identifies such acts with what the Bible calls *rahamim*, mercy, and claims that even Stalinism and the Holocaust cannot destroy the possibility of such acts. They are outside moral systems and political ideologies; they are not their product, nor do they "vindicate" them. They are not the results of motives we have every right to expect to be operating in the situations in question. Rather, the reality of such acts *testifies* to an old – permanent – feature of human existence, what he calls a "strange spirituality." It is this spirituality, this piety or moral sensibility, Levinas believes, that is all we can hope for, exactly what we can and should cultivate, and that comprises the central Biblical, that is, Jewish, teaching. When he says, moreover, that its future is unknown, what he means is that the chances of its realization, of individuals and societies now coming to shape their lives in tune with it, are beyond our calculation and certainly beyond our confidence. The twentieth century signals a massive suppression of such piety, of this sense of responsibility, and no one can tell if it is not only "invincible" but also resilient.[12] Can we reasonably envision the emergence of a world committed to generosity, justice, and goodness in the wake of Stalinism and Hitlerism – and subsequent atrocities and genocidal acts?

Levinas's point, in "The Bible and the Greeks," is not simply that the biblical teaching and the Greek world differ and yet collaborate in Europe, in Western culture, and that the horrors of the twentieth century make one dubious about the possibility of the biblical teaching becoming dominant or even effective. Levinas's little story is more Oedipal than that. As we have seen, he argues that the Greek world grows out of the biblical. The Bible teaches "the possibility of a responsibility for the alterity of the other

[11] Ibid., 135.

[12] One might contrast the optimism of Buber in "Dialogue between Heaven and Earth." More akin to Levinas's uncertainty is that of Eliezer Berkovits in *Faith after the Holocaust*.

person, for the stranger without domicile … for the material conditions of one who is hungry or thirsty, for the nakedness of the defenseless mortal."[13] It is the teaching of request and commandment, taught, for example, in the story of Genesis 24, as the rabbis read it, with the waters of Rebekah's well rising "in the service of mercy."[14] And out of this world of engagement with the face of the suffering other arises the Greek world, via the third party, the need for assessment, judgment, calculation, deliberation, knowledge, science, the state, and political authority. "The unique beings recognized by love … must be brought into the community, the world."[15] The connection is a derivation of a kind, as we have said, and the Bible a kind of condition for the Greek, a kind of parent. Levinas here focuses on its linguistic dimension: "Greek is Europe's inevitable discourse, recommended by the Bible itself," and hence as a kind of "metalanguage" – "which intends to translate – ever anew – the Bible itself."[16] And translation is a form of violence, of oppression, perhaps even repression.

The current crisis, then, is not just a tension between two aspects of one civilization. It reveals the suppression of the parent by the child's passions and drives, the willful assault of the child on the parent's hopes. Europe has become obsessed with definition, precision, universality, structure, and violence; it resists but still remains open to the ancient biblical spirituality, its sense of kindness and mercy. Body has come to dominate soul, reason to overwhelm love. Indeed, the lineage is precise: "a dehumanized humanity, surrounding institutions that were nonetheless the outgrowth of an initial revolutionary generosity and concern for the rights of man. …"[17] Hitlerism is the legacy of romanticism and even of Rousseau; Stalinism arose out of Marxism and its democratic, humanitarian roots. Levinas sees hope in Grossman's message, but he muses, how much hope, how deep, how resilient?

AN AUSTERE HUMANISM

This short, late piece expresses a good deal about Levinas's understanding of the role and content of Jewish life and Judaism. But it is only a short, late expression. To appreciate properly Levinas's views on Judaism,

[13] Levinas, "The Bible and the Greeks," in *In the Time of the Nations*, 133.
[14] Ibid., 133–134.
[15] Ibid., 134.
[16] Ibid.
[17] Levinas, "Beyond Memory," in *In the Time of the Nations*, 89; cf. 90.

we need first to look back at some of his early writings, from the postwar years, especially those collected in 1963 in *Difficult Freedom*.

After the Second World War, while representing the Zionist World Congress in Buenos Aires, Zvi Kolitz, a young journalist, was invited to contribute an article to the Yom Kippur edition of a local Yiddish newspaper, *Di Yiddishe Tsaytung*. He composed a fictional piece, in the form of a letter left in the rubble after the Warsaw Ghetto uprising, "Yosl Rakover Talks to God"; the story appeared on September 25, 1946.[18] Transmitted anonymously, the story surfaced in Tel Aviv, then in Germany and France, and was taken by some to be a genuine document, the impassioned religious testimony of a victim of the revolt. In 1955, it appeared in a French translation in a Zionist journal in Paris. Levinas gave a radio talk about the story on April 25, 1955, and it has become justifiably famous.[19] It is called "Loving the Torah More than God," a phrase that he appropriates from Yosl Rakover's prayer and that he takes to describe Judaism as what he calls an "austere humanism."[20]

Levinas presents the letter as "a text that is both beautiful and true," one that offers, he says, a "Jewish science." What is the content of this clear and true picture of Judaism?[21] What is Judaism's "austere humanism?" Levinas begins by noticing that "the suffering of the innocents" in the ghetto – and presumably also in the death camps – led many to deny God, to atheism. The problem of evil, theodicy, engaged in the face of such suffering, often leads to rejection. But, he notices, it does so because the conception of God that it refutes is "childish," a God of rewards and punishments. An empty heaven testifies to a childish mythology. Yossel is keener than this. His Judaism is adult, not childish. He does not reject God, but he does take His burdens upon himself. Yossel claims that God hid His face. Levinas takes this claim to be a true one. It says that the world has been turned over to savagery and that the time has come when the just suffer at the hands of the wicked, and there is no help. This image of God hiding His face, of *hester panim*, is not, Levinas says, "a theological abstraction or a poetic image." Rather, it is an accurate description of a time of utter destitution and failure. "It is the moment in which the just

[18] For the story, see Zvi Kolitz, *Yosl Rakover Talks to God*, translated and edited by Paul Badde, 48–54. This recent edition includes Levinas's essay on the piece.

[19] Levinas, "Loving the Torah More than God," in *Difficult Freedom*, 142–145.

[20] Ibid., 145. The phrase does not appear in all versions of the text, e.g., it is missing in the English translation that was published in Albert Friedlander (ed.), *Out of the Whirlwind*.

[21] Levinas knows that the piece is a work of fiction, but as fiction it nonetheless can disclose or hide the truth. It can speak to the primacy and character of the ethical in Judaism and in human life or can fail to do so. This text is "true" as well as "beautiful."

individual can find no help. No institution will protect him."[22] The good person suffers. The only hope is that others will respond to that suffering and stretch out a hand.

Moreover, the God who hides is Yossel's God, the God of the Jews, who are those who suffer, whose existence and whose teachings – whose Torah – calls for morality and conscience.[23] The suffering of the just person in behalf of a justice that struggles to realize itself "is physically lived out as Judaism." Judaism is not a confession, not an exclusive ideology. It is one way of living a life of suffering that teaches others what justice requires of all.

How can one believe such a thing or commit to such a fate? Levinas's answer is that it involves not a leap of faith but rather an education in Torah. In short, one learns to be a Jew by learning the teachings of the Bible. Levinas quotes Yossel; "I love him, but I love even more his Torah. …" One *learns* what suffering means and what justice or responsibility requires; one *learns* what Judaism is and appropriates it. The God who hides becomes *my* God, he says. "God is real and concrete not through incarnation but through Law." This is an adult view of God and Judaism, not a child's view; it is a "complete and austere humanism," for it means that the "adoration" of God is learned through the Torah and expressed through human kindness and generosity.[24]

Already in 1955, then, Levinas has in hand two major components of his conception of Judaism – that the suffering of the Jews is a plea for help and responsible concern, for justice, and that the primacy of ethics is the central teaching of the Torah. There is, that is, a conjunction of Jewish fate and Jewish soul; what the Jew teaches through his face, he also teaches with his mouth. A year later, in 1956, writing about the dilemmas of Jewish identity and the struggle of diaspora Jews for a "content" for their Judaism, Levinas calls it a "Jewish humanism."[25]

The core of that humanism is the Law that is taught by "the great texts of rabbinic Judaism, which are inseparable from the Bible." What these texts teach or, as Levinas puts it, "expose" is not rules or dogmas but rather "an entire world … a literature and a civilization."[26] Moreover, it is a world brought to life by "monotheism," the "vision of God [as] a moral act," or, as he says here, as later in *Totality and Infinity*, "this optics is an ethics."[27]

[22] Levinas, "Loving the Torah More than God," in *Difficult Freedom*, 143.
[23] Ibid., 144–145.
[24] Ibid., 145.
[25] Levinas, "For a Jewish Humanism," in *Difficult Freedom*, 273–276, especially 273.
[26] Ibid., 274; cf. "Judaism" (1953), in *Difficult Freedom*, 24–26.
[27] Levinas, "For a Jewish Humanism," in *Difficult Freedom*, 274–275; cf. *Totality and Infinity*, 23.

This monotheism, with these texts and their teaching about the primacy of goodness and response to the face of the other, is, he says, a "humanism," a "civilization built on justice."[28] Once, we might suppose, this task was called election or chosenness; Levinas calls it a "rare privilege" to promote "as one of the highest virtues the knowledge of its own sources," precisely because the content of that knowledge is ethics, justice, responsibility. The Jewish people, that is, is chosen to teach, to explore its own textual resources in order to "expose" their universalism. This is the sole purpose of diaspora Judaism.[29]

The most comprehensive of Levinas's early essays on Judaism, I think, was first delivered as a talk on education in 1957. It uses a motif we have already seen, the distinction between a childish and an adult religion, a distinction that has Kantian resonances. Indeed, its title employs the latter expression, "A Religion for Adults."[30] Like the other essays we have discussed, this one was written at the same time that Levinas was at work on *Totality and Infinity*. In the two works, he approaches the same goal from two points of view and shows how the same primary feature of human life is revealed through Judaism and through a philosophical exploration.

There is no need for us to review and consider every feature of this essay; rather, we should focus on the understanding it presents of Judaism, its character, its role. Judaism's "basic theses on man," or what he calls its "philosophical anthropology," are the central teaching of the Bible and also, in all their particularity and apparent parochialism, of the rabbinic texts.[31] Levinas calls this teaching "a link between man and the saintliness of God," but he makes a point of distinguishing the latter from God as a numinal or spiritual being.[32] He goes so far as to call such a numinal or sacred God "violent," an idol, and the Judaism of Abraham, freed of such mythology, an "atheism," that is, a non-theism.[33] The Judaism he is preparing for the reader is disenchanted, demystified, what we have seen to be ethical, responsible, and just – an "austere humanism." The core of this Judaism and the central teaching of Torah, Bible, and Talmud is the experience of the "presence of God through one's relation to man"; "through my relation to the Other, I am in touch with God." The other person is

[28] Levinas, "For a Jewish Humanism," in *Difficult Freedom*, 275.

[29] For these themes, see also Levinas, "Assimilation Today" (1954), 257; cf. "How Is Judaism Possible?" (1959), 250–254, and "Israel and Universalism" (1958), 175–176, all in *Difficult Freedom*.

[30] Levinas, "A Religion for Adults," in *Difficult Freedom*, 11–23.

[31] Ibid., 12–13.

[32] Ibid., 14.

[33] Ibid., 15.

"situated in a dimension of height, in the ideal, the Divine."[34] Once again, Levinas tells us that "ethics is an optic," which here means that "ethics is not the corollary of the vision of God, it is that very vision."[35] That is, what childish or immature religion takes to be seeing God is really, in life, our responses to others. This teaching is clearly manifest in Judaism's texts. It is what Maimonides means when, according to Levinas, he argues that the positive meanings of negative attributes should be read as imperatives: "God is merciful" means "Be merciful like Him."[36] Indeed, the coincidence of social justice with the relationship with the Divine is "the entire spirit of the Jewish Bible."[37]

Levinas acknowledges that this teaching is an "austere doctrine." It is demanding, exceedingly so, but it does not lead to despair.[38] What it expects is education and effort, and what it hopes for is an "aspiration to a just society … [through] religious action," a state of mind that Levinas says is "perhaps … [what] we normally call Jewish messianism." That is, Judaism accepts a severe teaching in a spirit of hope and opportunity, not one of frustration and despair.

This teaching, moreover, helps us grasp what the chosenness of the Jewish people means, and the centrality of ethics "allows us to understand the meaning of Jewish universalism."[39] Levinas explicitly argues that the traditional doctrine of election, the core of Judaism's particularism, is shown to incorporate a kind of universalism. Election is constituted by responsibility, and Levinas's notion of the face-to-face clarifies that while this responsibility for justice and generosity is universal, at the same time it is what the Jewish doctrine of election means. Each person has a moral duty to each and every other, for each of us is "elected" or "summoned" by each and every other. Judaism teaches the centrality of such duty. It is not unique to Jews, nor is Judaism its only advocate. But it is the core of Judaism and of Jewish particularity, so that when Jews speak of chosenness, what they mean is not some unique dispensation that comes from God but rather their ethical responsibility to others, an obligation binding upon each particular Jew but not only upon him or her.[40] The notion of the Jewish people being singled out and chosen by God is a "mythic" representation or image, as it were, of the ethical fact that each of us elects

[34] Ibid., 16, 17.
[35] Ibid., 17.
[36] Ibid.
[37] Ibid., 19.
[38] Ibid., 20–21.
[39] Ibid., 21.
[40] Ibid., 21–22.

and calls to responsibility every one of us. "Moral awareness," for the Jew, is "an awareness of being chosen." Levinas calls it a "particularism that conditions universality."[41] "Israel," as it were, is a moral notion – not an historical, national, or racial one, and this is part of its nature as landless, wandering, diasporic.[42] For Levinas, Judaism is primarily an inhabitant of time and not of space, and time means not history but "conscience," the call of justice, the hope and responsibility for a just society.

Why is this Judaism – ethical, universal, messianic, particular – a "religion for adults?" First, Levinas's Judaism is taken up with responsibility and justice, obligations that one must learn to understand, acknowledge, and accept for oneself. Children feel intensely their own needs; their desires are firm and full. Such desires dominate the child's world. In many ways, to outgrow childhood is to come to acknowledge others as independently important and to appreciate one's responsibility for and to them. It is to become educated, to learn the sense of obligation and concern, directed toward others, that is associated with adulthood. Secondly, Levinas is precise about calling this a "religion" for adults. It is not a religion of myth or fairy tale; it is not framed in terms of a patriarchal divinity, of rules and law, of rewards and punishments. Kant called such a religion "statutory" and suggested that it is demeaning and oppressive.[43] Levinas's religion is otherwise; it does not mystify the notion of the divine; it realizes that the language of God arises for us when we are aware of our responsibility to others and of the demands of justice. It treats such language not literally but indirectly or figuratively, as an expression of conscience, of our ethical sensibility. Such a religion is mature and not childish.

Furthermore, adulthood must leave behind the child, her enjoyments and pleasures, her naivete and innocence and selfishness. In short, adults must resign themselves to what they no longer have, what they have lost. They have learned to accept what they no longer have. Adult hopes are not childish ones; they are real and realistic. Judaism sees the past as gone and the future as genuine but neither too idealized nor wholly up to others. It is up to us, if we respond as we must and as we ought, with generosity and a sense of justice and concern. But this kind of Judaism has hope only

[41] Ibid., 22.

[42] Ibid., 22–23.

[43] In *Religion within the Limits of Reason Alone*, Kant claimed that Judaism was such a religion, that its legalism, otherworldly rewards, and heteronomy were characteristic of it and separated it dramatically and radically from the genuine history of moral development, the aim of which was a genuinely moral, rational faith.

because it realizes that the past, childhood, is gone, not to be recovered or reenacted, but mourned, genuinely and not mistakenly.[44]

Finally, Levinas's Judaism does not misconstrue, as a child might, the notion of election and the relation between Judaism's particularity and its universality. He has at least two mistakes in mind. One is to take election as a matter of privilege, when its real core is responsibility and hence a sense of burden or demand. The other is to take its responsibility only instrumentally, as if its particularity is its unique contribution to a universal goal, even if that goal is morality or the ideal moral community. Levinas rejects all of this.[45] Election is not a means to a universal goal; it is responsibility and therefore is itself universal. Jewish suffering and Talmudic teaching do call attention to the Jewish responsibility for others. But Jewish distinctiveness is an *historical* fact and *not* an *ethical or religious* one. Levinas is decisive about this. Ethics is not uniquely Jewish, of course; nor are its texts a unique resource for teaching goodness. Jews, like all persons, are each responsible to each and every other person, "elected" by the face of suffering and the need of the other. In a sense, then, the only justification for Jewish distinctiveness is the historical "accident" that Jewish teachings are an especially valuable resource for educating all humanity to an "austere humanism." At the same time, that distinctiveness is historically confirmed, as it were, by the suffering and persecution of the Jewish people.

Unlike Mordecai Kaplan, then, Levinas does not condemn chosenness altogether as an anachronism. Nor does he treat it as a decisive religious or theological fact grounded in divine will, a view shared by Joseph Soloveitchik, in his own way, and by Michael Wyschogrod and Emil Fackenheim.[46] In a way Levinas's view is akin to Spinoza's, that chosenness is an historical-political fact and not a theological-moral one.[47] The central difference between the two, with regard to chosenness, is that for Spinoza it exists only as a metaphor for the political and military success of the Jewish state, whereas for Levinas it is an ethical fact that, while shared by all, historically realizes itself in the life of the Jewish people as their central rabbinic teaching and their chief historical credential – suffering.

[44] See Espen Hammer, *Stanley Cavell*, 173. Cavell discusses this sense of maturity and growth, of education of the self to greater awareness and understanding of oneself and others, in many places, e.g., in *Conditions Handsome and Unhandsome*, *Pursuits of Happiness*, *Cities of Words*, and *Contesting Tears*. It is a central theme of what he calls "Emersonian or moral perfectionism."

[45] See Levinas, "Israel and Universalism," in *Difficult Freedom*, 176–177.

[46] See Joseph Soloveitchik, *The Lonely Man of Faith*; Michael Wyschogrod, *The Body of Faith*; and Emil L. Fackenheim, *What Is Judaism?* and *Quest for Past and Future*.

[47] See Benedict de Spinoza, *A Theologico-Political Treatise*, Chapter 5.

Levinas, in other words, does not try to defend Jewish particularity as much as he tries to understand it. The people and its texts exist. All people are nonetheless elected by the other to the demands of ethical responsibility. What, then, does the particularity of the Jewish people mean? This is the question Levinas seeks to answer.

From these early essays we can thus gain a basic picture of Judaism and Israel, the Jewish people. Much remains to be said, however. I select four themes: Levinas's treatment of the Holocaust and the problem of theodicy; his understanding of revelation, autonomy, and law; his understanding of messianism, eschatology, and prophecy; and his discussion of Zionism.

THE HOLOCAUST AND THE END OF THEODICY[48]

Earlier we saw that Levinas takes Stalinism and Hitler's fascism to mark a crisis in Western, European culture, a crisis that now accumulates the atrocities we associate with the genocidal acts in Iraq, Cambodia, Bosnia, Rwanda, Darfur and elsewhere during the late twentieth century. Both these regimes involved the oppression, persecution, and murder of millions of people; they engaged in horrific forms of torture and destruction. Stalinism was the outcome of Marxism and socialism and thereby, for Levinas, discredits the humanism invested in that tradition; it functions as a kind of historical *modus tollens*. Nazism realizes the worst nightmares of technological rationality and racist nationalism; the systematic murder machines, the killing squads and death camps mark a watershed in European culture. Levinas returns to the horrors again and again, if only in passing; the trauma never goes away.

Let me begin looking at Levinas on these matters by asking what is meant by the widely cited claim that for him, the Holocaust marks the "end of theodicy." Susan Neiman describes this view in these terms:

> The claim that whatever was left of religious faith before Auschwitz could not survive it became famous in works of witnesses like Elie Wiesel's *Night*, or of theologians like Richard Rubenstein's *After Auschwitz*. ... But unlike most contemporary thinkers, Levinas did not restrict the word *theodicy* to justifications

[48] On the role of the Holocaust for Levinas, see Susan Neiman, *Evil in Modern Thought*, 238–239, 291; Richard Cohen, *Ethics, Exegesis and Philosophy*, Chapter 8; and Richard Bernstein, *Radical Evil*, Chapter 6 (revised version of Chapter 12 in *The Cambridge Companion to Levinas*). See also Morgan, "Levinas, Suffering and the Holocaust" and Joshua Shaw, "Putting Ethics First: Emmanuel Levinas on the Priority of Ethics" (unpublished doctoral dissertation, 2004), Chapter 4. Robert Eaglestone "argues that his philosophy, throughout and in every way, from particular words and sentences to his overall aims, is a response to the Holocaust" (*The Holocaust and the Postmodern* [Oxford, 2004], 10) in Chapter 9, 249–278.

> of God's goodness that were modeled by Leibniz. Rather, he drew as much on secular forms of theodicy. … Theodicy, in the narrow sense, allows the believer to maintain faith in God in face of the world's evils. Theodicy, in the broad sense, is any way of giving meaning to evil that helps us face despair. Theodicies place evils within structures that allow us to go on in the world. Ideally, they should reconcile us to past evils while providing direction in preventing future ones. Levinas claimed that the first task could not be maintained in good conscience after Auschwitz. He thus gave philosophical expression to an idea shared by many: the forms of evil that appeared in the twentieth century made demands modern consciousness could not meet.[49]

Neiman takes Levinas to be using "theodicy" in a broad sense to refer to any intellectual way of placing and comprehending a past evil that also gives direction about how to prevent future ones. She takes him to be saying that we should abandon theodicies after Auschwitz. It – and other modern evils – are beyond our understanding.

Levinas's claim gives rise to a host of questions. What does Levinas think about theodicy, as the effort to place evils intellectually within structures or patterns in order to allow us to go on in the world, and to give evils meaning so that we can face and cope with despair? Is Neiman right that Levinas's rejection is tied precisely to modern evils, or perhaps even uniquely to Auschwitz? What does Levinas mean that the end of theodicy is the negative lesson of the Holocaust?

For Levinas, suffering – as a kind of evil – is beyond theodicy; it is untouched by it. For suffering by itself is wholly negative and beyond understanding. But theodicy is a matter of description and justification, of fitting evil into a structure or pattern that is part of our everyday or theoretical way of thinking and talking about the world and our experiences. Suffering as evil does take place in that world, and in one sense it can be described and explained, but in another it cannot. In its essence, evil lies beyond theodicy.[50]

Given what we know of Levinas, this would be a disappointing place for him to conclude. On the one hand, it would be unsatisfying to discover that in a sense – and a rather weak one – all suffering marks the limits of theodicy or explanation. And, on the other hand, it would be unsatisfying too if the only case of suffering that Levinas discussed were the self's own pain and suffering. Fortunately, however, Levinas takes a further, decisive step. He remarks: "one is surprised that there never appears on the

[49] Susan Neiman, *Evil in Modern Thought*, 239; also 291.

[50] Levinas gives his most elaborate account of suffering in "Transcendence and Evil," in *Collected Philosophical Papers*. He summarizes the account in "Useless Suffering."

foreground [of this commentary on the book of Job] the problem of the relationship between the suffering of the self and the suffering which a self can experience over the suffering of the other man."[51] He even suggests that in the book of Job itself there is a "secret indication" of this further issue. Levinas points out that God's challenge to Job at 38:4, "Where were you when I founded the earth?," is a "denunciation" of Job that assumes as background his fraternal solidarity with all creation and his "responsibility for everything and for all."[52] With these comments, then, we draw near to what is clearly of central concern to Levinas himself.[53]

Levinas then claims that even Nemo himself has *hinted* at the theme at the core of Levinas's thinking: transcendence as it is revealed in the "face of the other man."[54] In a crucial passage, he ties together Nemo's theme and his own:

> That in the evil that pursues me the evil suffered by the other man afflicts me, that it touches me, as though from the first the other was calling to me, putting into question my resting on myself and my *conatus essendi*, as though before lamenting over my evil here below, I had to answer for the other – is not this a breakthrough of the Good in the 'intention' of which I am in my woe so exclusively aimed at? Is it not theophany, and revelation? The horror of the evil that aims at me becomes horror over the evil in the other man.[55]

Much of this is familiar. What seems unusual is the emphasis on the way each of us, in response to the claim of the other person, suffers over his suffering – the evil suffered by the other afflicts me and touches me. Here is a real sense of the good that is deeper and fuller than my realization of a good other than the evil that assails me. Here is a good made up of my responsibility for the other and my obligation to assist him, help him, support him.

With this move, two important possibilities come into view. One is that Levinas can give a more profound meaning to the "end of theodicy," for he can take it to mean not every case of suffering in and of itself but rather a situation where the suffering of the other, to an extreme degree, is caused by and not alleviated by most people, that is, where the persecuted and afflicted are abandoned by the world. Another is that Levinas can now use the idea that the response to suffering is to assist the other, to respond to

[51] Levinas, "Transcendence and Evil," in *Collected Philosophical Papers*, 184.

[52] Ibid.

[53] Cohen fails to see the difference between the two. See *Ethics, Exegesis and Philosophy*, 271–275, where he collapses them. Bernstein also fails to note the distinction, in *Radical Evil*, 174–180.

[54] Levinas, "Transcendence and Evil," in *Collected Philosophical Papers*, 185.

[55] Ibid.

the plea and call directed to each of us by those in pain, to clarify how a post-Holocaust life should be conducted. It is in "Useless Suffering" (1982) that Levinas carries out this task.

In the opening section of this later essay, "Phenomenology," Levinas reviews the main features of his earlier account of suffering and evil.[56] The ethical problem of pain and suffering, the two of which are "useless" by nature, is what they mean as a call to others for aid and assistance, as a "demand for analgesia," "the original call for aid, for curative help, help from the other me."[57] Or, as he says, beyond pure suffering appears the "interhuman."[58] But if this is the ethical problem par excellence, then it is, he said, "high-minded" to think that as a civilization, bound to feed the hungry and heal the sick and lighten the suffering of others, we are indeed succeeding. Rather, the situation is much more "uncertain," at a point in modernity when we are "emerging at the end of a century of unutterable suffering."[59] With this comment, Levinas is on the brink of applying his analysis to the question of post-Holocaust life.

As in "Transcendence and Evil," Levinas calls attention to the "radical difference between *the suffering in the other*, where it is unforgivable to *me*, solicits me and calls me, and suffering *in me*, my own experience of suffering, whose constitutional or congenital uselessness can take on meaning, the only one of which suffering is capable, in becoming a suffering for the suffering (inexorable though it may be) of someone else." He calls this "the just suffering in me for the unjustifiable suffering of the other," an "attention to the suffering of the other" that is a "supreme ethical principle … commanding the practical discipline of vast human groups" both "despite [and] because of the cruelties of our century."[60] Moreover, "the consciousness of this inescapable obligation brings us close to God in a more difficult, but also a more spiritual, way than does confidence in any kind of theodicy." This is a provocative paragraph. Levinas shifts his focus from the experience of suffering to its impact on the self. He characterizes the self's attention and response to the other's suffering as itself an experience of suffering. Richard Cohen emphasizes Levinas's claim that my suffering, which is intrinsically useless or pointless, can "take on meaning" only by "becoming a suffering for the suffering of someone else." Cohen treats this as something that the self *can do*; it can *make* its suffering *compassion* for

56 Levinas, "Useless Suffering," in *Entre Nous*, 91–94.
57 Ibid., 93.
58 Ibid., 93–94.
59 Ibid., 94.
60 Ibid.

the other.[61] The self can set aside theodicy, the attempt to explain or understand suffering by making it an object, by externalizing it. Levinas, according to Cohen, is here claiming that "any attempt to erase the suffering of the sufferer by inserting an explanatory distance between the sufferer and his/her suffering … is not only a sham and hence futile, it is immorality itself."[62] The proper and moral thing to do is to take responsibility for the other. Such a commitment is the hallmark of a post-Holocaust Jewish faith and of a genuine human response to the atrocities of the twentieth century.

Levinas turns to the idea of theodicy next. It involves finding meaning in the experience of pain and suffering, by locating events in a large design or picture. Theodicy thereby seeks to give order to what is intrinsically absurd and meaningless. It is a "temptation," to find a place of intellectual satisfaction and a way of living in peace, even when there is pain and destitution. Theodicy is, moreover, an ancient tactic, and one that has taken many forms – religious consolation, philosophical resignation, political hopes, and utopian expectations. It contrives justifications in order to bring peace of mind or to direct our future.

What makes our age – after the horrors of world wars, totalitarianisms, Hitlerism, Stalinism, Hiroshima, the Gulag, and the genocides of Auschwitz and Cambodia (Levinas mentions them all, at one time or another) – the "end of theodicy?"[63] His answer: "perhaps the most revolutionary fact of our twentieth-century consciousness … is that of the destruction of balance between Western thought's explicit and implicit theodicy and the forms that suffering and its evil" have taken on in that century.[64] Here we have suffering inflicted deliberately with no rational limits under the aegis of politics divorced from ethics, "gratuitous human suffering in which evil appears in its diabolical horror," so that there is a manifest "disproportion between suffering and every theodicy." Auschwitz and "the Holocaust of the Jewish people under the reign of Hitler" are here the "paradigm." They show this imbalance, this disproportion or incommensurability between the amount and degree of suffering, on the one hand, and the capacity of explanatory frameworks to cope with it, on the

61 Cohen, *Ethics, Exegesis and Philosophy*, 276–277; see Levinas, "Useless Suffering," in *Entre Nous*, 100. On compassion, see Levinas, *Entre Nous*, 107.

62 Cohen, *Ethics, Exegesis and Philosophy*, 277.

63 Levinas, "Useless Suffering," in *Entre Nous*, 97. One might add now the Iraqi assault on the Kurds, the Serbian atrocities against the Bosnians, Rwanda and the genocidal acts against the Tutsis, and the genocide in Darfur.

64 Ibid.

other, "with a glaring, obvious clarity."[65] In short, for Levinas, the evil and horror of the atrocities of the twentieth century defy comprehension in thought.

It may be, as he claims, that all suffering is fundamentally meaningless and hence beyond theodicy. But what we have now, in the twentieth century and after, is a *crisis* in the "normal" way of coping with evil and suffering, for whatever success theodices once had, even if limited, today is destroyed. Recent evils defy *all* theodicy through and through. They do not simply *limit* theodicy; they *destroy* it. Hence, the need for an ethical response, the need to act in order to relieve suffering, is *emphasized* or *underscored*; it is highlighted and *dramatized*, for the old intellectual strategies are not merely shown to be insufficient; they are exposed as completely inappropriate and defective. It is not that recent atrocities are more deserving of attention and action in behalf of the suffering of the victims and of others. Rather, their character so cripples our capacity to become reconciled and to cope that our genuine and fundamental responsibilities are put in the most glaring, evident light. Theodicy may once have cast a shadow over those responsibilities, hidden or camouflaged them. But the cloud or mist is lifted, and the demands placed upon us are dramatically evident in a vivid way.

Although Levinas is not extremely precise in this account, he does help us to begin to answer several questions. First, theodicy is one way we use to cope with the evil of suffering; we seek to explain such occurrences and to satisfy our sense of anxiety by so doing. But the constellation of horrific events in the twentieth century is of such a kind that it thwarts all attempts at such explanations, and disables our intellectual satisfaction. Secondly, we are always, in every relationship with others, responsible for aid, assistance, and kindness. The atrocities of the twentieth century do not alter this dimension of our interpersonal relations; they do not increase the demand, create it, or elevate it. What they do is to remove the temptation of theodicy whereby such responsibility has been camouflaged or hidden. They discredit one possible response by exposing its failures as a response, even on its own terms. By realizing that we no longer can or should be tempted by explanations or rely on them, our responsibility emerges from the shadows and becomes vividly manifest. We see or should see, more clearly than ever before, what our humanity requires of us.

Finally, then, the Holocaust, Auschwitz, does not uniquely expose our responsibility in this way. It is a paradigm of the dissonance between

[65] Ibid.

our intellectual aspirations and the reality of suffering and evil. Perhaps most of all, its horrors resist the comfort of theodicy and explanation. In responding, we respond to others in our world, but we realize the centrality of our obligation because of Auschwitz and the other atrocities it stands for, from the Stalinist purges to the slaughter of Bosnians, Cambodians, Kurds, and Tutsis. Insofar as we realize our obligations and responsibilities more vividly, moreover, we do, in a sense, give *our* suffering a meaning it did not previously have, but only in a sense. For in another sense, that responsibility is present for us as long as the face of the other calls us into question and makes demands of us, which is a deep and permanent feature of all human social life. What we choose or do is to acknowledge those demands, first by not being tempted to theodicy and then by attending more vigorously and committedly than before to the obligations thereby disclosed. In this way, as Cohen claims, Levinas does charge us not to detach or distance ourselves from the suffering of others but rather to commit ourselves, to take upon ourselves compassionately, the task of alleviating it.[66] But our actions are not *directly* responses to Auschwitz, its victims, or the victims of other atrocities in the constellation of horrors.[67] We respond to the suffering of others *today*, in our own world, by recognizing that the suffering of those victims in the past disabled the capacity for theodicy, that this result makes dramatically prominent what our own deepest obligations are in the present, and that the extreme persecutions of the past century mark a period of abandonment that needs to be recognized and no longer allowed to continue.

RITUAL AND THE LAW

A central feature of Judaism is to cultivate justice and generosity, to care for the widow, the orphan, and the stranger.[68] This task is especially important, even if all the more difficult, after Auschwitz and the other

[66] See Cohen, *Ethics, Exegesis and Philosophy*, 276–278.

[67] In a way, insofar as they are an acknowledgment of the victims of those atrocities and hence a recognition of their place in our social lives, even though they are now dead. But in the most obvious way, as acts of reaching out to alleviate suffering and pain, our actions cannot in any way accomplish that for the victims themselves.

[68] See, for example, discussion of these themes in Emil Fackenheim, *What Is Judaism?*, Chapter 8, "The Ethics of Judaism – God's Love of Widows, Orphans, the Stranger, the Poor," 167–180. Fackenheim cites, as Biblical support, Deuteronomy 10:17–18 and Psalms 113:7–9. He takes caring for such figures to be central to Jewish ethics: "... since losers there are, and since God does love them, it is a *mitzve* [good deed] for us to love them as well, and to do what we can to relieve their condition. One might call this the mainspring of Jewish ethics. It is, at any rate, what gives it its special flavor." (169)

atrocities of the twentieth century. Moreover, while the suffering of the Jewish people makes the challenge all the more urgent for it, that suffering is a witness to others of how radical has been the abandonment of others and the indifference. But there is more to Jewish life than acting in behalf of others and representing the depth and significance of that obligation. Levinas takes the textual tradition of Israel to teach the centrality of such a task and what it means, so that study, teaching, and education are integral to Jewish life and to the Jewish mission to European civilization and the West. And there is the life of the *mitzvot*, of ritual and commandment. Why and how are these activities central to the vocation of Jewish life and especially of post-Holocaust Judaism?

Levinas says that "the most characteristic aspect of Jewish difficult freedom lies perhaps in the ritual that governs all the acts of daily life, in the famous 'yoke of the Law'." This might seem to be a strange thing for Levinas to say. As a descriptive statement about orthodox Judaism, it may be true. Surely the detail and extent of the ritual law is indicative of a traditional Jewish life. But even if it is true, can Levinas think that it should be? Indeed, can he find a significant place for Jewish ritual at all? It would be odd to be so immersed in the Talmud only to dismiss or ignore its legal, ritual dimension completely. To be sure, Levinas himself focuses on the Aggadic (interpretive) portions of the text, but he commends its primarily Halakhic (legal) character, and Jewish law regulates, among other things, ritual and ceremonial observance. In Wyschogrod's words, "what is the justification for Jewish ritual if ethical action is founded in the upsurge of the other and if such action is the way in which Judaism appears in the world? What, in short, accounts for the necessity of Jewish ritual *praxis*?"[69]

Let me start with Wyschogrod's answer: "According to Levinas, the obedience to ritual law constitutes a discipline that tends toward justice. In obeying ritual law, the demand of the other is recognized; the other, in this case God, has a right to suppress the egoity of the separated self."[70] For the moment, suppose that this answer is clear and acceptable: Jewish ritual is valuable as a regimen for everyday life that is a "discipline" in behalf of justice. Still, "why is ritual law necessary?"[71] Wyschogrod has no answer; Levinas seems to have none.

[69] Edith Wyschogrod, *Emmanuel Levinas*, 165. See Levinas, "The Name of God according to a Few Talmudic Passages," *Beyond the Verse*, 123–124.

[70] Ibid.

[71] Wyschogrod, *Emmanuel Levinas*, 166.

Tamra Wright, in *The Twilight of Jewish Philosophy*, discusses Wyschogrod's two questions and her understanding of Levinas's account of Jewish ritual as a "severe discipline" that "tends toward justice."[72] Wyschogrod drew on Levinas's "A Religion for Adults" for her interpretation of Levinas's justification for the ritual law. There Levinas explains that the law demands effort and regularity, and amounts to training; it cultivates "a courage that is calmer, nobler and greater than that of the warrior." In Judaism, goodness and legalism are in harmony, he says.[73] Wright accepts Wyschogrod's view and yet argues that the question of the law's necessity "loses its force" if we distinguish, as Levinas does, between recognizing one's ethical responsibility and acting on it or obeying the obligation to be just. It might seem that "ritual practice," Wright claims, "is needed not to enable us to hear [or recognize] the commandment, but to prepare us to respond to it in a positive fashion, acting in accordance with our responsibility."[74] She cites several comments that Levinas makes in the interview "The Paradox of Morality" where he distinguishes between the authority of the face and its force. Clearly, Levinas realizes that not all people, all the time, and with sufficient commitment, act in behalf of others. But Wright notes an ambiguity: Levinas admits that not all people "recognize" their responsibility to others, where "recognize" can mean both "are aware of" and "act on or obey." In the end, then, Wright's judgment regarding Jews, ritual, and the good is that "the commandment which issues from the face can always be recognized, but is not always obeyed, and the discipline of Jewish law can help prepare us to obey the Other. Whether or not there are other ways of preparing to welcome the Other remains an open question."[75] Indeed, one can easily suppose that there are and must be.

I am not convinced that separating the acknowledgment of the obligation to others, acceptance of them, from acting on one's responsibility toward them is in fact a wise strategy; indeed, it may be impossible. Outside of killing the other, all actions in relation to him or her involve some level of acknowledgment or acceptance, some responsiveness to the face. Even killing the other, as an act, involves such acceptance. The more one is conscious of that fact and of the responsibilities one owes, the more fully one can act in behalf of others. If Jewish ritual conduct disciplines or trains the Jew to greater attentiveness and greater sensitivity to others,

[72] Tamra Wright, *The Twilight of Jewish Philosophy*, 118–123.
[73] Levinas, "A Religion for Adults," in *Difficult Freedom*, 18–19.
[74] Wright, *The Twilight of Jewish Philosophy*, 120; see 119–121.
[75] Ibid., 121.

it serves a useful purpose. Indeed, it may do so in an especially effective way. In short, it may train the Jew to see things more clearly and to be sufficiently disciplined to act in behalf of what he or she sees to be right and good. But while the law is thereby valuable for the Jew, it hardly is uniquely valuable for these purposes, and it certainly cannot be so for all people, non-Jews included.

In his essay "Revelation in the Jewish Tradition," Levinas comments that Jewish ritual is "the most characteristic aspect of Jewish difficult freedom," and this might be taken as a descriptive point that what is most distinctive and manifest in Jewish life is ritual conduct. But this of course does not tell us why, nor does it tell us how ritual functions or what it means and accomplishes. Levinas goes on: "in ritual a distance is taken up *within* nature *in respect of* nature, and perhaps therefore it is precisely the waiting for the Most-High which is a relation to Him – or, if one prefers, a deference, a deference to the beyond which creates here the very concept of a beyond or a towards-God."[76] This is a difficult text, a perplexing and unclear one. Let me suggest a reading: ritual is explicitly, in Judaism, a response to divine command. Thus ritual acts constitute a kind of deference to God that serves to establish a sense of a beyond or other, which Levinas of course believes is the relation to the face of the other person. Jewish ritual, then, is a step on the way to seeing such a relationship, to our receptivity to it. Such ritual acts, which help train Jews to acknowledge otherness and transcendence and hence to recognize one's responsibility to others, do so by occurring in nature and by setting up a "distance" between the Jew and God as other. Ritual acts, that is, are part of the mythology of theology; they deal with Jews and God, but what they accomplish is a first step in the process of education that leads to the acknowledgment of the face of the other person.[77]

I would not want to claim that what Wyschogrod noticed and Wright elaborated should be replaced by this account. It is more likely that Levinas had a number of reasons for thinking Jewish ritual to be valuable and significant, all connected with the priority of the ethical but in different ways. What this interpretation adds, however, is the idea that ritual is not solely about motivation and obedience. It is also about awareness or recognition of the face as a commanding presence and in a very precise

[76] Levinas, "Revelation in the Jewish Tradition," in *Beyond the Verse*, 143.

[77] There is already an early anticipation of the idea that ritual acts are a training in acknowledging the transcendent in Peter Atterton, Matthew Calarco, and Joelle Hansel, "The Meaning of Religious Practice by Emmanuel Levinas: An Introduction and Translation," *Modern Judaism* 25:3 (2005), 285–289. This is a translation of an essay first published in 1937.

way. Operating within theological territory, ritual points beyond nature and totality and in this way, it prepares the Jew for an awareness of his or her ethical responsibilities. The dense life of ritual conduct may cultivate abilities that will ultimately serve ethical purposes; it may be a training for obedience. But it also encourages the Jew to acknowledge that which confronts her from outside nature, from beyond the everyday. That is, it trains her to see what lies hidden in concrete ordinary life, a dimension of responsibility, purpose, and meaning often hidden from view.

Wyschogrod asked whether ritual law and obedience to it is *necessary* for Jewish life. I think that Levinas would not be happy with the word "necessary" or with the way the question is framed. In an interview, he said that he could "accept the idea that the singular contributes to the universal." Even the pope, he said, recognized in Jewish existence "almost a character of necessity." But he then cautioned about the word "necessity." The point is that Jewish existence, its people, readings, and life, has a "permanent signification," that there is "a value to the survival of Judaism."[78] The same caution might be directed at the question of ritual in Jewish life. The issue is not whether it is necessary; rather, it is whether ritual is valuable and meaningful. Is it justified? Is there a point to it? And Levinas's answer is yes, for many reasons, insofar as it serves the greater purposes of human responsibility and justice.[79] Levinas, then, is not interested in justifying the necessity of Jewish survival or of the role of ritual in Jewish life, but he is concerned deeply about justifying the fact of Jewish existence and the fact of ritual. This is the task of finding meaning or value in them.

It should also be said that for Levinas the Bible and the Talmud, the chief texts of Judaism, do not include only Aggadic passages that speak of God and man and that incorporate the philosophical framework of Judaism. They also primarily include Halakhic or legal texts that prescribe obligations. It would be altogether strange if these norms, which command obedience, were in fact ignored as norms and if obedience to them were not meaningful and valuable. Moreover, since the central teaching of the former is a universal ethics, an austere humanism, surely obedience to those ritual norms should also contribute, in some way or ways, to the same universal ethical conception of human life. Levinas certainly indicates that it does, even if his account of how ritual contributes is neither comprehensive nor precise.

78 "Interview with Francois Poirié," in *Is It Righteous to Be?*, 69.

79 See "In the Name of the Other," in *Is It Righteous to Be?*, 198: "I take worship seriously, because those venerable gestures maintain and exalt man's humanity"; see also 258.

ETHICS AND EDUCATION

Judaism's most important role, however, is educational. If read properly, the Bible and the Talmud teach ethics and responsibility, that austere humanism. What is Levinas's hermeneutical method, and what are its products?

The Bible, the Talmud, and other Jewish texts are not the sole resources for teachings about the interhuman and ethical responsibility; ethical education is not restricted to translating Hebrew into Greek. This obvious point is well worth underscoring. Levinas takes Shakespeare, Dostoevsky, Pushkin, and many others to be valuable sources concerning the primacy of the ethical and the social.[80] Jewish and Hebrew texts may be exemplary and especially useful, but they are hardly unique. Like such fiction and poetry, religious texts can be shown to feature Levinas's ethical themes, and Jewish ones, on his reading, teach these themes everywhere, with nuance and conviction, although they are but one among many such resources. Nonetheless, because these themes *pervade* the Bible and its commentaries, and because they are the featured core, on his view, of that entire literary tradition, Levinas takes Hebrew and Hebrew literature to be virtually synonymous with awareness of the central ethical obligation to others.[81] Hence, as he often says, Jews have the responsibility to teach the Greek West to speak Hebrew. Jews, that is, must first learn what their own texts mean and then communicate that meaning to others, that is, to teach it to the world.[82]

The texts, preeminently the Bible and the Talmud, are not theological. Levinas is concerned primarily with the nonlegal or Aggadic passages, precisely those that thinkers like Fackenheim have taken to be theological.[83] For Levinas, however, even these passages are philosophical and not

[80] It is tempting to compare Levinas's engagement with Jewish texts – as well as with Shakespeare, Dostoevsky, and others – with Cavell's engagement with Shakespeare and Hollywood films. For the latter, see Anthony J. Cascardi, "'Disowning Knowledge': Cavell on Shakespeare," in Eldridge (ed.), *Stanley Cavell*, 190–205, especially 194: "... Cavell's work on Shakespeare shifts the ground of the analysis of tragedy [from action] to the questions of knowledge and doubt, which in turn point to the problems of acknowledgment and avoidance" and "the moral of skepticism." Similarly, one might say, Levinas's reading of the Talmud shifts the ground of the analysis from theology and law to what he calls the ethical, the primary responsibility of human social existence. On Dostoevsky's influence, see Val Vinokur, *The Trace of Judaism* (Northwestern University Press, 2008), Chapters 1 and 2.

[81] See Levinas, *Ethics and Infinity*, 117.

[82] See Putnam, "Levinas and Judaism," in *The Cambridge Companion to Levinas*, 45–53; and Jill Robbins, *Prodigal Son/Elder Brother*, Chapter 4. See also Cohen, Gibbs, and Handelman.

[83] See Cohen, *Ethics, Exegesis and Philosophy*, 217; Emil Fackenheim, *God's Presence in History*, Chapter 1; and Morgan (ed.), *The Jewish Thought of Emil Fackenheim*.

theoretical or ideological. Indeed, the legal passages also disclose, on careful reading, a philosophical core, the primacy of the ethical and responsibility.[84] And the task of the skilled interpreter is to unearth that core, to translate it into Greek – the language of Western philosophy – and then to communicate it, on the model of the original Greek translations of the Bible, the Septuagint.[85] Earlier we discussed how we must understand this effort at speaking about the face-to-face in a language not suited to it. Here what I want to emphasize is that Hebrew, in order to be understood, must be translated. This is what study requires, both the exploration that discloses the core meaning of the texts and the communication of that teaching in everyday terms.[86]

Furthermore, the real outcome of this process, and in fact the core that Jewish texts teach, is not a new theory, even an ethical one, but rather ethical action itself. The product of exegesis, in other words, is not a new interpretation of these old texts but rather a way of life that is aware of human responsibility and acts on behalf of others. Exegesis is a just life.[87]

In order to explore these themes, let me look at two essays by Levinas, "On the Jewish Reading of Scripture" (1979) and "From Ethics to Exegesis" (1985).[88] My goal is to understand what Levinas takes the method and role of such reading to be, and especially what part it plays in Jewish life.

In "A Religion for Adults" (1957), Levinas calls the Bible in "its specifically Jewish physiognomy," by which he means the Bible as interpreted in the Talmud and generally in rabbinic commentaries, a "route" that leads from Jewish particularity to its universalism.[89] That universalism and its meaning are constituted by the "ethical relation," for, as he puts it, that relation is "not the corollary of the vision of God, it is that very vision."[90] Throughout the essay Levinas uses Biblical, Talmudic, and other rabbinic texts to express and articulate that central teaching. In "From Ethics to Exegesis" (1985), Levinas returns to this same theme. "The reality of Israel" – which we find in the material and historical content of Judaism's documents and practices – is a "formation and expression of the universal."[91] This universal is what he calls the ethical, responsibility

84 Robbins, *Prodigal Son/Elder Brother*, 105.

85 Ibid., 105, 115–116.

86 See Ibid., 125–129.

87 I think that this is one of the central claims that Richard Cohen makes in *Ethics, Exegesis and Philosophy*.

88 See also the Talmudic reading "The Translation of the Scripture," in *In the Time of the Nations*, 35–54.

89 Levinas, "A Religion for Adults," in *Difficult Freedom*, 13.

90 Ibid., 17.

91 Levinas, "From Ethics to Exegesis," in *In the Time of the Nations*, 109.

toward the other, a "structure or modality" that is "hidden beneath consciousness" and is exposed by means of a phenomenology "attentive to the horizons of consciousness."[92] The Bible and Talmudic, rabbinic literature express this hidden structure theologically and narratively. Levinas calls these texts and interpretations a "*figure* in which a primordial mode of the human is revealed, in which, before any theology and outside any mythology, God comes to mind."[93] Alternatively, "the entire Torah, in its minute descriptions, is concentrated in the 'Thou shalt not kill' that the face of the other signifies. …"[94] These texts, that is, express God's Torah in the *language of human beings*, that is, in theological and mythological terms. Exegesis or hermeneutics is the way in which this secret, the teaching of the ethical, is revealed and "ever renewed."[95] He calls such exegesis "a solicitation" and an "appeal" to the Talmud and rabbinic commentaries, on behalf of a sense of prophecy that precedes theology, a "difficult universality."[96]

Levinas claims that the Bible and the Talmud have always contained this central teaching. But I think that he would argue that Jewish readers have not always appreciated this fact or grasped this message. Nor have others heard it from Jewish readers. To hear the "prophetic word" is to hear, from within Judaism, "the wisdom of the commentary of the masters." But Jews and others in the West have read the texts differently, and the outcome is the twentieth century, with its horror and atrocity. Now, in an especially urgent way, we live in a time when the "past refuses to be forgotten – a past of world wars and the camps of the twentieth century: Concentration and Death. A past of the Passion of Israel under Adolf Hitler." In such a time, the prophetic word of the Bible and its commentaries needs to be heard. The task of exegesis, of a life of hearing the message of responsibility, is indeed urgent.[97]

Levinas's commitment to reading the Bible through the prism of rabbinic commentaries not only aligns him with traditional Jewish hermeneutics – a point emphasized, for example, by Susan Handelman; it also suggests a comparison to Gershom Scholem and a contrast with readers as diverse as Spinoza, on the one hand, and Martin Buber and Franz Rosenzweig, on the other.[98] For one thing, several of these readers see the

[92] Ibid.
[93] Ibid., 110.
[94] Ibid., 111.
[95] Ibid., 112.
[96] Ibid., 112–113.
[97] Ibid., 113.
[98] See Susan Handelman, *Fragments of Redemption*; and Morgan, *Interim Judaism*, Chapter 2.

biblical text and commentaries on it in terms of their relation to revelation. For Buber and Rosenzweig, for example, that revelation is an event of divine-human encounter that is pre-conceptual and pre-literal, so that the Bible itself is the record or repository of the first Hebrew and Jewish literary responses to the formative revelatory events that established the history and destiny of the Jewish people. These texts incorporate the earliest articulations of the Jewish understanding of what a meaningful human life would be historically and what its character and goals should be. The aim of contemporary readers, then, should be to recover that pristine formulation and its content and to grasp what it means for Jewish life today. This recovery requires a reading that seeks to return to the text itself and its central teachings, which, for Buber and Rosenzweig, concern the shaping of genuine communities grounded in interpersonal love and concern. Buber privileges the biblical text and castigates the rabbinic commentaries, especially the tradition of Halakhic literature, as a later distortion of the original message. Hence, he calls for a return to the text itself in all its pristine purity, read in its original language. For very different reasons, Spinoza also denigrates rabbinic commentaries and calls for a return to the Bible itself, but his reading is not an attempt to disclose the original articulation of the meaning of a founding revelation. Rather, it is an effort to disclose the central, universal ethical teaching of the text by using historical-political and scientific methods to distinguish this abiding moral message from the historical contexts and personal rhetorical features that incorporate it.

Scholem, by contrast, rejects the Buberian commitment to a founding pre-linguistic revelation and the attack of Buber and Spinoza on traditional rabbinic interpretations. For him, and for his friend Walter Benjamin, the revelation itself is linguistic, and the Torah is not a response to it as much as it is its unique literary form. The vast legacy of commentaries and readings that constitute Jewish textuality is the bridge, the mediation, between every contemporary reader and that original revealed, divine, unique linguistic revelation. To recover that origin requires reading it through the layers and perspectives of that tradition, whether normative and rabbinic or non-normative and kabbalistic.[99]

Levinas's hermeneutics – its overall structure and its method – shares something with the readership of Buber, Rosenzweig, Spinoza, Scholem, and Benjamin. It also, of course, shares something with the method of

[99] See Morgan, *Interim Judaism*, Chapter 2; and Scholem, "Revelation and Tradition as Religious Categories in Judaism," in *The Messianic Idea in Judaism*.

traditional Talmudic interpretation.[100] Like them, he treats the Bible as basic and as the source of Jewish or Hebrew spirituality. But unlike Buber and Spinoza, he does not reject the vast textual tradition that stems from and reacts to the Bible; he respects it and studies it, especially the Talmud. As do Scholem, Benjamin, and the traditional readers, Levinas affirms the importance of rabbinic Judaism, "the oral tradition of exegesis which crystallized in the Talmud and its commentaries," which gives the Bible what he calls its "specifically Jewish physiognomy."[101] Without this tradition, the Bible is many books with many teachings. With it, the Bible pronounces and proclaims *one* message. In this regard, Levinas is most like Spinoza, whose momentous and important development of a historical reading of Scripture served to isolate and elevate the Bible's central ethical core, the obligation to act generously and justly, to love one's neighbor as oneself.[102] To be sure, Levinas casts his own reading of the Bible, the Talmud, and rabbinic Judaism as a teaching of ethics, as a traditional Jewish reading, and as what monotheism truly means. Ironically, it is a Spinozist content poured into an orthodox Jewish form, and in a bold, if not surprising, statement Levinas call the primacy of the ethical the Bible's "prophetic" teaching.[103]

Unlike these readers, however, Levinas was not really a theorist. He showed no interest in hermeneutics as a study of methods of interpretation. We have no treatise from him, like Gadamer's *Truth and Method*, nor essays like those of Buber and Rosenzweig.[104] Most of all, what we have – famously – are a series of readings, primarily of Talmudic texts and also of other Jewish writings. In fact, Levinas invested a great deal of himself in these readings, in learning and refining a way of reading the Talmud, and then in the actual readings themselves, which cover a period of at least thirty years, from 1960 to 1989.[105] Others have written about these

[100] Levinas often recalls his studies with the Talmudic genius Chouchani in the late 1940s and early 1950s; it is the method Chouchani taught him that Levinas employs in his Talmudic lessons. See Samuel Moyn, "Emmanuel Levinas's Talmudic Readings: Between Tradition and Invention," *Prooftexts* 23:3 (Fall 2003), 338–364.

[101] Levinas, "A Religion for Adults," in *Difficult Freedom*, 13; see also *Is It Righteous to Be?*, 275. See Cohen, *Ethics, Exegesis and Philosophy*, 243. For an excellent treatment of the rabbinic tradition, see Jay Harris, *How Do We Know This?* (SUNY Press, 1995).

[102] See Spinoza, *Theological-Political Treatise*. Cohen discusses Spinoza and compares him to Levinas in *Ethics, Exegesis and Philosophy*.

[103] See *Is It Righteous to Be?*, 283–285; and *Otherwise than Being*, 140–152.

[104] See Hans Gadamer, *Truth and Method*; Martin Buber and Franz Rosenzweig, *Scripture and Its Translation*; see also *Is It Righteous to Be?*, 161: "I have no rule for interpretation."

[105] Robert Gibbs gives a complete list of the published readings, from Levinas's annual presentations at the meetings of French Jewish intellectuals; see *Correlations*, 175. All but two have been

readings, especially the Talmudic lessons that he gave annually during these years, and there is no need to do so here, nor is there the space to discuss them properly.[106] But on two occasions his readings shed important light on the role and character of such textual interpretations.

READING JEWISH TEXTS

In the 1979 essay "On the Jewish Reading of Scriptures," Levinas seeks "to illustrate, by examples, certain ways of reading" the Bible within traditional Jewish texts.[107] Here Levinas elicits from traditional texts themselves insights about how to read those very texts and the Bible, of which they are themselves exegesis; this results in an "exegesis of the exegesis," as he calls it, a reading of a "commentary of the Scriptures" that "can take us on the path towards transcendence," that is, toward "the epiphany of God … involved in the human."[108] In the end, moreover, this reading requires "modern language" and reference to "the problems of today," to which these texts testify.[109] Let me say something here about this requirement.

The text Levinas looks at is Tractate Makkoth of the Babylonian Talmud, page 23b.[110] The issue in the text is whether flogging inflicted as a punishment by a court can affect the subject's atonement concerning his or her being excluded from eschatological rewards, which is a divine judgment. That is, can the result of a human act annul one of divine judgment?[111] Levinas says that his goal is to locate the "meaning" hidden behind and within the "antiquated language" of the text in its own "specific universe." To accomplish this goal requires raising "the anachronisms and local colour" like a curtain. He calls this concreteness and the way it hides generalities and meanings "the paradigmatic modality of Talmudic reflection."[112] Reading requires locating what is hidden behind that concreteness.

translated into English. In addition, Levinas gave regular Talmudic lessons while he was director of the Ecole in Paris.

106 For discussion, see the Introduction to *Nine Talmudic Lessons*; Robbins, *Prodigal Son/Elder Brother*; Wyshogrod, *Emmanuel Levinas*; Wright, *The Twilight of Jewish Philosophy*; and Handelman, *Fragments of Redemption*.

107 Levinas, "On the Jewish Reading of Scriptures," in *Beyond the Verse*, 101.

108 Ibid., 101, 102, 112.

109 Ibid., 102.

110 This text is also discussed in Levinas, *New Talmudic Readings*, translated by Richard Cohen, 47–77; the lesson is from 1974.

111 Ibid.

112 Levinas, "On the Jewish Reading of Scriptures," in *Beyond the Verse*, 103.

Levinas then reads the text and in the course of his reading shows how its meaning concerns the primacy of the face of the other and of responsibility, how it concerns "transcendence and height," and how it relates to the word "God."[113] Hence, as he puts it,

> the statement commented upon exceeds what it originally wants to say; that what it is capable of saying goes beyond what it wants to say; that it contains more than it contains; that perhaps an inexhaustible surplus of meaning remains locked in the syntactic structures of the sentence, in its word-groups, its actual words, phonemes and letters, in all this materiality of the saying which is potentially signifying all the time. Exegesis would come to free, in these signs, a bewitched significance that smoulders beneath the characters or coils up in all this literature of letters.[114]

Throughout this summation, the text in question is the Bible and the Talmudic comments, and the exegesis is the rabbinic exegesis of the Bible and Levinas's exegesis of the Talmud. But primarily the text is the Bible and the exegesis the Talmud and rabbinic commentaries.

Levinas asks: what makes the book divine, sacred? What is its "signature?" His answer concerns its "inspired" content, not its form. The divinity of the Bible derives from its inner meaning, from the meaning that "beckons" to a hearing that listens beyond the words, that "awakens" a genuine listening to the "meaning of meanings, to the face of the other man."[115] The Bible is sacred, and has its special status, because it disturbs our everyday, customary understanding and grips us with the call to a realization of our responsibility to others. Its message is its medium or at least its significance. For others, from traditional Jewish readers to those like Buber and even Scholem, the Bible is sacred because it is revealed, or it is taken to be sacred because it is either taken to be revealed or taken to be an original response to revelation and thus grounded in revelation. And in all these cases, revelation is an event of divine-human encounter or divine-human communication. For Levinas, on the contrary, the voice that speaks to the reader through the words of the Bible is the voice of suffering and responsibility; the Bible articulates the meaning of the other's face, and that is what makes it divine or why the reader should take it to be so. Even when the Bible does not use the word "God," as in the Book of Esther, there is this ethical awakening when the "ontological rest of being" is "torn and sobered up."[116] For Levinas, the status and

113 Ibid., 103–107.
114 Ibid., 109; see also 110–111.
115 Ibid., 111.
116 Ibid., 112.

authority of the text derive from its message and not from its origin or source.

The *right* reading of the Bible, then, responds to its call by listening and by hearing its message, to respond to the face. As Levinas would have it, Talmudic and rabbinic commentary, in *its* listening and responding, in *its* exegesis, confirms to today's reader the central meaning of the Bible. Indeed, we might say, each act of exegesis, when it reveals various modalities of that central ethical message, confirms, through an act of listening that is also an act of reading, the voice that speaks through the texts and to the reader.

But is this the right reading? Indeed, might this transcendence not be just the outcome of "man's interiority, his creativity or subconscious?"[117] This is an obvious criticism, what Levinas calls a "modern-day resistance." The objection is that his reading might be just his own subjective response to the text. Such a criticism goes to the heart of Levinas's worry about totality and idealism. He sees this: he paraphrases the question, about whether his reading takes the Bible and Talmud to disclose transcendence, as a general question about ethics itself. He asks: "is not ethics basically autonomous?" Let us be clear. Levinas is not asking about whether *any* reading can be said to be the right one;[118] rather, he is asking about whether *his* reading can be the right one. Does the *text itself* appreciate this objection, that there is *no transcendence*, and respond to it or anticipate it? Levinas thinks that it does. The text juxtaposes two views, one that reason is sufficient and the other that along with reason, divine judgment intervenes. According to one view, reason is solely human; according to the other, it is human and also divine. Yet, while tradition records that the latter is retained, the former rejected, both are "written down." That is, as Levinas puts it, the text may appear to retain an ambiguity, and "would not the man of today [i.e., today's reader] recognize in this ambiguity the alternating movements of his own thought?"[119] Today's reader may take the texts, the Bible and its commentaries, either with Levinas's openness to an ethical spirituality or with the stepticism of historians and philologists who seek to naturalize and demystify them. The text itself calls on us at least to alternate back and forth, to take it to be open to transcendence or to be closed to it. Its ambiguity would result in an "alternation" of perspectives that can be hesitant and incredulous but that also can be open – awaiting

[117] Ibid., 113.

[118] Levinas may think that tradition supports his reading as the most likely one, but he has no argument for there being only *one* correct reading. See *Is It Righteous to Be?*, 164.

[119] Levinas, "On the Jewish Reading of Scriptures," in *Beyond the Verse*, 114.

a hermeneutic, as he puts it.[120] The text does not guarantee that Levinas's reading is correct, but it does itself acknowledge its possibility, and it even encourages an openness to it. The Talmud, in this light, is not dogmatic. It underscores the possibility of its own receptivity.

This is a valuable conclusion, one that is all the more appealing because it is not dogmatic but rather open and even suggestive. Levinas realizes that our culture and our language are unavoidable features of our lives. The Bible and the Talmud cannot call upon us to reject them totally, nor should they call upon us to read these texts reductively and narrowly. And once we realize that the ethical teaching he calls "transcendence" is unavoidable, we can see the case it makes for its significance and how the texts in their own way disclose that case. The alternating of readings matches the fact that in life both transcendence and totality are unavoidable; we ought to appreciate that our social life is grounded in responsibility but also that it requires language, thought, argument, theory, institutions, principles, and policies. Philology is as necessary as the third party and the practices of justice.

TRANSLATING THE BIBLE AND THE TALMUD

We noted earlier that for Levinas our contemporary readers require a "modern language" that calls attention to the "problems of today."[121] He also notes that the Bible and Talmud couch their teachings in an ancient vocabulary and in concrete issues of a bygone culture. The point of these requirements is that transcendence is revealed in texts in language, and if Hebrew is more attuned to expose it, our modern language surely is not. For that we need translation, a translation of Hebrew into Greek – of the ancient texts into modern terms – and even more fundamentally of the grounds of the ethical into language itself. Levinas's best account of this issue is the Talmudic lesson "The Translation of the Scripture."[122]

The lesson deals with passages from the Tractate Megillah (8b and 9a–9b), and its subject is the question "whether or not [Jewish religious] law authorizes the translation of the very verses in which it is framed, and thus the presentation of the Scriptures, the Hebrew text of the tradition, in a foreign language, without compromising their dignity and spiritual significance."[123] Levinas takes the Greek language to represent European

[120] Ibid., 115.

[121] Ibid., 102.

[122] Levinas, "The Translation of the Scripture," in *In the Time of the Nations*, 33–54; see Gibbs, *Correlations*, 164–167.

[123] Levinas, "The Translation of the Scripture," in *In the Time of the Nations*, 36.

and Western civilization, the domain of theory, of the everyday, and of the shapes of consciousness that life takes for us.[124] To learn from the Bible and its commentaries requires exploring it in our own terms, relating it to modern problems, and hence translating its stories, motifs, and figures into our language, what "Greek" stands for.[125]

The lesson is about what the Talmud itself says about such a translation of Hebrew spirituality into Greek terms. Can it be done? Does it sacrifice the meaning of the original or distort it? The text refers to the legend about the origin of the Septuagint, the first Greek translation of the Pentateuch; Levinas claims that for all its fantastical character and "anecdotal value ... [the story] contains a truth independent of its historical reality and is a teaching ... [whose] truth is what interests us."[126]

Let me attend only to the central points that Levinas makes. First, the Talmud, as so often, records contending views. There are those who hold a "universalist stance, which recommends a 'translatable Judaism,' open to the language of the nations" without losing its sacred, that is, ethical, character, and there are those who claim that "there is no universal meaning of Judaism separable from the traditional forms. An untranslatable Judaism."[127] Second, the text distinguishes between "cult and culture," as Levinas puts it, between the books and the universal teaching of Judaism, on the one hand, and the "unalterable Judaism ... of the synagogue" with its ceremony and ritual. The latter is untranslatable and internal; the former is "a Judaism open to modernity."[128] Third, there is something unique about the "exceptional relationship between biblical wisdom and Greek."[129] The Torah retains its sacred character when translated into Greek; there is a sense in which "rabbinic Judaism wishes to be a part of Europe."[130] Levinas calls this an "assimilation into Europe" but only "up to a point," an "alliance between the Hebrew and the Greek Bible, [an]

[124] See *Is It Righteous to Be?*, 161; Gibbs, *Correlations*, 156–157.

[125] Indeed, the deeper issue is whether the face-to-face can be "translated" into language at all. Is it or is it not beyond expressibility altogether? See Michael L. Morgan, *Discovering Levinas* (Cambridge, 2007), Chapter 10.

[126] Levinas, "The Translation of the Scripture," in *In the Time of the Nations*, 38.

[127] Ibid., 40, 41.

[128] Ibid., 44.

[129] Ibid., 47.

[130] Ibid., 48. The problem of translation is closely related to the relationship between totality or ontology and infinity or ethics. I have tried to show that for Levinas, they are dimensions of one human life, so to speak. There is no infinity without totality; infinity is the most fundamental dimension of ordinary life. Hence, the central teaching of the Bible, its Hebrew message, must be translated into Greek, the language of the everyday. We shall say more about these issues shortly.

assimilation – that page 9b of the Megillah 'authorizes' by relating the miracle of the agreement of the seventy-two translators."[131]

Fifth, this assimilation, this alliance and translation, is limited. It exists but only "up to a point." The Talmud records, and Levinas discusses, fifteen cases where the Septuagint, the Greek, "corrects" and does not strictly translate the Hebrew. The point of these corrections, Levinas claims, is to show that "there is a domain of the untranslatable at the heart of the Pentateuch itself." Why? In some cases, he argues, the corrections are made for historical or political reasons; they are intentional alterations to avoid confusion or misreading or worse. But in other cases, the corrections reveal what he calls "more subtle reflections." In certain texts, the literal meaning calls out for interpretation, and gives rise to *midrash* and a tradition of interpretation. The written meaning is elaborated by a tradition of reading. Hence, translating the Torah into Greek can be a "trial" that exposes moments when the written text cannot or ought not be grasped without that tradition. It is a challenge to the biblical teaching to "welcome" Western philosophy and culture, while exalting its own "genius." Translation, that is, is not simple or easy; it marks a task: how to communicate to modern culture this ancient teaching and yet to maintain one's integrity, to know when "correction" is necessary or expedient and when it is impossible.[132]

Finally, "perhaps also [the Bible] *must* be translated into Greek."[133] Greek brings with it clarity. It brings method; it deciphers, demystifies, demythologizes, and depoeticizes. It is the heart of our academic discourse; it is conceptual and prosaic. And these functions, as Levinas hints, are necessary for the Bible and its ethical core. Without them, the message may remain hidden, elusive, and obscure. It may be a risk to translate the Bible, but without taking that risk, there is no hope of learning what it teaches and living by it.

For Levinas, there is something about the face-to-face that is transcendent and hence beyond linguistic expression; the face as trace, as the epiphany of what is beyond being, of the absolutely absent, is somehow beyond thought and expressibility. There is at least an analogue between that problem and the question of translating the Hebrew Bible into Greek discourse. Indeed, it may be that the problem is more than an analogue; it may be the original, founding case of such a translation question.[134]

131 Ibid., 48–49.
132 Ibid., 51–52; for Levinas's comments, see *Is It Righteous to Be?*, 274–275.
133 Levinas, "The Translation of the Scripture," in *In the Time of the Nations*, 52.
134 For an excellent discussion of the text, see Robert Gibbs, *Correlations*, 164–167.

"Greek" stands for theoretical discourse but also for the ordinary language of everyday life; it stands, that is, for all the ways in which we normally articulate, describe, or express our everyday interpersonal relations. By extension, it stands for the ways in which our relationships are lived and conducted. Moreover, we live in these articulable relations, and to the degree that we recognize our responsibility for the other person and seek to realize it, we do so through these relations and in everyday social acts. As we have so often argued, the ethical and the everyday are not alternative ways of relating to others, as if we could choose to live only in exclusively ethical relations. The problem we face is whether and to what degree we are aware of our responsibilities and whether and to what degree we live our relations with others as responsive to them, out of acknowledgment, acceptance, and respect. Hence, just as the face-to-face *requires* everyday life, so Hebrew, the mode of thought that identifies our responsibility, *requires* Greek, the mode of thought and discourse that gives responsibility its expression. In a sense, when it comes to our discourse and thought, Hebrew is the *content*, while Greek is the *form*. Neither can do without the other or does do without the other. This may not be exactly right, but it is close: it is at least true that there is no Hebrew without Greek, and that no Greek is genuinely meaningful without Hebrew.

In the case of the Bible, the Talmud, rabbinic commentaries, and other Jewish texts, there is a chain of tradition, of exegesis and reinterpretation that is marked by renewal and recovery. There is, as I mentioned earlier, a homogeneity or continuity that unites that tradition as an enunciation and elaboration of a core teaching. That continuity confirms the reading and, increasingly, the correctness of it.[135] But there are needs – social, political, and even internal and interpretive – for opening those texts and that tradition to the rest of life, to Greek language and Western culture. The risks are obvious. In this Talmudic lesson Levinas spends more time on the benefits, as plentiful internally as externally. He affirms the particularity and the universality of Judaism. Translation is a bridge between them, a major one but not the only one. It is one vehicle for the educational role of Judaism in Western culture and today in modern culture. As we have pointed out, the suffering of the Jewish people, as a barometer of the failings of civilization, is one dimension of that educational role. A more positive dimension is the role of teacher, of educating others through the exegesis of the Bible and rabbinic texts, of preaching the word

[135] On this issue of objectivity, see Wright, *The Twilight of Jewish Philosophy*, 164–169; there are many readings – *Is It Righteous to Be?*, 164; Cohen, *Ethics, Exegesis and Philosophy*, 257–258.

in the "language of humankind."[136] Indeed, when we ask ourselves how Levinas conceives his own role as a philosopher, as a Jew, and as an ethical agent, education about responsibility and justice is certainly of central importance.

MESSIANIC ESCHATOLOGY, ETHICS, AND POLITICS

The ultimate goal of such reading and of Jewish life, indeed of all life, is to feed the hungry and clothe the naked, to reduce suffering and practice justice. Levinas sees this goal or task or responsibility as akin to ethics and politics, to be sure, but his favored expressions for it, as a goal, are religious and Jewish. He calls it "messianism" and "prophetic eschatology." He also calls it "peace."[137]

Many of the biblical motifs and much of the Hebraic vocabulary – from "election" and even "face" to "glory," "holiness," and "prophecy" – that Levinas appropriates have many purposes, among them to signal the close association he sees between ethics and human responsibility and all that we call "religious." In the twentieth century and certainly from Weimar through the postwar period, as philosophy and Western culture have become increasingly "disenchanted" and secularized, this terminology and these motifs have taken on a very restricted venue. To transport them into philosophical discourse was and remains a challenging, surprising, and even shocking accomplishment, and it is safe to think that Levinas knew exactly how dramatic it was and what risks he ran in so doing. On the one hand, he could easily have been misunderstood as abandoning philosophy altogether for some kind of parochial or even confessional stance. Indeed, he has often been misread in just this way. On the other, he could have simply been dismissed as misguided or anachronistic or both. We could take one of these attitudes and find many sympathetic readers, but I am inclined to be more charitable and to take Levinas to be saying something important about religious life, morality, everyday experience, and philosophy and to be seeking a new perspective on all of them. Levinas is no reductionist, no Spinoza or Kant or Hegel. But just as he feels that religion harbors something of importance, so he believes that philosophy needs religious resources in order to call attention to its most important teaching.[138]

[136] See Wright, *The Twilight of Jewish Philosophy*, 141–169; she gives a reading of "The Translation of the Scripture" on pp. 149–156; see also Wyschogrod, *Emmanuel Levinas*, 168–171.

[137] See, for example, Levinas, *Totality and Infinity*, 22–26, 304–307; see also 149–152.

[138] Hermann Cohen, more than a century ago, claimed that a neo-Kantian ethics required the biblical idea of "messianism," without which it would not be complete. Fackenheim argues for

Levinas's use of the expressions "eschatology" and "messianism," however, occurs in a more complex context. These terms, in the twentieth century and especially in German and continental thought, have not been so narrowly restricted to religious or theological venues. From the beginning of the century and certainly after World War I, they have been widely employed by philosophers, poets, social and cultural critics, literary theorists and critics, political thinkers, and historians. Levinas's work emerges out of modernist culture, and the discourse of messianism and redemption was a prominent feature of that culture. From Simmel, Buber, Rilke, and Kafka to Bloch, Benjamin, Kracauer, Adorno, Lukács, and Rosenzweig, reflection on the fragmentation and nihilism of Western civilization, on alienation and a crisis of values, was mixed with new ways of thinking about history, hope, and the messianic.[139] Levinas's appropriation of this vocabulary, then, was not idiosyncratic. As in the case of many others, moreover, his use of the terms and his interpretation of them arose out of both philosophical reflection and Jewish sensibility.

We might be confused, as we approach Levinas on messianism, about what issues concerning this idea and this theme interest him. There are a host of questions that he, or we, might find difficult and worth exploring. What is the relation between the messianic and history? Is there a messianism without teleology or some narrative view of history? How is the messianic related to human conduct, to divine action, or to both? What is the character of the messianic? What kind of a state or condition is it? Is the messianic an object of hope or a task to be accomplished? Do we live in a period after the "end of messianism" and the "demise of eschatology?" What is the nature of "messianic peace"? What is the relationship between time and the messianic?[140]

Levinas's messianism is not necessarily associated (and perhaps not at all) with a linear or teleological account of history. In his fragments on the concept of history, Walter Benjamin articulated an episodic, discontinuous conception of the messianic and associated it with traditional Jewish messianism, albeit according to his own, somewhat eccentric interpretation.

the contribution Judaism can make to philosophy in *Encounters between Judaism and Modern Philosophy* and *To Mend the World.*

139 For discussion of these features of Weimar culture and their impact throughout the twentieth century, see Morgan, *Interim Judaism*; Anson Rabinbach, *In the Shadow of Catastrophe*; and Michael Löwy, *Redemption and Utopia*.

140 In the last section of this chapter I will turn to Levinas's discussion of Zionism and, in terms of it, his views on messianism and the political. For now, however, I focus on issues that are relatively independent of his account of Zionism and politics. See also Theodore de Boer, "Beyond Being, Ontology and Eschatology in the Philosophy of Emmanuel Levinas," in *The Rationality of Transcendence*, Chapter 2, 33–55.

As I have suggested, Levinas might usefully be viewed as part of that tradition of messianic reflection that developed before and after World War I. Some of these figures were religious anarchists, some socialists, some antipolitical, others political through and through. Their thinking was regularly tied to some narrative about the decline of Western civilization and a crisis of values, and each in his or her own way proposed a solution, through revolution, art, religion, or some combination of them, or proposed that the times were apocalyptic and beyond redemption. Benjamin, in current discussion, is a core member of this tradition, along with Bloch, Lukács, Rosenzweig, and a host of others – Buber, Scholem, Spengler, Heidegger, and Landauer among them.[141] Many, but not all, were secular or religious Jews, whose thinking achieved a synergy of traditional Jewish messianic ideas with post-Hegelian and Neo-Romantic idealism, and who challenged the ideal of *Bildung*, of bourgeois progress and optimism, and of the alignment of Judaism with this German idealism.[142]

In an outstanding essay on this "new Jewish sensibility," Anson Rabinbach characterizes it as a "modern Jewish messianism: radical, uncompromising, and comprised of an esoteric intellectualism that is as uncomfortable with the Enlightenment as it is enamored of apocalyptic visions – whether revolutionary or purely redemptive in the spiritual sense."[143] The central feature of this view was a novel view of messianism, which, according to Rabinbach, "demanded a complete repudiation of the world as it is, placing its hope in a future whose realization can only be brought about by the destruction of the old order." It was a vision that was "apocalyptic, catastrophic, utopian, and pessimistic."[144] It was about recognizing the fragmentation and alienation of society and envisioning a recovery of its wholeness only through destruction, about a new view of European culture and politics.[145]

In his essay Rabinbach explores the messianic thinking of Bloch, Benjamin, and a number of others, and he concludes that Benjamin, for one, formulates a view that is apocalyptic, that rejects normal politics and "historical activism" in favor of an esoteric, redemptive intellectualism, and that is genuinely anarchic and radically utopian.[146] For Benjamin the

141 See Michael Löwy, *Redemption and Utopia*; and Richard Wolin, *The Frankfurt School Revisited.*

142 See Rabinbach, *In the Shadow of Catastrophe*, 27–28.

143 Rabinbach, "Between Apocalypse and Enlightenment: Benjamin, Bloch, and Modern German-Jewish Messianism," in *In the Shadow of Catastrophe*, Chapter 1, 27–65, especially 28; originally published in *New German Critique* 34 (Winter 1985).

144 Rabinbach, *In the Shadow of Catastrophe*, 29, 30.

145 Ibid., 29.

146 See ibid., 62–65.

redemption of Western culture from fascism will involve a destructive leap and a rupture, and furthermore it will not be the result of historical and political activism. Rather, it will require episodic revelations of the cause and character of urgencies and danger and subsequent response to such "knowledge." That knowledge is got by genuine historical inquiry, that of the literary critic, who "establishes a conception of the present as the 'time of the now' which is shot through with chips of Messianic time."[147] And that redemption occurs in order to make that present instant – *any* present – messianic, "for every second of time was the strait gate through which the Messiah might enter."

For Levinas, prophetic eschatology and messianism, although not apocalyptic and catastrophic, are similarly redemptive and episodic or momentary.[148] They are the ethical as it occurs at any moment in acts of responsibility, of kindness and generosity (or ethical acts that are as pure as one could imagine, given the situation).[149] And they are the ethical when it transforms social practice and political policy into justice. Levinas is not apocalyptic, nor is he intellectualist, but he is redemptive and utopian. In some ways, moreover, like Benjamin, he conceives of the messianic as outside the historical and the political, if we take them to be constructed according to traditional narratives. But in other ways, Levinas does not reject social and political institutions as much as he fears their corruption and appreciates the extraordinary failures of Western civilization, particularly in the twentieth century. He does not despair; he retains some hope, but only if individuals can understand their infinite responsibilities and if they can learn to live by them.[150] In his valuable essay "Different Styles of Eschatology: Derrida's Take on Levinas's Political Messianism," Robert Bernasconi calls attention to this nonteleological way in which Levinas takes the messianic to interrupt history: "Messianic eschatology is not a doctrine of last things. … The 'beyond history' is … that which interrupts history. … Eschatology in Levinas is not a question of the future, but a disturbance or interruption of the present."[151] Messianic peace and

[147] Walter Benjamin, "Theses on the Philosophy of History," in *Illuminations*, 265, 266; see also the recent translation "On the Concept of History," in *Walter Benjamin, Selected Writings, Volume 4, 1938–1940* (Harvard, 2003), 397.

[148] See Robert Bernasconi, "Different Styles of Eschatology: Derrida's Take on Levinas's Political Messianism," *Research in Phenomenology* 28 (1998), 7 and following.

[149] One thinks of the action of the Russian woman, described by Grossman in *Life and Fate*.

[150] There are times when Levinas has hopes of this kind for Marxism; see Simon Critchley, "Persecution before Exploitation: A Non-Jewish Israel?" *Parallax* 24 8,3 (July–September 2002), 71–77.

[151] Bernasconi, "Different Styles of Eschatology," 7.

prophetic eschatology are not teleological themes.[152] But they do involve human acts, acts of kindness and of justice.

LEVINAS'S ZIONISM

There are a number of perspectives one might take on Levinas's Zionist writings – in terms of their place in the tradition of Zionist thought within Judaism, their relationship to Western views of Judaism and politics, their relation to thinking about political institutions and ethical theory, and what they say that is related to traditional Jewish thinking about messianism and the Land of Israel. I do not want here to conduct a full-scale inquiry into Levinas's Zionist thinking in terms of these issues and more. Rather, I want to ask two questions: how does Levinas see the relationship between Jewish universalism with its central focus on the ethical and justice, on the one hand, and the State of Israel, on the other? And is there any connection between his conception of the ethical as messianic, as prophetic eschatology, and the Jewish state? In "Different Styles of Eschatology," Robert Bernasconi discusses these issues in the light of Levinas's three essays on Zionism collected in *Beyond the Verse*.[153]

In his early writings on the State of Israel, Levinas clearly claims that the State of Israel, to live up to the ideals of the state, should be religious, and this means that it must be committed to the "difficult and erudite work of justice." The land and the state are the venue and opportunity for the Jewish people to carry out its work, the "execution of justice." As Levinas puts it, the genuinely religious Jews are "those who seek to have a State *in order to have justice*"(my italics).[154] Levinas accepts the functional role of the political, of government, but sees it as requiring an ethical character. For Jews, then, the State of Israel is like a sculptor's marble or clay, to be shaped and molded in a way that exemplifies justice and generosity. The material itself is of no intrinsic value. It becomes valuable as the setting and opportunity for people to realize a society of justice and goodness.

But if the state is a necessary venue for Jews to engage in the practice of justice, it is not an unproblematic one, and Levinas is very clear about the

[152] See Levinas, *Totality and Infinity*, 22–23; see also "Revelation in the Jewish Tradition," in *Beyond the Verse*, 143.

[153] Bernasconi, "Different Styles of Eschatology," 12–16; Howard Caygill, *Levinas and the Political*, 170–198 and generally Chapter 5, 159–198.

[154] Levinas, "The State of Israel and the Religion of Israel," in *Difficult Freedom*, 216–220; compare Caygill, *Levinas and the Political*, 160–161.

dangers. The State of Israel could lapse into a nationalist program and take on the character of power politics. All states run this danger, and Israel, after the Holocaust, motivated by practical, political concerns as much as – and perhaps even more than – religious and moral ones, is surely not immune from such a lapse.[155] Ideally, the State of Israel was "the heir to the vocation of protecting 'Israel's ethics' that was previously undertaken by the reading of the Torah."[156] But the pressures, external and internal, on a modern state endangered this project; the state of Israel could easily "betray … its religious vocation to Israel. The risk that now emerges is … the destruction of Israel by the actions of the state of Israel."[157]

As Howard Caygill argues, this danger of corruption is explored in the essay "From the Rise of Nihilism to the Carnal Jew."[158] The risk is one of reducing Israel entirely "to political categories," to a form of political realism, and to forgetting the "eschatological dream" and sliding into "nihilism." For Levinas, the risk, that is, concerns "assimilation," becoming a state like others, without a sense of conscience. He calls this the difference between the Universal Israel – spiritual, ethical, seeking the truth of justice – and an Israel of Fact, that for all its reality risks abandoning its prophetic vocation.[159] Once again, Levinas takes the State of Israel as an opportunity and not an end in itself, and as an opportunity it can fail. It is at risk. Political practices can serve to realize justice, or they can ignore or impede it. As Caygill underlines, the core of Israel's opportunity is that it be "worthy of an ultimate sacrifice." Levinas then says: "The State of Israel, in this sense, constitutes the greatest event in modern Judaism."[160]

Caygill takes Levinas to mean that Israel bears the responsibility to sacrifice, but I am not sure that he has understood Levinas correctly. Levinas takes Israel's vocation, its destiny, to be its universalism. That is, Israel is like each and every nation; it is *chosen*. "Each nation worthy of the name is chosen" and has an "ability to carry out the common task. … Each nation must behave as though it alone had to answer for all."[161] Levinas calls this a limitation of "political sovereignty" on behalf of "moral sovereignty." This means being willing to die for an idea, and that is what the ideas of abnegation and sacrifice mean to Levinas. The State of Israel is

155 Caygill, *Levinas and the Political*, 162–166.

156 Levinas, *Beyond the Verse*, 9; see Caygill, *Levinas and the Political*, 164.

157 Caygill, *Levinas and the Political*, 164.

158 Ibid., 164–166; see Levinas, "From the Rise of Nihilism to the Carnal Jew," in *Difficult Freedom*, 221–225.

159 Levinas, "From the Rise of Nihilism to the Carnal Jew," in *Difficult Freedom*, 223–224.

160 Ibid., 225; compare "The State of Caesar and the State of David," in *Beyond the Verse*, 187.

161 Levinas, "From the Rise of Nihilism to the Carnal Jew," in *Difficult Freedom*, 224.

"the greatest event in modern Judaism" because it is the Jewish people's opportunity, as a people, to die for a principle, for justice. To Levinas, secular Jews, who have abandoned Judaism and its texts, do not see this opportunity or this task. Of course, not all Jews see it either. If the State of Israel, then, is modern Judaism's "greatest event," it is not because it gives Jews a chance to engage in power politics or to become imperialists or to fight for their own physical survival. It is because it gives Jews a chance to live socially and politically in accord with what responsibility and justice require, to live an ethical life as a society. In a twist, at the end of the essay, and perhaps in an incautious way, Levinas calls this responsibility for the other person Israel's – that is, the Jewish people's – "invisible universality," its "carnal essence," and "its innate predisposition to involuntary sacrifice, its exposure to persecution."[162] Its essence, that is, is to recognize its obligations to others, to realize concretely its "original responsibility." Its worldly persecutions are an emblem of its primordial persecution, which we know, for him, is its original ethical obligation and responsibility to and for others.

The Jewish state could become a total corruption of the ethical ideal. Becoming a political state is certainly a threat and could itself become an object of veneration and ultimate respect. Clearly Levinas opposes all such situations as distortions. But since social life and hence politics are necessary features of our lives, no matter how fully we must accommodate, still the genuine political goal ought to be to increase justice. This is true for all people and all states. It is especially true for the State of Israel insofar as the Jewish people's tradition carries the ethical message as the central feature of the Bible, the Talmud, and the commentaries as well. Caygill claims that this is one of the central lessons of Levinas's comments on the "messianic dream" in his Talmudic lessons, to illuminate "the State of Israel as bearing witness to the promise of a new kind of state."[163] He makes the nice point that investing in the political and pinning one's hopes on it might be a matter of making alliances with assassins – and hence of being "duped by morality."[164] But Levinas seems to realize that it is nonetheless worth the risk and even *necessary* to accept it. What is called for is vigilance.[165]

Politics is politics, but messianism is ethics. In "Space is Not One-Dimensional" (1968), reflecting on the French Jewish response to the Six

[162] Ibid., 225; compare "Space Is Not One-Dimensional," in *Difficult Freedom*, 263.
[163] Caygill, *Levinas and the Political*, 167.
[164] Ibid., 168.
[165] Ibid., 170–172.

Day War, Levinas says that what brings the "Reign of the Messiah closer" is not the fact of Israel's being a state "but because the men [sic] who inhabit it try to resist the temptations of politics … [and] because this state … embraces the teaching of the prophets."[166] Allegiance to Israel, then, by French Jews – and, by implication, by others as well – is allegiance to this prophetic, ethical, universal vocation and not just to another political entity.[167] It is not a matter of dual loyalty. Indeed, this is true even for those who care about Israel's Arab enemies. What holds for French Jews and for us all, the need to care most about justice and the other, holds, he says, for "you too, my Muslim friend, my unhated enemy of the Six-Day War!"[168] We will return to this theme of friends and enemies, but not until we have considered further the risks and dangers politics poses for the realization of ethics in political and social life.[169]

Levinas published *Beyond the Verse* in 1982. In the Foreword, he notes that the last three pieces, called collectively "Zionisms," deal explicitly with the relation between politics and ethics and with the conflict between Israelis and Arabs.[170] I want to look at the essays first with regard to the larger themes, the relation between politics and religion or ethics, the necessity of the political, and the risks of political corruption. "The State of Caesar and the State of David" was written in 1971 and, as Caygill notes, summarizes Levinas's thinking of the 1960s.[171] Levinas begins by discussing texts that acknowledge the need for the state. But, he says, "the State of Caesar, despite its participation in the pure essence of the State, is also the place of corruption *par excellence* and, perhaps, the ultimate refuge of idolatry."[172] Levinas does not, in concrete and analytic terms, spell out these corruptions. This is not his style, nor would such enumeration lend itself to the textual and interpretive tactics of the essays. We can nonetheless look for hints.

166 Levinas, "Space is Not One-Dimensional," in *Difficult Freedom*, 263–264.

167 Ibid., 264.

168 Ibid.

169 Critics might well take this to be apologetics and even disingenuous. But Levinas is a universalist, as we have seen, and one who takes the ethical as determinative for how one ought to live. Social, political, and economic institutions are necessary, but they do not deserve our most fundamental allegiance. Levinas's point here seems to be that loyalty to France is not in conflict with loyalty to Israel insofar as both should be vehicles to the same ultimate goal, the most just society possible. Indeed, as long as there is evidence that a given nation's heritage aspires to just and benevolent treatment of all people, both within and outside its domain, it deserves our allegiance. Without that evidence, one would be hard put to claim that the nation in question aspires to such a goal. It might represent a commitment to power and domination for its own sake.

170 Levinas, Foreword to *Beyond the Verse*, xv.

171 Caygill, *Levinas and the Political*, 170.

172 Levinas, "The State of Caesar and the State of David," in *Beyond the Verse*, 183.

For example, Levinas recognizes that according to certain Talmudic scholars, the form of the pagan state involves various features that are in tension with the messianic ideal: the state is jealous of its sovereignty; constantly seeks hegemony; is imperialist, totalitarian, and conquering; can be oppressive; and is attached to a realist egoism.[173] It seeks adoration and fidelity. Furthermore, the state is grounded in a contradiction; it "subordinat[es] some men to others in order to liberate them."[174] Thus, Levinas recognizes that all forms of government, even those grounded in a social contract, involve subordination of some by others and run the risk of oppression, domination, and persecution. "By serving the state, one serves repression; by serving repression, one becomes a member of the police force."[175] Domination and conflict are endemic to political life. If they can be mitigated or reduced, then the state and the lives of its citizens are bettered, but the risk is always present that they will not be mitigated. In social networks, justice can never be perfect, but it can be the plumb line for institutions, policies, and practices. When it is not, division and enmity dominate. Still, in public life, politics is required to organize and distribute, to protect and control, to act in behalf of goodness, and to facilitate acts of kindness and concern. Levinas notes that one does not save oneself by rejecting the political altogether, for the tension between freedom and exploitation is something "against which the very person who refuses the political order is not protected, since in abstaining from all collaboration with the ruling power, he makes himself party to the obscure powers that the State represses."[176]

At the end of the essay, Levinas calls attention to comments of Dan Avni-Segré, an Italian Jew teaching in Haifa, which he had heard at the IXth Colloquium of French Jewish intellectuals. Segré had discussed the infancy of Jewish politics in Israel and the hopes for the future; he had spoken of a "monotheistic politics" as the "culmination of Zionism" – a task "beyond the concern to ensure a refuge for those who are persecuted."[177] This messianic ideal of what, for Levinas, would be a just state marks out a place between corrupt power politics and a facile and careless moralism.[178] In 1971 it was one way of talking about what messianism could bring to politics in the Jewish state.

173 Levinas, "The State of Caesar and the State of David," in *Beyond the Verse*, 184. For me, there are resonances of Dostoevsky in these worries; see Frank, *Dostoevsky*, passim.

174 Levinas, "The State of Caesar and the State of David," in *Beyond the Verse*, 184.

175 Ibid.

176 Ibid.

177 Ibid., 187.

178 Ibid.

I do not think that Levinas's conception of messianism and politics is unique to Judaism and the State of Israel. Messianism involves all those commitments that are concerned with our responsibilities to others; it is about realizing ethics in our lives. Politics is about the institutions of organized social life that enable us to live together and with one another. Politics should have a messianic vision; it should be guided by ethical conscience and by the hope that its institutions and its citizens will live just lives. Messianism and politics are both unavoidable features of all of our lives.

In the life of the Jewish people and in Zionism, these ideas do operate in a specific way. For Levinas, the Bible and the Talmud often reflect on the engagement of the political and the messianic, and, after the Nazi destruction and with the establishment of the modern State of Israel, these issues have a precise, concrete reference. Israel is not a unique state in many ways, but it does arise with a great weight of historical specificity. Its challenges are not its alone.[179] But they are emblematic of what modern states ought to confront and ought to meet. On Levinas's reading, the Jewish people carries a special burden to enact its persecution through just institutions and, in the State of Israel, to embody them. Israel is the name of this people's return into history and, at the same time, of the political and messianic opportunities for us all.

For these reasons, the concrete problems that face Israel are of signal importance, and it is important to see how Levinas grapples with them. Here the central issue is how Levinas deals with engagement with the face of one's enemy, and this means how Israel ought to deal with her Arab neighbors in general and with the Palestinians in particular. As Caygill puts it, "if the State of Israel ignores human rights, then this means that through a brutal irony of history the prophetic mission of Israel becomes endangered by its own adoption of the form of the state."[180] The two major texts in which this challenge is most markedly faced, if at all, are "Politics After!" (1979) and the radio interview "Ethics and Politics" (1982), with Alain Finkelkraut.

Caygill argues that in these texts Levinas's judgment of the Palestinians and Arab nationalism is ambivalent.[181] At one point, commenting on "Politics After!," Caygill says that we have every right "to expect a more

[179] See the reference to "the society of Western countries, which remain faithful, after the horrors of Hitler, to the nostalgic longing for the Just City and a merciful justice," in *In the Time of the Nations*, 8.

[180] Caygill, *Levinas and the Political*, 174; see 186–194.

[181] Ibid., 186.

nuanced sense of historical development from Levinas, and a more explicit acknowledgment of the possibility that the past and present of the State of Israel is capable of ruining the promises of the future."[182] That is, Levinas may take politics to be necessary for ethical messianism and Israel to be historically devoted to creating a just social and political order, but no state is immune to corruption or failure, Israel included. Can Levinas recognize such a possibility? Even if the Holocaust recommends a special role for Jewish self-defense in Israel, surely, by Levinas's own very high standards, self-defense cannot be a blanket justification for all political practices, even repressive and horrific ones. As Caygill accurately points out, the issue came to a head for Levinas with the massacre of Palestinian refugees – men, women, and children – at the camps at Sabra and Shatila in September 1982.[183] In a radio conversation with Shlomo Malka and Alain Finkelkraut, less than two weeks after the events, Levinas was called upon to say something about responsibility and, to say the least, he was evasive. One wonders if there is significance even in this evasiveness.[184]

Levinas considers explicitly, in the Foreword to *Beyond the Verse* (1982), the question whether our passions and ideas are not at risk "in the purely political sense" if they are divorced "from their prophetic and ethical depths."[185] And, as I read him, he charges the Jewish people not to evade its responsibilities and moral conscience by claiming its status as chosen. It must, and hence Israel must, face the question: "Can we understand the suffering of others?"[186] Levinas notes that we cannot tolerate any weighing up of sufferings. Sufferings do not have discrete measures. Still, the Holocaust is a benchmark, a radical break – and the outcome of "a millenial history of outrages and tears, of permanent insecurity and of the shedding of real, warm blood." Levinas calls *this* "the concrete cause and real *raison d'etre* of Zionism," not, he says, domination and persecution. That is, Zionism is a movement to acknowledge Jewish suffering and reduce it. It is politics constituted to reach out to the afflicted, to the hurt, to the abandoned; it is about helping Jews and not oppressing others. What, however, will that require? What must be done in order for the State of Israel, in its situation, to protect Jews from suffering and to secure itself?

182 Ibid., 190.
183 See ibid., 190–194; compare Levinas, "Ethics and Politics," in *A Levinas Reader*, 289–297.
184 In tune with this critical spirit, Simon Critchley gives a brief sketch of the political problems that face Levinas; see his editor's introduction to *Parallax* 24, 1–3.
185 Levinas, Foreword to *Beyond the Verse*, xv.
186 Ibid., xvi.

Levinas says that Zionism is not about what Israel's neighbors do or ought to do; it is about "the necessity for the Jewish people, in peace with its neighbors, not to continue being a minority in its political structure."[187] This is not, Levinas adds, just a matter of "historical necessity" or of what we might call political expediency in order to guarantee Jewish survival. It is about recognizing that ethics as responsibility applies "*to me*, to the individual and the person that I am,"[188] but it cannot mean that in order to be ethical I must be willing to martyr myself. That is, I should not exclude, from the parameters of my ethical responsibility, those others who are close to me, my kin, my family: "those near to me are also my neighbors."[189] Some might take this to be callous and insensitive, but others might take this response to be sober. We should recall Bernard Williams's famous remark that a man whose wife is drowning and yet who deliberates about whether to save her or another person is guilty of having one thought too many.[190] In part, Williams is criticizing moral theory and warning against too much philosophizing. Levinas is clear that in the context of society, where we are responsible for everyone, judgments are necessary and hence accommodation, and to accommodate in favor of those close to you is, depending upon the situation, beyond reproach.[191] Without details, Levinas's comment, and the suggestion that the Palestinians may need to remain a minority and may not deferentially have *their* suffering reduced, may be difficult to appreciate fully. But the overall point is, I think, clear: that modern Zionism should remain ethical to the degree that it can, remembering its role for Jews in the aftermath of a history of enormous suffering and persecution and especially of the Holocaust.

Let me turn to "Politics After!," which is an overview of Zionism and a specific response to Anwar Sadat's peace initiative of 1977.[192] Levinas in this essay raises explicitly the problem that the conflict between Jews and Arabs is grounded in the fact that the state was created on land claimed by the Jewish people, yet "lived on for centuries by those who call themselves Palestinians, who are surrounded on all parts and over vast expanses by the great Arab people of which they are a part."[193] This is not, he claims, simply a "political" problem; there are moral and psychological features that need to be considered. Jews should "wish and hope for

[187] Ibid., xvii.
[188] Ibid.
[189] Ibid.
[190] Bernard Williams, "Persons, Character and Morality," in *Moral Luck*, 18.
[191] For a different critical attitude, see Caygill, *Levinas and the Political*, 189–190.
[192] See ibid., 190.
[193] Levinas, "Politics After!," in *Beyond the Verse*, 188.

a reconciliation between Jews and Arabs" and should "foresee it, above and beyond becoming peaceful neighbors, as a fraternal community."[194] Levinas, that is, sets a lofty moral goal, and he takes Sadat's trip to Jerusalem on November 19, 1977, as a momentous step on the way to realizing it. It is momentous because, for Levinas, it involved Sadat's recognizing the ethical character of anti-Semitism and of one's responsibility to the other. It was a realization of what is necessary for "social living itself,"[195] and in its own way an acknowledgment of all that Hitler and the death camps meant for ethical, social life. Zionism is an ethical and not a narrowly political movement, and hence the reconciliation of Jews and Arabs in the land is an ethical matter, rooted in the universalism of Zionism and its ethical core.[196]

In political terms, Zionism and the establishment of the modern Jewish state on a land already occupied may seem like nationalist imperialism, callous and belligerent. But Levinas takes its import to be ethical, to express an attempt to realize in fact a political-ethical society in behalf of all. It is not a matter of "an armed and dominating State … [pitted] against the unarmed Palestinian people whose existence Israel does not recognize." Rather, it is about Israel, "the most fragile, the most vulnerable thing in the world, in the midst of its neighbors, undisputed nations, rich in natural allies, and surrounded by their lands."[197] This is what makes Sadat's visit such an "exceptional transhistorical event. … For a moment, political standards and clichés were forgotten. … Cautiousness and precautions were forgotten. …"[198] No one knows whether Sadat saw Israel clearly, in its moral role. Levinas surely does not know; he wonders what Sadat sensed in Zionism, whether he grasped the opportunities and heard the "prophetic promises," whether he was aware that Israel could not live its vocation without a state and a land and yet "a State which will have to incarnate the prophetic moral code and the idea of its peace."[199] Nonetheless, regardless of his intentions, which may have been wholly political and diplomatic, Sadat provided an opportunity, "the suggestion that peace is a concept which goes beyond purely political thought." The peace Levinas has in mind, of course, is not merely the cessation of war; rather, it is the realization of a fundamental cooperation, of fraternity, mutual acceptance and concern.

194 Ibid., 189.
195 Ibid., 190.
196 Ibid., 191–192.
197 Ibid., 193.
198 Ibid.
199 Ibid., 193–194.

In this essay, then, Levinas does not raise the question what Israel should do vis-à-vis its Arab neighbors, the occupied territories, and its Palestinian citizens, at least not in any explicit way. He assumes that every Jew, every Israeli Jew, should want reconciliation and peace with these groups. What he does, instead of asking what *should* have been done, is to characterize what Sadat *has achieved*. He sees the event of Sadat's visit and the peace as an offer, as an act of acceptance, of recognition, and by implication he urges that Israel act in kind, that it reach out to secure the offer and help to advance the opportunity. He makes no reference, of a specific kind, about what this might involve or what it might mean for dealing with the Palestinian problem as a political problem. But he does imply that such an act must elicit a response and that no genuine one, out of the heritage of Zionism, should degrade the act into a political one and fail to appreciate its ethical importance.

Levinas's thinking about the State of Israel is complex. Like many others, he sees Zionism and the state in terms of the long history of Jewish suffering and persecution and in the shadow of Hitler and the Nazi destruction. At the same time, he takes Zionism to be grounded in a prophetic vision, of a desire to realize a just and humane society and to organize and conduct politics in order to express what justice requires. Furthermore, he is realistic about the historical situation of the land, the state, and the Arab world. There is a need, he realizes, to create a "fraternal community" with Israel's neighbors, but at the same time – in order to respond to Israel's ethical calling and to its millenial suffering – the Jewish people cannot, in his eyes, risk its majority control over Israel's future and over its promise. The conflict with the Palestinians may be intractable; it certainly can expect no easy solutions. Just as, in a sense, all are responsible for the horrors and atrocities of the twentieth century, so Jews and Israelis are responsible for the pain and suffering of their Palestinian citizens and neighbors. But, as we have seen, no one can act on all one's responsibilities; justice is *always* a matter of degree and accommodation. Yet concrete events, particular events, may shape and alter the balance. In his most explicit public encounter with such events, the radio conversation after the massacres at Sabra and Shatila, Levinas says as much as he ever does about these matters.[200]

[200] To be sure, it may not be enough. Levinas, as we shall see, does not make a clear and precise judgment about who is right and who is wrong and especially about whether Israel is guilty for the massacres and what should be done in response to that guilt. Given who Levinas is and the circumstances at the time of the interview, if Levinas was evasive or negligent or irresponsibile, can he be forgiven? By whom?

If Levinas's treatment of Israel and the problem of Palestinian rights seems to many to be morally irresponsible, his statements about Asia and Asian civilizations have been judged by

Levinas here claims that ethics is fundamental but that politics, self-defense, and concern for oneself and one's neighbors are not just possible but even necessary. But, as Alain Finkelkraut then points out, the question arises about conflict between the two. What about an apparent confrontation between ethics and "political necessities" or *raison d'etat*?[201] Or, to put it more clearly: in recent times, have not political necessities, or the pleas on their behalf, taken priority? Have we not become obsessed with politics, too willing to accommodate or compromise our moral conscience to political necessity? In this case, the *we* are Jews and Israelis, concerning the affairs of the state.

To this, Levinas argues that the "Zionist idea ... is a political idea" that has an ethical justification, to "put an end to the arbitrariness which marked the Jewish condition, and to all the spilt blood which for centuries has flowed with impunity across the world."[202] For Levinas, this means "a political unity with a Jewish majority," what he calls the "essence of Zionism," "a State with an army and arms, an army which can have a deterrent and if necessary a defensive significance." And, as we have heard before, he justifies this morally, since "my people and my kin are still my neighbours."[203] But – and now Levinas faces the critical issue – "[t]here is also an ethical limit to this ethically necessary political existence. But what is this limit?"[204] The issue, of course, is an historical and not a philosophical one; it involves in this case, with these events, a people with an ethical tradition and an ethical conscience. What needs to occur is for events that should not have happened to affect "the concrete consciousness of those who suffer and struggle."[205] Levinas's point, I take it, is that here philosophy is not relevant, although it is Levinas's judgment to make, about what has been done and what now should be done, because it is everyone's judgment to make.

Levinas is explicit: Sabra and Shatila are "the place where everything is interrupted, where everything is disrupted, where everyone's moral responsibility comes into play."[206] He then says, enigmatically, "Everyone's

at least one commentator to be virtually "insane." See C. Fred Alford, "Levinas and Political Theory," *Political Theory* 32:2 (April 2004), 159–161, where Alford cites Levinas's essay on the conflict between the Soviet Union and China as evidence of Levinas's complete lack of understanding of the cultures of Asia: "Le Débat Russo-Chinois et la dialéctique," *Les imprévus de l'histoire* (Fata Morgana, 1994), 171–172. The essay is now translated in Levinas, *Unforeseen History*, trans. Nidra Poller (University of Illinois Press, 2004), 107–109.

201 Levinas, "Ethics and Politics," in *A Levinas Reader*, 293.
202 Ibid.
203 Ibid.
204 Ibid.
205 Ibid.
206 Ibid.

responsibility." I do not think that Levinas means directly that the massacre at Sabra and Shatila was everyone's responsibility in the sense that everyone brought it about or that everyone was equally guilty of perpetrating the massacre. What I think he means is that, in his eyes, these events register on or interrupt, as he says, everyone's moral responsibility, everyone's conscience, everyone's ethical sensibility. The events matter ethically to us all, and hence they are significant for everyone near and far.

Then, when asked directly whether for the Israeli the Palestinian is not "above all" the other, Levinas demurs. His answer is that the other is the neighbor, and that this can mean your kin. "If your neighbor attacks another neighbor," he says, "or treats him unjustly, what can you do?"[207] In such a situation one must at least try to determine who is right, who wrong. But for Levinas the central point is that these events "disturb" everyone and challenge everyone. In particular, they threaten the Jewish soul and, as he goes on to note, Jewish books, the books that carry the central ethical teachings of Judaism and mean more to Israel than the land. Levinas ends the conversation by affirming this point, recalling a passage from the Talmud that "a person is more holy than a land, even a holy land." This comment may be indirect and muted, but it expresses, to my ears, distress and worry in the midst of a deep fidelity. Levinas clearly understands Zionism as a movement meant to rectify a heritage of suffering, and yet the massacres at Sabra and Shatila have registered in him a worry that the mission of Israel is in jeopardy. But he is not a politician or a political commentator. He makes no precise judgment or recommendation. Perhaps he is reluctant to express more concern because there is too much he does not know, or perhaps because his worries are too deep. Nonetheless, he does not hide his anxiety as much as he lives with it, as he recommends we all do – and indeed must.[208]

ETHICAL MESSIANISM

The messianic occurs, at concrete moments, when a person or an institution enacts the ethical, and lives with others in justice and with responsibility. This kind of messianism, beyond war and peace, is a central theme of Levinas's thought and of his conception of Judaism. The two are intimately entwined for him, and increasingly so, as the years go by.

[207] Ibid., 294.

[208] For a much more negative appraisal of Levinas's responses in the radio conversation, see Caygill, *Levinas and the Political*, 192–194.

More and more, especially in essays, talks, and interviews, he recalls Talmudic teachings in order to express the centrality of responsibility and its nuances. But at the same time that he calls on his Jewish heritage to illuminate his ethical vision, so his understanding of responsibility certainly determines his reading of Jewish life, ritual, books, and politics. Prophetic eschatology, Zionism, the Bible and the Talmud, all mingle in a way that calls for a deep rethinking and modification of Western philosophy and European culture. Commentators regularly refer to this conglomerate as Levinas's effort to teach the Greek West to speak Hebrew or to remind Greek philosophy and culture of the teachings of the Bible, of Scripture. However one interprets these metaphors, they signify – all of them – the fact that Western culture, with all the trappings of philosophy, literature, science, and art, both hides and yet is grounded in an ethical sensibility that is biblical in character, as Levinas sees it. That biblical heritage is vital to our living full human lives, but it is not sufficient on its own. Western culture, with its Greek roots, is necessary for life, but it too is inadequate, bereft of the understanding of social interaction and responsibility to others without which the risks of domination, persecution, violence, and suffering are very high indeed. In Levinas's vocabulary, terms like "assimilation" and "universalism," while reminiscent of the Enlightenment, carry different meanings, similar to those of earlier rationalists and modern thinkers but unique nonetheless. They are the hallmark of his vision of the Jewish people, historically distinctive and yet with a universal soul, a prophetic soul, whose central vision is a life of kindness and justice for one and all.

Throughout this book I have argued that the face-to-face and human responsibility for the other, primordial and determinative, are features – if often occluded – of all our social interaction; they are what is fundamental to all social life. As Levinas himself declares, this contemporaneity, which is also a diachrony, is a central theme of *Otherwise than Being*. In the essay "Essence and Disinterestedness" (later revised as the first chapter), after distinguishing between the Saying and the Said, Levinas asks: "can this *saying* and this *unsaying* be assembled, can they be at the same time?"[209] That is, when we realize that ethics is a feature or dimension of all ontology, of all human existence, is this not a betrayal of the special character of the ethical? Is there not here a risk of idealism or naturalism? Or, in his terms, does not this "simultaneity" reduce the *other* to *being*, ethics to ontology?[210]

209 Levinas, "Essence and Disinterestedness," in *Basic Philosophical Writings*, 114.

210 Ibid.

The same problem arises for Levinas's understanding of Judaism, the Bible, the Talmud, and Jewish life. When we realize that Judaism is simultaneous with, if often hidden or distorted by, Western culture and civilization, is it also betrayed? Is it *necessarily* betrayed? Is the translation not itself a distortion? Of course, Levinas does not think so. In the case of responsibility, what prevents such necessary betrayal is diachrony, that the face is always a trace of an absolute absence, of *illeity*. One might say the same about Judaism and its central teaching: it is always present in our lives as a "trace" of an absent Revelation. Sinai is not an historical event in the life of the Jewish people as much as it is a symbol of what is primordial for all human life. Indeed, it is more than a symbol; it is the way of life of Jews and thereby a reality within Western society and Western life. In this way, as I have claimed, terms such as "Hebrew," "Greek," "Jew," "Israel," and "Zionism" ultimately are metaphors for Levinas, signifying fundamental features of the human condition, and the Jewish people is, as it were, a living metaphor.

To be sure, like "eros," "femininity," "paternity," and others, they are contested. They have their own connotations that upset and disturb at the same time that they illuminate and resonate. But Levinas's affinity for concreteness and particularity alongside universality and abstractness is something he does not avoid. Nor does he elude what is difficult. But what he does say – especially in his comments on Zionism – often seems disturbing. Nonetheless, there is reason to respect his candor and his reticence, for the specific situations in question are not simple.

Indirectly, the State of Israel, then, is not exclusively a Jewish concern, in Levinas's eyes, nor indeed is Judaism – its books and central teachings – an exclusively Jewish matter. Judaism and the Jewish people are one historical manifestation of a central truth about humanity. "Judaism is valid not because of the 'happy end' of its history, but because of the faithfulness of this history to the teachings of the Torah." Judaism is not about a divine promise, whether fulfilled or not, whether renounced or not. The history that matters is one of commitment to ethics and to a real messianism. It is "a history which cannot get through our time, nor testify to its truth without taking on, somewhere, political conditions. That is why the State of Israel is important today to the Torah of Israel and to its meaning for all men."[211] And what is important to Israel's teaching is in fact important to all humankind. For all its brute particularity, its life, its suffering, the Jewish people is the soul of humanity, and its essence is universalism. And

[211] Levinas, "Dialogue on Thinking-of-the-Other," in *Entre Nous*, 206.

to the degree that its messianic, ethical purpose requires a political reality, to that degree too is that political reality of importance to all humankind. To some, this may seem narrow, parochial, and even self-serving, but to Levinas it is noble and elevating. Nor should we forget that in his own eyes, Jews are not the only Jews, nor is Israel the only Jewish state. All people are Jews, and all states are Israel, but no less than all Jews speak Greek and live in the Greek West.[212]

[212] Here I am alluding to a comment, frequently cited, of Bernard Malamud, that all people are Jews, only they don't know it.

Conclusions, Puzzles, Problems

To a great degree, Levinas's philosophical commitment to the primacy of ethics is a response to intellectual and historical challenges to morality in the nineteenth and twentieth centuries. Viewed in this way, Levinas's thought is a contribution to moral philosophy. Examining it, one can ask what he says about the grounds of moral obligation and value, the nature of morality, its normative content, and such. But we have seen that to read Levinas in this way is too narrow. It is more appropriate to take his philosophy as a contribution to understanding human existence in the broadest sense. It is, in this way, a philosophical anthropology or a philosophy of human existence, and Levinas's central teaching is that ethical matters are fundamental or central to human existence. He is not, of course, the first person to make this claim, but the way in which he argues for this position is distinctive. He claims that as human beings we are social beings, that is, that we have direct, first-person/second-person, face-to-face relationships with others, and that as social beings our relationships have an ethical character that is the most determinative feature of our existence with others in the world. This is at least part of what he means by the claim that "ethics is first philosophy."

In traditional forms of Western philosophy, metaphysics or theology identified the most fundamental entities or principles on which all of reality is founded. Whether these entities were conceived as divine or material or abstract or formal or whatever, metaphysics was conceived as the enterprise of identifying these most basic things and of showing what they are and how they are related to everything else that exists. After Descartes, this project required attention to the primacy of the mind or of conscious thought in this enterprise. Hence, metaphysics became preoccupied or at least seriously occupied with mental phenomena and the mind. Metaphysics became psychology.

Levinas's response to this metaphysical tradition is twofold. On the one hand, Levinas argues that the most primary or fundamental features of the world as human beings experience it are features of interpersonal relationships and actions; the world makes sense to human beings most fundamentally in terms of how human beings are related to one another as they live in the world together, rather than merely in terms of how they think. On the other hand, Levinas argues that all human relationships have an ethical core that is determinative of their significance, of what they mean. Hence, if Levinas is right, then what once functioned as metaphysics or first philosophy should be replaced in our thinking with ethics as that is manifest in interpersonal encounters of one person with another living in the world. This is what it means for "ethics to be first philosophy." In brief, metaphysics is grounded in how human beings live in the world together, and human existence is fundamentally ethical. Moreover, ethics is not a cognitive matter; it is not theory. It is what goes on in human interactions in the world.

As we have seen, the content of this thought or this claim is that there is a dimension of all our relationships with all people that involves the other person's dependence upon us for acknowledgment, acceptance, and assistance or aid and our responsiveness to these claims. These claims upon us make of us centers of responsibility to others – indeed, to all others. But this responsibility to others is embedded in a complex, infinitely ramified network of relationships that we have with others, so that in daily life we are always "negotiating" our responsibilities; we give to some and not to others, we share with some more, others less, and so on. Hence, this layer or dimension of claim and responsibility is always present for us, but in everyday life we respond differentially, deliberating and choosing to acknowledge and care about some people but not others, all the time, day in and day out. Moreover, everything we do, all the domains of our life, our vocational lives and religious lives, our family lives and our public or civic ones, are venues in which the policies, plans, and programs we devise reflect to one degree or another how we manage what for Levinas is this claim to justice. In this book, I have tried to set out some of the basic features of this situation – how Levinas understands the face-to-face and its ethical character, how it is related – as a kind of transcendental structure – to all the "totalities" or domains that make up our lives, what role it plays for our conception of ourselves as persons, where traditional notions of God and religion fit into his conception of the ethical, and what it means for our sense of history and of time. I have also tried to show why he pays special attention to his Jewish background, in part to show how his philosophical anthropology helps Levinas to understand what Judaism means to him and in part to give an example of how the ethical is related to a particular domain of ordinary life, a Jew's experience of his or her Judaism.

As commentators have noticed, however, there are a number of puzzles that seem to arise for Levinas and a number of objections that can be raised against his view. I cannot deal with them fully here, but it is important, as we close, to indicate, if only briefly, some difficulties that have been raised. One puzzle concerns the notion of totality or totalization. Levinas argues against the ill effects, the violence and domination, that are characteristic of totalities, and yet his claim that all of our existence is grounded, as it were, in one single ethical obligation appears to some to have created a new totalization that risks being as oppressive and distorting as any other. It looks, that is, as if Levinas is simply replacing any number of traditional totalities with another. To be sure, one can answer this criticism. Levinas does say that, unlike the features that characterize others in our daily relationships with them, the face-to-face involves transcendence or otherness, and this separateness is part of what makes each relationship with another person utterly particular. In short, Levinas, if he is right, is not interested in human beings as a species or in types of persons; he is interested in how we relate to each other, face to face, in an utterly particular way and in a way that nonetheless is grounded in how we differ from one another. But such an answer may not satisfy the critics, who see Levinas as someone who claims that there is difference but in the end never goes beyond unity or homogeneity, and with distorting results for human existence.

I have addressed another puzzle, regarding the relationship between the primacy of the claim of the other person and the self's freedom, in Chapter 5. Levinas exaggerates the passivity of the self, the way in which it is under the influence of the other's claim prior to being free itself. We are, as he says, heteronomous – determined by an other – before we are autonomous – determined by ourselves. But some have argued that making the self a pure or unqualified receiver before it is active or responsive is incoherent. And in fact, they claim, Levinas slips again and again into using active language for the self, a slip that they argue is unavoidable. Even if the other person initiates a claim against me, for example, in receiving that claim surely I already exist and at that moment engage in the act of reception. It simply makes no sense to talk about the determination of another person on me without my first being there to receive that determination or to be affected by it. In response, as I have tried to show, Levinas in fact does not take this issue to be a temporal one; structurally, in ordinary life, the self has a host of features and roles and characteristics, and it is this ordinary self that is the subject of responsibility, of the claim of the other.

What Levinas is saying is that the meaning of the self's existence – what makes it the kind of being for whom things matter and what makes it a being that cares about others and whose life has a point – is always already there for the self as the other's claim upon it. It is, as it were, "conceptually" prior to all the other features the self has. This may not satisfy all the critics, but it is the beginning of a response to their concern that Levinas has lapsed into incoherence.

Perhaps the most telling puzzle raised for Levinas is that his claim about the other person's transcendence, about its having a face that is somehow inconceivable and inexpressible, is itself regularly defeated by his own continual discourse about it. That is, if the face is genuinely transcendent, then it is beyond thought and expressibility. But if it is, then how can Levinas talk so much about it? What does his terminology mean? To what do his novel expressions refer? If "the face" designates something that is beyond being, how can he say that it "is" or "exists"? This kind of criticism of Levinas is associated, in the minds of many, with the criticism of Jacques Derrida, in his influential review of *Totality and Infinity*, "Violence and Metaphysics." There has been a great deal of discussion of Derrida and Levinas, and I have nothing to add to it. But let me say that in order to understand what Levinas actually accomplishes and to avoid taking him to have made an obvious error, one must be attentive to his use of language and his understanding of how language can function. Furthermore, one would have to consider his indebtedness to figures like Plato, Plotinus, and Descartes, as well as his links to figures like Karl Barth and Franz Rosenzweig, what he takes "transcendence" to mean and whether one is willing to accept the very possibility of acknowledging and accepting such a notion. This would lead one to consider the criticisms of some that Levinas is really a religious thinker and not a philosopher. I would like to warn the reader that it is tendentious to assume a rigid separation between these categories. Simply to assume that philosophy and theology or religious thought exclude one another is to accept a very narrow view of what philosophy is, and a very partisan one at that. Clearly, Levinas is not a rigid or extreme naturalist, but not all philosophers are or have been resistant to a sensibility for the transcendent. Indeed, what distinguishes Levinas's notion of transcendence may be that his conception of interpersonal relations and his sense of what religion is at its deepest level converge in a particularly compelling way, a way that is different from traditional theism and even different from modern developments associated with figures like Paul Tillich, Karl Barth, Martin Buber, and Franz Rosenzweig.

These puzzles for Levinas have a rather abstract character. Several problems that have been raised are more concrete. For example, it is tempting to read Levinas as someone who gives pride of place to altruism and our obligations to other people. If so, what does he have to say about obligations to ourselves or about interests of his own that a person might have? Does Levinas require that in every situation, a person should sacrifice himself to others? Is his an ethics of extreme self-sacrifice? Secondly, is not such an ethic too demanding to be reasonable and plausible? Indeed, Levinas seems to be saying that ethics is infinitely demanding; we are infinitely responsible to each and every person in every way all the time. This by itself would make ethical accomplishment impossible for us, and even if we were to accept this level of demand – a standard exceeding anything we could every meet – is it not also too demanding to hold that in conflicts between our own interests and those of others, we should always abandon or override our own in order to help others? Hence, for two reasons at least, Levinas's ethics seems beyond anything we would conceive as possible or reasonable for normal human beings.

Once again, these are large questions, and to deal with them adequately would require a good deal of time, but let me say this. As so often with objections to Levinas, one must be very careful about what Levinas means by "ethics" and what its relation is to our ordinary everyday lives. While the face-to-face or responsibility is fundamental to all our human encounters with one another, we never – or at least normally do not – experience such a relationship purely or by itself in our everyday lives. Levinas realizes, and for this there is a great deal of evidence, that in our everyday lives we are always responsive to others in different ways; this means that there may be very good reasons for us to do a great deal for one person and less for another. Our resources are limited; our time is limited; and there are all kinds of pressures on us at any given time. Furthermore, we do have genuine responsibilities to ourselves. These are rooted in our nature, as natural beings living in the world, a world there for our use, nourishment, and enjoyment. There is nothing wrong with this; it is a significant part of who and what we are. Hence, just as we must and should evaluate how much to give to one person, how much to another, we must also evaluate how much to use ourselves and how much to give away. To be sure, these responsibilities – to ourselves and to others – may be grounded in different ways, but they are both real responsibilities that are constitutive of who and what we are. Moreover, if we were to ignore our own personal needs and desires all of the time, it would not be long before we would have nothing to give to others at all, and in this sense we would be putting ourselves in a position to negate our responsibilities. That is, even if we thought that our only ultimate responsibilities were to others, we would still have intermediate or instrumental ones to ourselves, without which we could not continue to execute the ones directed to others. In a sense, accepting others requires accepting ourselves and always weighing the needs of others against our own. Our embodied existence demands no less of us.

Many ask: what kinds of beings have a face? Do animals have a face? Does nature or do natural beings? And what of future generations or those who have died? How extensive or how limited is the reach of our responsibilities? With whom can we in principle have a face-to-face encounter? Students and scholars alike have regularly asked such questions of Levinas, and to many he is ill-equipped to answer them. To be sure, there is Levinas's short, famous piece that mentions his experience in a Nazi prisoner-of-war camp of a friendly dog that recognized in him and his fellow prisoners their humanity.[1] But it is not clear what the piece implies about the face of nonhuman animals. Arguments have been made that support the apparent anthropocentrism of Levinas's view and others that claim that he is not insensitive to animal rights and such matters.[2] Once again, however, I think that the key to unlocking this problematic issue is to realize something about how Levinas's thinking is phenomenological and transcendental. For Levinas the account of the face-to-face and responsibility as a transcendental and real feature of all human encounters with genuine others does not legislate who is a genuine other; rather, it begins with those encounters and then attempts to disclose dimensions of those relationships that are often hidden from view or obscured or forgotten their particularity and ethical character. It may be that in our everyday lives most of our moral relationships, so to speak, are with other persons; hence to disclose the ethical core of such encounters is to disclose the way the claim of other persons on us involves the plea and demand I have described. But if situations arise in which we have to deliberate about how to treat animals or natural resources or unborn persons, then it is not a question of how or whether these beings have faces for us, as if the face were a feature or trait or characteristic, or of asking whether we are responsible to them or for them. Rather, it is incumbent upon us to consider how the complex network of relationships in which we find ourselves – which includes our relationships with other persons of all kinds,

[1] Levinas, "The Name of a Dog, or Natural Rights," in *Difficult Freedom*, 151–153.

[2] For an excellent recent account, with which I have much sympathy, see Diane Perpich, "Scarce Resources? Levinas, Animals, and the Environment," in *The Ethics of Emmanuel Levinas*, 150–176.

animals, and so forth – bears upon us and what kinds of responsibilities we have and what the particular situation seems to require of us. These are everyday matters; they do not constitute a metaphysical question about what kind of thing an animal or a natural resource is. The issue is about giving some weight to a relationship that already exists and figuring that weight into a network of considerations that bear upon us. It is a matter of weighing reasons and coming to a decision. What this means is that the issue of what beings play a role in our moral and practical decisions occurs at the ordinary everyday level; it is a matter of deliberation and decision, not a matter of philosophical disclosure. It may not be possible to explain why we feel such responsibilities except by saying, if we seek a philosophical clarification, that we do have a kind of face-to-face with a particular animal or indeed with every particular animal. Naturalisms may have an easier route to explaining why this is so than Levinas does, but he may not feel bound to explain where such sensibilities come from as much as how they figure into our everyday lives.

Levinas is often criticized for his irrelevance. In particular, some argue that he is so opposed to rules or programs or policies that his conception of ethics is unhelpful or inapplicable or at least of no significance for our ordinary lives. For these lives are social and political, and society and politics require institutions, bureaucracies, and laws. I have tried to show, from the outset, that Levinas is surely opposed to bad institutions, ones that are oppressive, dominating, and harmful, ones that lead to pain and suffering, but he is not opposed to all institutions and laws and practices. In fact, he is – in *Totality and Infinity* and later in *Otherwise than Being* – fully aware that our ordinary lives require regularized patterns of behavior, institutions, organizations, and such. Excessively oppressive or inflexible ones will restrict freedom and cause suffering, but better ones will maximize people's well-being and enable them to flourish and to care for one another as they would like to do. Ordinary life always involves compromises, and every situation is distinctive. Often we can treat each situation discretely and with sufficient attention; sometimes we cannot and have to trust policies or programs. But it is clear that for Levinas room should always be made for very particular deliberations about what to do and how to act, even within frameworks and institutions with normal structures. Moreover, even when we follow rules or acknowledge obligations, we should never forget that in acting we are related responsibly to particular other persons. Hence, for him, politics is not always bad. It can be, but it need not be. For him the word "politics" is generally used in a very broad way; it means how we live in the *polis*, that is, how we live together with others in everyday life. In this broad sense and also in the narrow sense, in which politics is the domain of power and the use of violence or force to protect, serve, and control members of a society, there can be good expressions of it and bad ones. What disclosing the fundamentally responsible character of our relations to particular others does is to show what considerations politics should take most seriously. Keeping ethics in mind brings a standard of goodness to bear on our political lives.

Finally, Levinas's conception of the ethical character of all social existence may seem so single-minded and focused that it leaves little room for other aspects of our lives that we regularly take to be valuable. That is, there are things we do that we take to enrich our lives and to be valuable – producing and enjoying works of art, engaging in athletic activities, playing games, reading a good book; we desire such activities and engage in them not simply because they contribute to other ends, but because we find them intrinsically valuable or worthwhile. As Hilary Putnam notices, an Aristotelian view of human flourishing allows for a wide variety of activities as contributing to a good life; Levinas seems to be denying this variety in favor of a life devoted single-mindedly to ethics or at least one in which everything we do is judged according to whether or not it contributes to ethical results. Such a view, however, seems blind to the richness of our identities and to life itself.

This objection gives content to the puzzle about Levinas's introducing a new form of totality. Any effort to confront this worry about Levinas's single-mindedness, however, must first of all consider what he does say about art, poetry, and literature, and the way his views about such activities and their products seem to have changed throughout his career. There is a moment when he does seem to denigrate, in Platonic fashion, poetry and the arts; his relatively early essay "Reality and Its Shadow" has often been read to point in this direction.[3] But later his treatment of authors as diverse as Proust and S. Y. Agnon reflects a more positive evaluation, although one that clearly suggests the relationship between their works and the ethical character of our lives.[4] The first step in evaluating Levinas's attitude toward the production of works of art and toward an assessment

[3] Emmanuel Levinas, "Reality and Its Shadow," in *Collected Philosophical Papers*, translated by Alphonso Lingis (Duquesne University Press, 1987), 1–13; also in Seán Hand (ed.), *A Levinas Reader* (Basil Blackwell, 1989), 129–143. See also Jill Robbins, *Altered Reading*, and Peter Atterton, "Art, Religion, and Ethics *Post Mortem Dei*: Levinas and Dostoevsky," *Levinas Studies* 2 (May 2007), 104–132.

[4] See Emmanuel Levinas, "Poetry and Resurrection: Notes on Agnon" and "The Other in Proust," in *Proper Names*, 7–16 and 99–105. See also Seán Hand, *Emmanuel Levinas*, Chapter 5, 63–78.

of their value and purpose would be to consider what he did say about such matters. A second, however, is to keep in mind that the ethical for Levinas, as we have regularly pointed out, is not a restricted domain. It is not a restricted domain of moral value and certainly not the domain of moral obligations or moral virtues. Rather, ethics is another word for that feature of human relationships and encounters that gives point and purpose to human existence itself. It is not the whole of human social existence, but it is a basic and determinative feature of it. Hence, one should not be so quick to judge Levinas's single-minded attention to it. If he is excessive about it, his passion is no doubt driven by a sense of urgency about Western culture and history and about our lives. To say that art, as well as leisure, hobbies, and personal projects, ought all to be somehow involved with our ethical character as social beings is not to demean these activities. It is no more, but also no less, than to say that our engagement in these types of activities ought to be evaluated and determined by how much or how little it contributes to our lives as human beings.

With this comment, I arrive at the conclusion of our introduction to Levinas's philosophy. For us, it may be that the next step would be to probe his works more fully and more deeply in order to clarify these difficulties and others and to determine for ourselves the limits of his insight. For him, the step that follows understanding what he says about our lives is to act toward others with concern and love and a sense of justice. Both steps are worth taking.

Recommended Readings

WORKS BY LEVINAS

Levinas, Emmanuel. *Basic Philosophical Writings*. Adriaan T. Peperzak, Simon Critchley, and Robert Bernasconi (eds.). (Bloomington: Indiana University Press, 1996). Excellent collection of nine important philosophical essays, with helpful introductions; includes "Is Ontology Fundamental?," "Transcendence and Height," and "Substitution." The best available place to begin reading Levinas's philosophical works.

Ethics and Infinity. Conversations with Philippe Nemo (Pittsburgh, PA: Duquesne University Press, 1985). Very helpful set of interviews, broadcast in 1981, on various themes. A good place to begin reading Levinas.

Time and the Other. Richard A. Cohen (trans.). (Pittsburgh, PA: Duquesne University Press, 1987). Early set of lectures that forms the skeleton for the systematic structure of *Totality and Infinity*.

Totality and Infinity (Pittsburgh, PA: Duquesne University Press, 1969). Published in 1961, Levinas's great early systematic work; very challenging.

Robbins, Jill (ed.). *Is It Righteous to Be? Interviews with Emmanuel Levinas* (Stanford, CA: Stanford University Press, 2001). Excellent collection of many interviews conducted during the 1980s and 1990s. A good place to become acquainted with Levinas.

Levinas, Emmanuel. *A Levinas Reader*. Ed. Seán Hand (Oxford: Basil Blackwell, Inc., 1989). Helpful collection of pieces of various kinds, some selections from works, others articles and occasional writings; includes an important radio interview after the Lebanon War with Alain Finkelkraut.

Difficult Freedom. Seán Hand (trans.). (Baltimore, MD: The Johns Hopkins University Press, 1990). Important collection of Jewish writings, originally published in 1963 and 1976; includes "A Religion for Adults," "Loving the Torah More than God," and "Signature."

Nine Talmudic Readings. Annette Aronowicz (trans.). (Bloomington: Indiana University Press, 1990). Important collection of Levinas's Talmudic lessons.

SECONDARY WORKS

Caygill, Howard. *Levinas and the Political* (London: Routledge, 2002). Important study of Levinas's implications for themes in political philosophy.

Chanter, Tina (ed.). *Feminist Interpretations of Emmanuel Levinas* (University Park: The Pennsylvania State University Press, 2001). Useful collection of essays on Levinas and gender issues.

Cohen, Richard A. *Elevations: The Height of the Good in Rosenzweig and Levinas* (Chicago: University of Chicago Press, 1994). Helpful set of essays on these two figures, as philosophers and as Jewish thinkers.

Cohen, Richard A. (ed.). *Face to Face with Levinas* (Albany, NY: SUNY Press, 1986). Earliest collection of essays in English on Levinas, with an extremely helpful interview by Richard Kearney and important papers by Theodore de Boer, Jean-Francois Lyotard, Robert Bernasconi, and Luce Irigaray.

Critchley, Simon. *The Ethics of Deconstruction: Derrida and Levinas*. 2nd edition. (West Lafayette, IN: Purdue University Press, 1999; orig. 1992). Major study of Derrida and Levinas on ethics and politics.

Critchley, Simon, and Robert Bernasconi (eds.). *The Cambridge Companion to Levinas* (Cambridge: Cambridge University Press, 2002). Outstanding collection of essays on all aspects of Levinas's work; includes an excellent introduction by Critchley and essays by Hilary Putnam on Levinas and Judaism, Robert Bernasconi on substitution, Gerald Bruns on art and poetry, Richard Bernstein on evil, and other valuable essays.

Davis, Colin. *Levinas: An Introduction* (Cambridge: Polity Press, 1996). Helpful brief introduction to Levinas's major works.

Drabinski, John E. *Sensibility and Singularity: The Problem of Phenomenology in Levinas* (Albany: SUNY Press, 2001). Excellent study of selfhood in Levinas and the role of phenomenology in his thinking.

Gibbs, Robert. *Correlations in Rosenzweig and Levinas* (Princeton, NJ: Princeton University Press, 1992). Challenging but valuable study of Rosenzweig and Levinas.

Hand, Seán. *Emmanuel Levinas* (London: Routledge, 2008). Short introduction to Levinas's works and main themes.

Kosky, Jeffrey L. *Levinas and the Philosophy of Religion* (Bloomington: Indiana University Press, 2001). Excellent study of Levinas's treatment of religion and theology.

Morgan, Michael L. *Discovering Levinas* (Cambridge: Cambridge University Press, 2007). An attempt to explore Levinas's thought in conversation with Anglo-American analytic philosophy.

Moyn, Samuel. *Origin of the Other: Emmanuel Levinas between Revelation and Ethics* (Ithaca, NY: Cornell University Press, 2005). Important study of the influence of theology in Weimar Germany on Levinas's understanding of transcendence and ethics.

Peperzak, Adriaan. *To the Other: An Introduction to the Philosophy of Emmanuel Levinas* (West Lafayette, IN: Purdue University Press, 1993). A translation of and detailed commentary on Levinas's "Philosophy and the Idea of the Infinite" and an introduction to *Totality and Infinity*.

Perpich, Diane. *The Ethics of Emmanuel Levinas* (Stanford, CA: Stanford University Press, 2008). Outstanding recent study of Levinas's understanding of the face and its ethical significance; excellent chapters on animal rights, natural resources, and gender issues.

Robbins, Jill. *Altered Reading: Levinas and Literature* (Chicago: University of Chicago Press, 1999). Important study of Levinas on literature.

Wyschogrod, Edith. *Emmanuel Levinas: The Problem of Ethical Metaphysics* (The Hague: Martinus Nijhoff, 1974). Early influential study of Levinas that addresses many central themes.

SELECTED BIBLIOGRAPHY

ENGLISH TRANSLATIONS OF ADDITIONAL WORKS OF EMMANUEL LEVINAS

Levinas, Emmanuel. *Beyond the Verse: Talmudic Readings and Lectures.* Bloomington: Indiana University Press, 1994.

Existence and Existents (Pittsburgh, PA: Duquesne University Press, 2001; orig. 1978).

Proper Names (Stanford, CA: Stanford University Press, 1996).

"Useless Suffering." Trans. Richard A. Cohen. In Bernasconi and Woods, pp. 156–167.

Otherwise than Being (Pittsburgh, PA: Duquesne University Press, 1998; orig. 1981).

The Theory of Intuition in Husserl's Phenomenology (Evanston, IL: Northwestern University Press, 1973).

Entre Nous: Thinking-of-the-Other (New York: Columbia University Press, 1998).

Outside the Subject (Stanford, CA: Stanford University Press, 1993).

Collected Philosophical Papers. Alphonso Lingis (trans.). (Pittsburgh, PA: Duquesne University Press, 1998; orig. 1987).

In the Time of the Nations (Bloomington: Indiana University Press, 1994).

Unforeseen History (Urbana: University of Illinois Press, 2004).

Humanism of the Other (Urbana: University of Illinois Press, 2003).

Discovering Existence with Husserl. Richard A. Cohen and Michael B. Smith (trans.). (Evanston, IL: Northwestern University Press, 1998).

God, Death, and Time (Stanford, CA: Stanford University Press, 2000).

Of God Who Comes to Mind (Stanford, CA: Stanford University Press, 1998).

"As If Consenting to Horror." *Critical Inquiry* 15 (Winter 1989), pp. 485–488.

"The Meaning of Religious Practice." Trans. Peter Atterton, Matthew Calarco, and Joelle Hansel. *Modern Judaism* 25:3 (2005), pp. 285–289. [Orig. 1937].

"Reflections on the Philosophy of Hitlerism." *Critical Inquiry* 17 (Autumn 1990), pp. 63–71.

On Escape (Stanford, CA: Stanford University Press, 2003).

Alterity and Transcendence (New York: Columbia University Press, 1999).

ADDITIONAL SECONDARY SOURCES

Alford, C. Fred. "Levinas and Political Theory." *Political Theory* 32:2 (2004), pp. 146–171.

Atterton, Peter, and Matthew Calarco. *On Levinas*. Belmont, CA: Wadsworth, 2005.

Batnitzky, Leora. *Leo Strauss and Emmanuel Levinas: Philosophy and the Politics of Revelation* (Cambridge: Cambridge University Press, 2006).

Bauman, Zygmunt. *Postmodern Ethics* (Oxford: Blackwell Publishers, 1993).

Bernasconi, Robert. "Rereading *Totality and Infinity*." In Charles Scott and Arleen Dallery (eds.), *The Question of the Other* (Albany: SUNY Press, 1989), pp. 23–24 and 225–226.

"The Trace of Levinas in Derrida." In Wood and Bernasconi, pp. 13–29.

"Different Styles of Eschatology: Derrida's Take on Levinas's Political Messianism." *Research in Phenomenology* 28 (1998), pp. 3–19.

Bernasconi, Robert, and D. Woods (eds.). *The Provocation of Levinas* (London: Routledge, 1988).

Bernasconi, Robert, and Simon Critchley (eds.). *Re-Reading Levinas* (Bloomington: Indiana University Press, 1991).

Bernstein, Richard J. *Radical Evil: A Philosophical Interrogation* (Cambridge: Polity Press, 2002).

Blanchot, Maurice. *The Infinite Conversation* (Minneapolis: University of Minnesota Press, 1992).

Bloechl, Jeffrey. *Liturgy and the Neighbor: Emmanuel Levinas and the Religion of Responsibility* (Pittsburgh, PA: Duquesne University Press, 2000).

Bloechl, Jeffrey (ed.). *The Face of the Other and the Trace of God* (New York: Fordham University Press, 2000).

Blum, Roland Paul. "Emmanuel Levinas' Theory of Commitment." *Philosophy and Phenomenological Research* 46:2 (1983), pp. 145–168.

Chalier, Catherine. *What Ought I to Do? Morality in Kant and Levinas*. Trans. Jane Marie Todd. (Ithaca, NY: Cornell University Press, 2002; orig. 1998).

Chanter, Tina. *Time, Death, and the Feminine: Levinas with Heidegger* (Stanford, CA: Stanford University Press, 2001).

Cohen, Richard A. *Ethics, Exegesis and Philosophy: Interpretation after Levinas* (Cambridge: Cambridge University Press, 2001).

Critchley, Simon. *Ethics – Politics – Subjectivity: Essays on Derrida, Levinas and Contemporary French Thought* (London: Verso, 1999).

Very Little . . . Almost Nothing: Death, Philosophy, Literature (London: Routledge, 1997).

"Five Problems in Levinas's View of Politics and the Sketch of a Solution to Them." *Political Theory* 32:2 (2004), pp. 172–185.

De Boer, Theodore. *The Rationality of Transcendence: Studies in the Philosophy of Emmanuel Levinas* (Amsterdam: J.C. Giehen, 1997).

Derrida, Jacques. *Adieu to Emmanuel Levinas* (Stanford, CA: Stanford University Press, 1999).

The Gift of Death (Chicago: University of Chicago Press, 1995).
Drabinski, John. "The Possibility of an Ethical Politics: From Peace to Liturgy." *Philosophy and Social Criticism* 26:4 (2000), pp. 49–73.
Dudiak, Jeffrey. *The Intrigue of Ethics: A Reading of the Idea of Discourse in the Thought of Emmanuel Levinas* (New York: Fordham University Press, 2001).
Eaglestone, Robert. *Ethical Criticism: Reading after Levinas* (Edinburgh: Edinburgh University Press, 1997).
Fagenblat, Michael. *A Covenant of Creatures: Levinas's Philosophy of Judaism* (Stanford, CA: Stanford University Press, 2010).
Fryer, David Ross. *The Intervention of the Other: Ethical Subjectivity in Levinas and Lacan* (New York: Other Press, 2004).
Grossman, Vasily. *Life and Fate*. Trans. Robert Chandler. (New York: Harper & Row, 1985).
Hand, Seán (ed.). *Facing the Other: The Ethics of Emmanuel Levinas* (Richmond, Surrey, UK: Curzon, 1996).
Hendley, Steven. *From Communicative Action to the Face of the Other: Levinas and Habermas on Language, Obligation, and Community* (Lanham, MD: Lexington Books, 2000).
Herzog, Annabel. "Is Liberalism 'All We Need'?: Levinas's Politics of Surplus." *Political Theory* 30:2 (2002), pp. 204–227.
Hutchens, B. C. *Levinas: A Guide for the Perplexed* (New York and London: Continuum, 2004).
Kleinberg, Ethan. *Generation Existential: Heidegger's Philosophy in France, 1927–1961* (Ithaca, NY: Cornell University Press, 2005).
Llewelyn, John. *Emmanuel Levinas: The Geneology of Ethics* (London: Routledge, 1995).
Manning, Robert John Sheffler. *Interpreting Otherwise than Heidegger: Emmanuel Levinas's Ethics as First Philosophy* (Pittsburgh, PA: Dusquene University Press, 1993).
Nemo, Philippe. *Job and the Excess of Evil* (Pittsburgh, PA: Duquesne University Press, 1998).
New, Melvyn, with Robert Bernasconi and Richard A. Cohen (eds.). *In Proximity: Emmanuel Levinas and the 18th Century* (Lubbock: Texas Tech University Press, 2001).
Peperzak, Adriaan Theodoor. *Beyond: The Philosophy of Emmanuel Levinas* (Evanston, IL: Northwestern University Press, 1997).
Peperzak, Adriaan T. (ed.). *Ethics as First Philosophy: The Significance of Emmanuel Levinas for Philosophy, Literature and Religion* (London: Routledge, 1995).
Plant, Bob. *Wittgenstein and Levinas: Ethical and Religious Thought* (London: Routledge, 2005).
"Ethics without Exit: Levinas and Murdoch." *Philosophy and Literature* 27 (2003), pp. 456–470.
Purcell, Michael. *Levinas and Theology* (Cambridge: Cambridge University Press, 2006).

Reinhard, Kenneth. "Kant with Sade, Lacan with Levinas." *MLN* 110:4 (1995), pp. 785–808.

Robbins, Jill. *Prodigal Son/ Elder Brother* (Chicago: University of Chicago Press, 1991).

Sandford, Stella. *The Metaphysics of Love* (London and New Brunswick, NJ: The Athlone Press, 2000).

Simmons, William Paul. "The Third: Levinas' theoretical move from an-archical ethics to the realm of justice and politics." *Philosophy and Social Criticism* 25:6 (1999), pp. 83–104.

Smith, Steven G. *The Argument to the Other: Reason beyond Reason in the Thought of Karl Barth and Emmanuel Levinas* (Chico, CA: Scholars Press, 1983).

Toumayan, Alain P. *Encountering the Other: The Artwork and the Problem of Difference in Blanchot and Levinas* (Pittsburgh, PA: Duquesne University Press, 2004).

Wood, David, and Robert Bernasconi (eds.). *Derrida and Diffèrance* (Evanston, IL: Northwestern University Press, 1988).

Wright, Tamra. *The Twilight of Jewish Philosophy: Emmanuel Levinas' Ethical Hermeneutics* (Amsterdam: Harwood Academic Publishers, 1999).

Index

Lightning Source UK Ltd.
Milton Keynes UK
UKOW04f2220201114

241901UK00001B/153/P